University of
Hertfordshire

College Lane, Hatfield, Herts. AL10 9AB

Learning and Information Services

For renewal of Standard and One Week Loans,
please visit the web site **http://www.voyager.herts.ac.uk**

This item must be returned or the loan renewed by the due date.
The University reserves the right to recall items from loan at any time.
A fine will be charged for the late return of items.

Political Communications Transformed

Also by John Bartle

POLITICAL COMMUNICATIONS: Why Labour Won the General Election of 1997 (*co-editor with Ivor Crewe and Brian Gosschalk*)

Also by Dylan Griffiths

THATCHERISM AND TERRITORIAL POLITICS

Political Communications Transformed

From Morrison to Mandelson

Edited by

John Bartle
Lecturer in Government
British Academy Post-Doctoral Fellow
University of Essex

and

Dylan Griffiths
Senior Research Fellow
Constitution Unit
University College London

First published 2001 by
PALGRAVE
Houndmills, Basingstoke, Hampshire RG21 6XS and
175 Fifth Avenue, New York, N. Y. 10010
Companies and representatives throughout the world

PALGRAVE is the new global academic imprint of
St. Martin's Press LLC Scholarly and Reference Division and
Palgrave Publishers Ltd (formerly Macmillan Press Ltd).

ISBN 0–333–77676–3

This book is printed on paper suitable for recycling and
made from fully managed and sustained forest sources.

A catalogue record for this book is available
from the British Library.

Library of Congress Cataloging-in-Publication Data
Political communications transformed : from Morrison to
Mandelson / edited by John Bartle and Dylan Griffiths.
       p. cm.
    Includes bibliographical references and index.
    ISBN 0–333–77676–3
    1. Communication in politics—Great Britain. 2. Mass
media—Political aspects—Great Britain. 3. Great Britain–
–Politics and government—1945– I. Bartle, John, lecturer.
II. Griffiths, Dylan.
    JA85.2.G7 P65 2000
    320'.01'4—dc21
                                                    00–066883

10   9   8   7   6   5   4   3   2   1
10   09   08   07   06   05   04   03   02   01

Printed in Great Britain by Antony Rowe Ltd, Chippenham, Wiltshire

Contents

List of Tables

List of Figures

Acknowledgements

The editors gratefully acknowledge the help of the following individuals: Professor Ivor Crewe of the University of Essex, who gave advice on the project at an early stage; Samantha Laycock and Jack Kneeshaw of the University of Essex for their comments on drafts of Chapters 1 and 2; and Professor Pippa Norris for her advice and encouragement throughout this project. We also wish to thank Sunder Katwala, formerly of Palgrave, and Alison Howson, our commissioning editors, for their assistance in guiding us toward publication.

Notes on the Contributors

John Bartle is Lecturer in Government and British Academy Post Doctoral Fellow at the University of Essex. His research interests include voting behaviour, British political parties and political knowledge. He has published articles in the *British Journal of Political Science*, *Political Studies* and *British Elections and Parties Review*. Recent publications include *Political Communications: Why Labour Won the General Election of 1997* (London: Frank Cass, 1998) which he edited together with Ivor Crewe and Brian Gosschalk.

David Denver is Professor of Politics at the University of Lancaster. He is the author of *Elections and Voting Behaviour in Britain* (Hemel Hempstead: Harvester Wheatsheaf, 1994) and (with Gordon Hands) *Modern Constituency Electioneering* (London: Frank Cass, 1997). He has also edited (again with Gordon Hands) *Issues and Controversies in British Electoral Behaviour* (Harvester Wheatsheaf, 1992). Professor Denver is co-convenor of the Elections, Public Opinion and Parties (EPOP) Group of the UK Political Studies Association and is a frequent commentator on elections in the press, and on radio and television. He has a forthcoming book on the 1997 Scottish referendum, and is researching candidates in the Welsh Assembly and Scottish Parliment elections.

Peter Goddard researches and teaches in the School of Politics and Communication Studies at the University of Liverpool. His research interests include media history and institutions, news, current affairs and politics on television. He has contributed chapters to books including Neil T. Gavin (ed.), *Economy, Media and Public Knowledge* (Leicester University Press, 1998), and Ivor Crewe et al. (eds), *Political Communications: Why Labour Won the General Election of 1997* (London: Frank Cass, 1998), and has published articles in journals including *Media, Culture and Society* and *Parliamentary Affairs*. At present, he is undertaking research into *World In Action*, the long-running British current affairs series.

Dylan Griffiths is a Senior Research Fellow at the Constitution Unit based at University College London. His main responsibility is the management of the Nations and Regions programme, investigating devolution across the United Kingdom. He was formerly a Lecturer in Politics at the University of Newcastle. His research interests include Welsh government, devolution and political marketing. He has published articles on the government of Wales, voting behaviour and devolution, together with *Thatcherism and Territorial Politics* (Avebury, 1996).

Gordon Hands is Head of the Department of Politics at the University of Lancaster. He is the co-author (with David Denver) of *Modern Constituency Electioneering* (London: Frank Cass, 1997). He has also edited (again with David Denver) *Issues and Controversies in British Electoral Behaviour* (Harvester Wheatsheaf, 1992). He has written widely on British electoral politics and political sociology. He is currently involved with David Denver in an ESRC-funded study of local election campaigning.

Martin Harrop is a Senior Lecturer in Politics at the University of Newcastle. His research interests include electoral behaviour, the media, political communications and comparative politics. He has published extensively in all these areas, contributing a co-authored chapter on the press in *The British General Election of 1997* by David Butler and Dennis Kavanagh (London: Macmillan, 1997).

Pippa Norris is Associate Director (Research) of the Shorenstein Center on the Press, Politics and Public Policy and she lectures at the Kennedy School of Government, Harvard University. She has published many books on comparative political behaviour in elections, gender politics and political communications. Current research focuses on a global comparison of the digital divide in the Internet age. Recent books include *A Virtuous Circle: Political Communications in Post-Industrial Democracies* (New York: Cambridge University Press, 2000).

Colin Seymour-Ure is Professor of Government at the University of Kent at Canterbury. His research interests include political communications and the British press. He has written about a variety of aspects of media and British elections since first contributing a chapter about the press to *The British General Election of 1966* by David Butler and Anthony King (London: Macmillan, 1966).

Dominic Wring is a Lecturer in Communication and Media Studies at the University of Loughborough where he has been completing a book on the historical development of Labour Party campaigning (Palgrave, forthcoming). Reflecting his research interests in political marketing and communication, he co-convenes the UK Political Studies Association's Media and Politics Group.

List of Acronyms

BBC	British Broadcasting Corporation
BEPS	British Election Panel Study
BES	British Election Study
BMP	Boase, Massimi, Pollitt
BSA	British Social Attitudes
CCO	Conservative Party Central Office
CPV	Colman, Prentis, Varley
EEC	European Economic Community
ERM	European Exchange Rate Mechanism
EU	European Union
FPTP	First Past the Post
IBA	Independent Broadcasting Authority
ITA	Independent Television Authority
ITC	Independent Television Commission
ITN	Independent Television News
ITV	Independent Television
MORI	Market Operations and Research International
MTV	Music Television
NEC	National Executive Committee (Labour Party)
NES	National Election Study
NOP	National Opinion Polls
NPB	National Publicity Bureau
PEB	Party Election Broadcast
PORD	Public Opinion Research Department
PPB	Party Political Broadcast
RPA	Representation of the People Act
SCA	Shadow Communications Agency
SDP	Social Democratic Party
SNP	Scottish National Party

1
Introduction

John Bartle and Dylan Griffiths

This book examines the transformation of political communications in Britain over a period running roughly from 1945 to 1997. We begin by dividing the system into three component parts: its citizens, parties and media, and then examine how each of these has responded to technological, social and cultural change. We examine how processes within these component parts, such as technological innovation in the broadcast media, competition between the major political parties, or between ITN and the BBC, have transformed the system. In addition, we demonstrate how political actors have responded to change – whether real or imagined – in the other component parts of the system. In Chapter 3 for example, we document the increasing importance of marketing specialists that resulted from the growing conviction that voters were becoming more volatile, less loyal and increasingly behaving like 'informed consumers'. In Chapter 7, we describe how television has responded to the increasing sophistication of the parties' media operations by adopting a more sceptical and aggressive approach to political broadcasting. In Chapter 5, we chart *both* the death *and* the apparent resurrection of the local election campaign in response to shifting theories of voting behaviour. In all these cases, we aim to demonstrate the fundamental interconnectedness of the political communications system. If we are to fully understand the nature of the changes, no component part of the system can be studied in isolation.

Political communications

The term 'political communications' has been widely interpreted. Some scholars tend to emphasize the importance of institutions and the legal regulation of broadcasting and the press.[1] Scholars working in the field of cognitive psychology tend to focus on how subjects select and evaluate new information.[2] Those working within a sociological tradition tend to focus on the 'meaning' which people attach to information and their emotional responses to stimuli.[3] Some think that the study of political communications should focus primarily on the impact of the media on voters and parties,[4] while yet another group emphasizes the fundamental importance of social group contacts.[5]

In this book, we focus primarily on political communications as they relate to elections in general and to general elections in particular. We do so for the obvious reason that general elections are widely thought to most closely approximate the 'voice of the people' and the source of political legitimacy in democratic societies. Free and competitive elections represent the most important means of communication between the rulers and the ruled. Parties communicate their intentions, priorities and competence to voters who in turn communicate their overall judgements of the parties at the ballot box.[6] Shifts in the way in which parties communicate with voters or the way in which the media deals with parties and presents information to voters are therefore of potentially great importance to democratic politics.

Why choose 1945 as a starting point?

Any study of change must begin by selecting some relevant baseline from which to compare a state of affairs in another period. We have settled on 1945 as the most appropriate starting point for a variety of reasons. The first of these is simply historical convention. No single datum, with the possible exception of 1979, is regarded as being quite so important in British politics, since it marks the beginning of the postwar consensus, the acceptance of the mixed economy and welfare state. The second reason is that, as we have already emphasized, the transformation of political communications has taken place over a long time as a result of glacial social, cultural and technological change. It follows that we must select a relatively lengthy period in order to appreciate the cumulative impact of these changes. Yet if we extended our scope much beyond 1945, it would compel us to examine the effect of the extension of the franchise and constitutional changes such as those brought about by the Secret Ballot Act 1872, the Corrupt Practices Act 1883 and the Redistribution Act 1884.[7] The period 1945 to 1997 did not witness major constitutional change, except for Britain's entry into the European Community in 1973 and this does not appear to have had much effect on political campaigning. To be sure, recent reforms introduced by the New Labour government, such as the increased use of referendums, devolution to Scotland and Wales and directly elected mayors, may have some impact on campaigning, but their implications are – as yet – far from clear. The third reason for using 1945 as our base is that it was one of the final elections fought before television assumed such a dominant role in the campaign. This enables us to contrast the 'pre-modern', 'modern' and 'post-modern' election campaigns – or what we will later call the 'Morrisonian', 'Wilsonian' and 'Mandelsonian' eras. The fourth and final reason for choosing 1945 as our approximate starting point is that this election witnessed the appearance of one of the most valuable works of reference in the English language: the 'Nuffield' studies. These volumes, published shortly after each general election, have provided information on the political, economic and social context and have carefully documented each campaign in detail. Moreover, since 1959 David Butler and his colleagues have been granted access to the 'key players': the leading politicians, the pollsters and advertisers.[8] These studies have given us a view of elections from 'inside the belly of the beast' so to speak. They therefore represent invaluable evidence for anyone interested in the 'transformation' of political communications. However, this book represents more than a distillation of the 15 Nuffield volumes that have already appeared. Our contributors have consulted a wide range of evidence and though most contributors to this volume take 1945 as their approximate starting point, some have had to extend their temporal perspective in order to fully describe the transformation that has taken place. Nevertheless, the editors and the contributors to this book would like to acknowledge the fundamental importance of the Nuffield studies to their thinking about the development of political communications in Britain.

The transformation of political communications

In this book we make the claim that political communications have been 'transformed' or fundamentally changed since 1945. However, we do not claim that this change has occurred overnight: evolution rather than revolution has very much been the order of the day. The best way to demonstrate these changes is to provide a brief description of three general elections: those of 1945, 1959 and 1997. The first and third of these elections were chosen simply because they cover the period under consideration. The election of 1959 was chosen as a marker election because it seemed to us – from our reading of various studies – that this undoubtedly represented the first 'television election'.[9] To be sure, it could be argued that the 1979 election or 1992 elections also constituted 'marker' elections. The former saw the rise of the advertising agency and Saatchi & Saatchi's formidable relationship with the Conservative Party (see Chapter 4), while the latter arguably witnessed the application of the marketing paradigm by both the major parties (see Chapter 3). However, since our aim is merely to provide a broad description of the political communications system, we do not feel our choice of elections will do much violence to reality.

1945: the Morrisonian era

The election of 1945 was unusual in some respects. It took place after the end of the war in Western Europe, but before the end of war in the Far East. The election itself took place on 5 July 1945, but the results were delayed until the 26 July in order to count the forces vote. However, in most other respects the election was typical of what might be called the 'pre-modern' campaign. The campaign itself was a short ad hoc affair organized by the party leader and a few colleagues.[10] It was dominated by a series of well-attended public meetings across the country addressed by prominent leaders such as Churchill and Eden for the Conservatives and Attlee and Morrison for Labour. While Churchill was conveyed around Britain in a chauffeur-driven motorcade, Attlee made his own way around the country driven by his wife, with just a single journalist in the back seat to monitor his progress. Though the deputy leader of the Labour Party, Herbert Morrison, was given formal responsibility for the Labour campaign. His role was limited since there were few telephones and the mail system was slow. Strategic coordination of the campaign was difficult – if not impossible – and senior politicians were largely left to fight their own campaign as best they could.

The election on the ground was typical of the pre-modern campaign too. In every one of the 640 constituencies hundreds (and sometimes thousands) of party members sought to inform voters where the polling stations were located, canvass their support, deliver leaflets and – on the election day itself – arrange for voters to be taken to vote. With the abolition of the hustings, all sides largely avoided direct debate with their opponents.[11] Indeed, David Butler has described the parties as 'manoeuvring on a battlefield of their own devising'.[12] In 1945 debate between the parties was rarely joined. Nor was any effort made to find out what the voters wanted or what were their priorities. The few opinion polls that appeared in the national press were scarcely commented upon by the newspapers that had commissioned them and were certainly not acted upon by the parties themselves. Some politicians like Nye Bevan despised them, claiming that they took 'the poetry out of politics', while others such as Harold Macmillan were sceptical as to their accuracy.[13] During the campaign the flow of communications was therefore almost entirely unidirectional: propaganda flowed from party to voter.

The national press played a prominent role in the 1945 election. Most newspapers remained deeply partisan in their outlook, giving virtually unqualified support to their party. The Beaverbrook press offered strong support for the Conservatives while the *Daily Mirror* and *Daily Herald* offered equally strong support for the Labour Party. Television was in a state of arrested development after the war, but national radio offered politicians the opportunity to reach a large portion of the electorate. Some 49 per cent of the electorate listened to Churchill's broadcasts, a figure that only slightly exceeded that for Attlee. The authors of the first Nuffield study speculated that radio would lead to more rational debate than was associated with large party meetings.[14] Fifty years later, however, critics of television were less sanguine about the effects of broadcasting (see Chapter 10).

Unsurprisingly the 1945 general election was a relatively low-cost affair. It is estimated that central expenditure by the Conservative Party amounted to just £50 000–100 000 while Labour spent a total of £51 000.[15] However, features of the 1945 election deserve notice. First, the election campaign tended – then as now – to focus on the activities of the party leaders. The idea that elections have since become increasingly 'presidential' has – on the whole – been somewhat exaggerated.[16] Second, parties did make some effort to coordinate their campaign and ensure that party members 'sung from the same hymn-sheet'. Herbert Morrison, for example, warned a conference of Labour candidates 'not to make unauthorised promises which would not be honoured by the party', especially in relation to housing policy.[17] Third, although the parties' tactics in 1945 were primarily decided by the politicians themselves, the parties had recently used outside 'experts' to help them with their campaigns. The Conservatives established a relationship with the firm of S. H. Benson in the 1930s, while Herbert Morrison himself had used sympathizers from journalism and advertising to devise his successful campaigns for the London County Council (see Chapter 3). The absence of 'experts' in this particular election gives the false impression that features of the 1959 election were entirely new. They were not. Fourth, although debate was limited, there were some sharp exchanges between the parties. The most famous example is the 'Laski episode' when the then Chairman of the National Executive Committee (NEC) of the Labour Party, Harold Laski, stated that Attlee would be unable to accept responsibility for agreements on the British side which have been conducted by Mr Churchill as Prime Minister.[18] This led to a sharp exchange between the party leaders about the relationship between Labour leaders and Annual Conference throughout the campaign. Thus many of the features we associate with the 'modern' campaign were already present in 1945, albeit to a lesser extent.

1959: the Wilsonian era

While the next three postwar elections remained very similar to that of 1945, the 1959 election was clearly very different from all those that followed in one important sense: the extent to which it was dominated by television. Postwar affluence and technological innovation meant that sets had become affordable by most families in Britain. By 1959, almost three-quarters of the electorate had access to a television. For the very first time viewers could experience the election from the comfort of their own armchairs. Moreover, with the arrival of ITV, viewers now had a choice of channels and the BBC was forced to drop its self-imposed ban on campaign coverage (see Chapter 7). The style of political reporting and analysis was transformed as ITV eschewed the tradition of deference that had been established by Lord Reith at the BBC. In the face of this increased competition, journalists at the BBC followed suit. The print media again offered strong support for their parties. However, newspaper sales had begun to decline and they found themselves largely superseded by television both as sources of information for the voter and as channels of influence for the parties (see Chapter 6). Power and influence within the media shifted decisively from newspapers to television.

Like radio before it, television found itself charged with further nationalizing politics and ensuring the declining importance of the local campaign. Voters in Bromley and Barnsley were exposed to the same information: much of it – in stark contrast to the information provided by newspapers – non-partisan in nature. The various Representation of the People Acts (RPA) also helped to further nationalize the campaign. While prominent party politicians could be interviewed in their capacity as party politicians – rather than as candidates in their constituency – other candidates could not appear on television without the consent of all other candidates.[19] In practice, this meant it was not possible to focus on 'local issues'. Moreover, most journalists were simply more interested in the 'big issues' of national politics and happily focused on these to the exclusion of smaller local issues.

Features of the consumer society – market research and advertising – also intruded into the 1959 election. The parties began to invest heavily in opinion polling in order to find out what groups of 'target' voters wanted of parties. In doing so, they abandoned the assumption that the flow of communications during a campaign was unidirectional. The Conservatives in particular employed the services of Colman, Prentis & Varley (CPV) who identified the party's strengths (their association with prosperity) and weaknesses (their association with privilege).[20] They then produced posters designed to strengthen their association with prosperity ('Life's Better with the Conservatives: Don't Let Labour Ruin It') and weaken their association with privilege by showing photographs of ordinary people ('You're looking at a Conservative'). This campaign was begun long before the election itself in order to have some impact on voters' predispositions.[21] The Nuffield study of that year devoted a full chapter to the 'projection of party images' and noted that – by contrast – 'Labour continued to rely upon policy debates and party organisation to develop popular support'.[22] Social democrats within the party bitterly attacked its 'cloth-cap' image in the wake of their defeat.[23]

The parties responded to the growing importance of television by initiating daily morning conferences in order to ensure that their favoured issues and their interpretations of news dominated the media's agenda.[24] They even began to mimic the style of television in their broadcasts and make use of politicians with television experience such as Tony Benn, Christopher Mayhew and Woodrow Wyatt.[25] Labour broadcast its Party Election Broadcasts (PEBs) from their very own 'Television and Radio Operations Room' and some astute politicians began tailoring their speeches to the requirements of television, littering them with 'sound bites' that would appeal to both news editors and voters alike.[26] The presence of television also helped to increase the speed of politics. This worked to the advantage of those astute politicians, such as Harold Macmillan and Harold Wilson, who could think on their feet and provide journalists with exactly what they needed: short, memorable comments that could be slotted into the news bulletins. Some politicians even had the foresight to visit and learn from American campaigns, where consumerism was most advanced. Political communications therefore became associated with an 'instinctive, self-reliant' or 'seat of their pants' style of campaigning exemplified by Wilson.[27]

The growing dominance of television and the rise of the morning conferences were both factors that contributed to greater debate between the parties – at least as mediated by the journalists, who increasingly demanded that party spokespersons respond to their opponents' charges *before* presenting their own case. In 1959, this allowed sharp exchanges to take place in a couple of days between Macmillan and Gaitskell over Labour's tax policies.[28] For example, on 28 September the Labour leader, Hugh Gaitskell, pledged that Labour would not raise income tax despite its promises to raise pensions by ten shillings a week.[29] On 29 September the Conservative leader, Harold Macmillan, was able to suggest that Labour had plans to raise other types of tax.[30] When, on 1 October, Harold Wilson promised to remove purchase tax from essential goods, the Conservatives and their press allies alleged that Labour were trying to buy their way into office. Parties no longer manoeuvred on a battlefield of their own devising; they had well-defined targets in the shape of their opponents. The authors of the 1959 Nuffield study went so far as to suggest that Labour's tax pledges represented the 'turning point' of the campaign: the moment when the tide turned against Labour.[31]

The media also made increasing use of public opinion polls to monitor the 'horse race'. Four of the nine daily papers published polls on a weekly basis. Moreover, since each was published on a different day of the week it was possible to take the electorate's temperature on an almost daily basis.[32] The parties also began commissioning private opinion polls on a larger scale. This, together with greater use of newspaper advertising, resulted in a major increase in campaign expenditure. Central expenditure by the Conservative Party amounted to £631 000, while Labour spent a total of £239 000.[33] Moreover, these figures concealed some of the real cost of the election campaign, since the Conservatives may have spent some £468 000 and Labour some £103 000 on pre-election advertising.[34] Political communications had taken a large step toward the 'modern' campaign and modernity was expensive.

1997: the Mandelsonian era

Political communications continued to evolve over the next thirty years. Progress was often erratic, especially in the case of the Labour Party, which – between 1979 and 1983 – all but abandoned 'modern' campaign methods, partly as a reaction to the perceived failures of the Wilson and Callaghan governments.[35] However, overall, both parties and broadcasters adopted an increasingly 'professional' approach to election campaigning.

Indeed, were we writing this book a few years ago, we may well have settled on either 1979 or 1992 as representing 'marker' elections akin to 1959 in their importance for political communications. However, it seems generally agreed that this honour is more appropriately reserved for the 1997 election. The authors of the Nuffield study, for example, argue that:

> It was not just that, for the first time in [eighteen] years, it led to a change in government. It was also because the way in which it was conducted marked a change in style on a scale unmatched in any post-war election except one. In 1959, the advent of intensive television coverage, of large-scale advertising, of press conferences, and of private polls transformed the nature of campaigning. In 1997, the Labour Party brought an altogether new pitch, the sophisticated presentation of its messages, nationally and locally.[36]

While many of Labour's specific innovations were not startlingly novel in themselves, their strategic integration was truly impressive. 'New Labour' seemed to adapt simultaneously to meet the demands of the electorate, intensified party competition and the new media environment. The whole process was overseen by Tony Blair, Gordon Brown and John Prescott, with the advice and support of advisers such as Alistair Campbell and Peter Mandelson, the grandson of Herbert Morrison.

Before considering the effect of political communications on New Labour's victory, it is worth remembering that Labour's victory also resulted from substantive political change. The creation of 'New Labour' began with the rewriting of the statement of its aims and values in Clause Four of the party's constitution. The party abandoned its historic commitment to public ownership in an effort 'modernize' itself and appeal to 'middle England'. While the practical effect of this change was minimal (Labour had effectively abandoned the commitment to public ownership as a result of Kinnock's Policy Review),[37] its symbolic effect was substantial. It said to the world: 'We have changed. We are new. We are no longer the party we were. You can put your trust in us again.'[38] The party tried to shed its 'tax and spend' image by pledging not to increase the standard or top rates of income tax. At the same time, it stressed its commitment to reforming its own internal procedures, reducing the power of the trade unions and empowering individual members.[39] Many commentators sensed that this had more to do with 'image' than substance. This cynical view of New Labour was reinforced by New Labour's use of extensive polling and focus groups in the run-up to the election itself in order to craft policy that appealed to voters.[40] The party had appeared to abandon any commitment to the notion of politics as a 'moral crusade'. Even the notoriously rowdy Annual Conference was transformed into a 'love in' by organizational reforms which focused on presenting a united image.[41] Many Labour MPs were left to wonder whether the 'ruthless' pursuit of power meant that Labour was becoming like the Democrats in the US: a party bereft of an ideology and electoral base.[42]

The technology of political communications was undoubtedly taken to new levels of sophistication in the 1997 election. The BBC invested millions of pounds in a new political unit (like Labour's, based in the thoroughly modern Millbank tower) in order to monitor the campaign and provide instant expert advice on issues as diverse as election law, economics, social policy and defence.[43] Just about every aspect of Labour's campaign was planned with television in mind. The major parties monitored the claims of their opponents and issued press releases attacking them and giving journalists ideas for stories. Both Labour and the Conservatives invested in rapid rebuttal systems to enable them to respond to allegations from either their opponents or the media (see Chapter 3). However, only Labour's machine – Excalibur – actually worked. The Conservatives invested some £5 million in a machine that did not work because the software did not interface properly.[44] Yet far more impressive than the technology was the political desire of the Labour Party to unite and win the election. Its spokespersons were provided with pagers and mobile phones to keep them in touch with campaign headquarters in order to ensure that the party spoke with one voice. Consequently, power within political parties seems to have been redistributed towards the leaders and their media advisers (see Chapter 3). However, as the Conservative campaign proved, changes in technology do not always facilitate coordination. Some 'Euro-sceptic' Tories evaded efforts at coordination by the simple expedient of switching their pagers off![45]

Both sides prepared for the election long in advance, compiling 'war books' stuffed full of material that could be used to attack their opponents. They also employed advisers or 'spin doctors' in order to control the agenda and influence the presentation of news on television. If some commentators are to be believed, Labour's masters of the 'black arts' of spin are to be given considerable credit for the way in which they set the agenda and bullied their way to the front page or to the news headlines.[46] Journalists responded by adopting increasingly cynical attitudes to the claims of the various parties. News reports often gave prominence to the activities of the spin doctors and, in an effort to separate fact from fiction for viewers, journalists gave their own assessments on the validity of the various allegations. Both journalists and parties began to blame each other for the apparent growing disillusion of the electorate with politics. The former claimed that politicians were inveterate simplifiers who hid behind sound bites and ducked difficult questions. The latter claimed that journalists asked impossible questions, adopted sneering attitudes toward politics and sought to advance their own reputations and careers. It appears that the increased velocity of politics has increased friction but provided little light. Yet as we shall see in Chapters 9 and 10, there is little evidence that political communications during the campaign had much effect on the people who mattered most: the voters themselves.

In contrast to previous elections, the national press offered substantial support for Labour. Six out of nine daily titles backed New Labour (see Chapter 6). The conversion of the *Sun* was widely regarded to be of particular significance.[47] Newspapers appeared to be following – rather than leading – their readers. Some took this apparent 'dealignment' as a further indication that Britain had entered the era of the post-modern campaign.[48] However, it is far from clear whether this represents a permanent set of affairs in which papers follow their 'media logic' or a temporary blip. The *Sun* in particular has often been bitterly critical of the New Labour government and especially of its European policy.

Much about the 1997 general election appeared new and innovative, but a great deal was old and traditional. In some respects there was a distinctly 'retro' feel to some of the innovations. Television tried to focus on 'local issues' or examine national issues from a local perspective.[49] There were fewer polls in the national press – though this was partly as a response to the 'Waterloo of the Polls' in 1992.[50] The election of 1997 saw the strange rebirth of the local campaign – especially among Labour and the Liberal Democrats – though this was complicated by strategic coordination from the centre (see Chapter 5). Moreover, as in 1992, John Major made great play of his attempts to communicate directly with the people by the use of his 'soap box' and his old-fashioned 'straight to camera' broadcast on Europe.

The 1997 campaign was enormously expensive to the major parties. Evidence presented to the Neill Committee suggested that the Labour Party spent some £14.9 million on their campaign in 1997, compared with £8.4 million in 1992, while the Conservatives spent £28.3 million in 1997 compared with £11.2 million in 1992.[51] The Neill Committee has since recommended capping expenditure at some £20 million: a policy that might find a lot of support in the cash-strapped parties.[52]

It is difficult to say whether 1997 does indeed represent a marker election akin to 1959. In truth, we will only know with the advantage of hindsight. However, it is clear that the belief that New Labour's communications strategy was – at least in part – responsible for their victory in 1997 will continue to shape the development of political communications. The Conservative Party has moved rapidly to improve their communications strategy. The apparent success of Labour's targeting strategy has encouraged the Conservative Party Central Office (CCO) to obtain new powers to coordinate their campaigns and led to some erosion of the local autonomy of Conservative Associations.[53] Journalists have adopted an increasingly cynical attitude to Labour in office. One thing is certain: political communications have been transformed over the last fifty years or so and political communications will continue to evolve in the next fifty years. Moreover, among those who follow such things, it is generally assumed that the best guide to the future is the United States. In the next section we will therefore briefly examine the American system and consider whether it does offer a glimpse into the future of British political communications.

The American example

British political communications have always appeared to be heavily influenced by American experiences. This is no surprise. Britain often looks to the United States for leads in popular culture, fashion, entertainment, design and sport. George Gallup introduced the opinion poll to Britain in the 1930s. British politicians went West to study campaigning methods in the early 1950s. Heath and his advisers sought to learn from Nixon's campaign in 1968. Mrs Thatcher's advisers admired the Reagan campaigns in 1980 and 1984.[54] It was therefore entirely unsurprising that Blair and his advisers followed the progress of Clinton and the 'New Democrats' with equal interest.

Experience appears to suggest that as goes the United States so goes the United Kingdom. Our vision of American politics comprises an electorate that is dealigned and susceptible to influence, parties that are weak and non-ideological, candidates that are chosen for their film-star good looks rather than their political skills, a media that broadcasts 24-hour news and is eager for incident and 'professional advisers' who use 'negative' or 'attack' advertisements to attack their opponents. Candidates are marketed in just the same way as a motor car. The market is carefully segmented. Polling is used to find out what voters want. The candidate adopts his or her position on the basis of this information and uses the media or direct mail to communicate that position.[55]

Before we go much further, it must be noted that this is very much a stereotyped view of American politics. Research suggests, among other things, that party plays a strong role in structuring vote, that 'going negative' does not necessarily lead to victory, nor does spending – in itself – guarantee electoral success.[56] Moreover, Britain is different for several reasons. First, broadcasting is much more heavily regulated than in the United States. British television is required to produce fair and balanced coverage of all parties and cannot engage in partisan editorializing.[57] Research suggests that television meets these objectives.[58] Second, British parties are not allowed to buy airtime to broadcast short advertisements. Instead, they are allocated free airtime in the form of Party Political Broadcasts (PPBs) and Party Election Broadcasts (PEBs) whose minimum length is five minutes. This minimum length makes it difficult to rely on purely emotional appeals of the sort used in the United States.[59] Instead some sort of sustained argument is required and – since the broadcast is preceded by statements such as, 'There now follows a broadcast by the Conservative Party' – people can switch off. Third, the broadcast media continues to have a strong public service ethos. Journalists take very seriously the idea that they should entertain, *educate* and *inform*. Recent elections have witnessed brave attempts to examine the substantive issues and explain them in a way that ordinary voters can understand.[60] Fourth, British campaigns tend – on the whole – to be far shorter than those in the United States. To be sure, the 1997 campaign lasted a full 45 days, but this is far shorter than most American campaigns. We are still far from the 'permanent campaign'. Fifth, parties are undoubtedly far stronger in Britain. Until the creation of the Mayor of London, there were no directly elected posts in British politics and so politicians rely on party endorsements for their career. The parties tend to be programmatic and select their candidates internally. There is therefore less scope for candidates to adopt their own positions and party discipline remains strong. Moreover, local campaign expenditure is capped, and it is therefore the national organization that spends most campaign resources. When Martin Bell was elected as the MP for Tatton in 1997, he was the first independent MP to be elected to the House of Commons since 1974, when Dick Taverne won the Lincoln by-election and he had the advantage of being a sitting MP.[61] Finally, it must be noted that some of the influence goes the other way: East to West. Philip Gould worked on both the Labour campaigns in 1992 and 1997 and the Democrats' campaign in 1992.[62] Moreover, Peter Mandelson himself never visited the Clinton 'War Room', and claimed that 'They learnt more from us than we did from them'.[63]

The British system of campaigns and communications is continuously evolving and it is important to document these changes. In a recent development, political campaigning has moved into cyberspace, with most political parties creating a website.[64] In 1999, 20 per cent of the British public had access to the Internet: a figure that appears about to expand rapidly in the future. All the major parties have used the Internet to gather the views of voters (or those that surf the net and read political websites). It may well be that some changes, such as increased competition in the media and the creation of directly elected mayors will reduce differences between Britain and the United States. Yet, at the moment, these differences are large enough to make any simple projection from America to Britain at best problematic and – at worst – wholly inappropriate. Moreover, decisions such as the Neill Committee's recommendation to limit campaign expenditure and the retention of the PPB and PEB systems are likely to insulate Britain from the dangers of 'Americanization'. Looking at the example of the United States therefore provides clues as to possible developments, but does not provide a blueprint for the future of British political communications.

Outline of the book

Given our interest in general elections voters are at the centre of our concerns. Chapter 2 therefore offers a synthesis of a massive range of voting behaviour studies and builds a model of voting behaviour that campaigners might find useful. It also surveys the literature on electoral change and concludes that – contrary to a great deal of literature in the 1970s and 1980s – there is little evidence that the electorate has been fundamentally transformed.

Chapters 3, 4 and 5 examine how parties have changed since 1945. Chapter 3 adopts a historical approach similar to the one outlined in this introduction and then examines the effect of this on the distribution of power within the party. Chapter 4 provides much more detail on the impact of 'campaign professionals' and highlights several differences between Britain and the United States. It suggests that their rise has been by no means as remorseless or inevitable. Moreover, rather than directing the campaign itself, professionals are increasingly called upon to implement strategies *already* decided by senior politicians. Chapter 5 concludes our examination of the parties by examining changing perceptions of the effectiveness of 'local campaigning' and provides considerable evidence as to their continued relevance. Chapters 6 and 7 examine changes within the media. Chapter 6 documents the declining influence of the press, variations in their political allegiances and speculates whether the 1997 general election really represents a 'dealignment' of the press. Chapter 7 examines the rise of television from its infancy in the 1950s to its growing maturity at the start of the millennium. It demonstrates how the forces of competition, regulation and journalistic culture transformed the broadcasting system and examines how the system may continue to evolve.

Chapters 8, 9 and 10 examine complex issues about the relationship between political communications and democracy. Chapter 8 examines the use of political communications in referendums, taking the recent examples of the 1975 referendum on British membership of the EEC and the recent referendum on a Welsh assembly. Chapter 9 examines how both politicians and political scientists have tried to assess the impact of political communications on voters. Finally, Chapter 10 examines the impact of media exposure on voters' engagement with politics and finds that – contrary to theories of 'videomalaise' – greater exposure to the media is positively associated with greater knowledge and participation.

2
Changing Voters or Changing Models of Voting?

John Bartle

Introduction

Commentators have frequently suggested that the political communications system has been transformed, at least in part, because of changes among its citizenry.[1] These commentators contrast the apparent stability of voting behaviour in the 1940s and 1950s with the 'volatility' of the modern electorate.[2] They suggest that voters have become less constrained by their social characteristics and less loyal to the parties than in the past. They suggest that voters have become more knowledgeable, more sophisticated and better able to choose between the parties on the basis of those issues discussed during the campaign.[3] This rise of 'issue voting' has forced the parties to pay much greater attention to the conduct of campaigns and the quality of their communications.

Before I examine these propositions in detail, it is useful to examine the history of research into voting behaviour in Britain. I begin by presenting the 'aligned voter' model that is associated with the work of Butler and Stokes. This emphasizes the importance of group identities to the study of voting behaviour. It suggests voters often seek to express their identity as group members through their voting. It also suggests a particular role for political communications. I will then examine a series of 'issue-voting models' associated with rational choice approaches to voting behaviour. These models suggest that voters are largely goal-oriented and that different forms of communication are required to motivate voters. I will then assess the contention that groups in general – and class and parties in particular – have become less important to voters. Finally, I will assess whether voters have become more knowledgeable, more volatile and better able to decide how to vote on the issues raised by the parties during the campaign.

The aligned voter model

The remoteness of politics

The most influential book ever written on British voting behaviour is David Butler and Donald Stokes's *Political Change in Britain*. One of its most striking findings about the British electorate in the 1960s was just how remote the world of politics was for the average citizen. While most voters could name the party leaders, knowledge of secondary party leaders was at best sketchy and at worst non-existent.[4] Sizeable portions of the electorate could not match policies to the correct parties or attach any meaning to the basic ideological terms such as 'Left' and 'Right'.[5] More disturbingly, few voters appeared to hold meaningful opinions themselves, since their responses to related issues did not correlate highly with each other. Indeed, even their responses to the same item appeared to fluctuate randomly over time.[6] Butler and Stokes therefore concluded that voters' opinions were not constrained by any discernible structuring principle and that few were capable of deciding how to vote based on the issues emphasized during the campaign. Much of the detail of politics simply flew over the heads of voters.

The continuity of political preferences

Despite this unflattering portrait of the electorate, Butler and Stokes found considerable evidence of continuity of political preferences. Indeed, many voters appeared to have supported the same party at just about every election they could remember. While the degree of continuity may have been overstated as a result of warped recollections of earlier behaviour, Butler and Stokes had little doubt that 'millions of British electors remain anchored to one of the parties for very long periods of time'.[7] Their general findings are confirmed in Table 2.1, which displays the turnover of the vote at two pairs of elections (1987–92 and 1992–97) using BEPS panel survey data. Most voters lie on the main diagonal running from left to right, indicating considerable continuity of behaviour. In fact 65 per cent of people acted in exactly the same way in 1992 as they did five years previously: either voting for the same party or abstaining on both occasions. Even in the landslide election of 1997, some 61 per cent acted in the same way as five years previously. If non-voters in either election are ignored this rises to 70 per cent. Moreover, in the 'long campaign', in the year running up to the 1997 election, fully 82 per cent (again excluding non-voters) supported the same party. Evidence from BEPS (1992–97) suggests that an astonishing 57 per cent of those who gave

Table 2.1   The turnover of the vote 1987–92 and 1992–97

Vote in 1987	Vote in 1992					
	Did not vote	Con	Lab	Lib	Other	Total
Did not vote	3.5	3.0	2.5	1.0	0.2	10.2
Con	2.2	30.0	2.1	3.3	0.4	38.0
Lab	2.2	1.0	21.5	2.1	0.8	27.6
Lib Dem	1.2	3.6	5.8	11.6	0.6	22.8
Other	0.2	0.1	0.1	0.2	0.8	1.5
Total	9.3	37.7	32.0	18.2	2.9	

Vote in 1992	Vote in 1997					
	Did not vote	Con	Lab	Lib	Other	Total
Did not vote	3.7	1.5	2.2	0.9	0.3	8.6
Con	4.4	22.9	5.2	4.7	0.4	37.6
Lab	2.8	0.5	26.1	1.3	0.6	31.3
Lib Dem	1.1	0.9	5.2	8.7	0.6	16.5
Other	0.7	–	2.2	0.3	2.9	6.1
Total	12.8	25.7	40.9	15.9	4.5	

Note: The figures in the table do not add up to 100 per cent, since some voters moved between 'other' parties.

Source: British Election Panel Studies, 1987–92 and 1992–97.

a vote intention in each of five successive interviews indicated support for the same party.

Additional evidence as to the continuity of political preferences comes from questions about when voters decided how to vote.[8] In election after election around 60 per cent of respondents indicate that they had decided long before the campaign itself got under way, compared with around 25 per cent 'during the campaign'. This, together with the panel study evidence, suggests that most voters have decided how to vote long before a PEB is broadcast, a leaflet is printed or a campaign speech is made.

The social alignment

Butler and Stokes sought to account for this well-documented stability of political preferences by reference to those enduring features of voters' everyday lives: their social class, religious affiliations, education, their neighbourhood and housing tenure.[9] They argued that membership of such groups established voters' identities and shaped perceptions of their interests. This is reflected in the vote model in Figure 2.1. Many groups had 'norms' of behaviour to which loyal members were expected to conform,

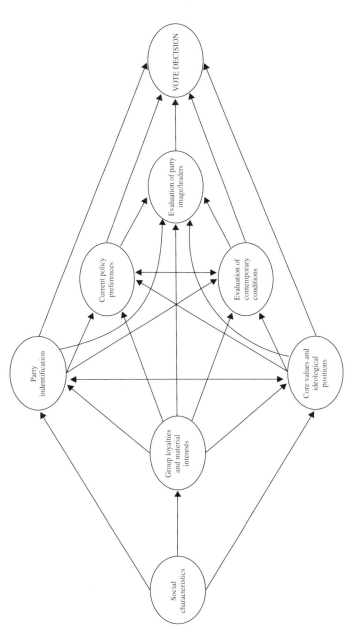

Figure 2.1 A vote model.

and these often included norms of partisanship. Since people spent a great deal of time in these groups, they obtained many of their ideas and feelings about politics from them. The stronger the sense of identification with the group and the greater the partisan consistency of voters' social characteristics, the more likely the voter was to vote in accordance with those norms.[10] A middle-class homeowner who was not a member of a trade union was highly likely to vote Conservative, since all these groups were aligned with that party. However, those voters who had inconsistent partisan characteristics were subject to cross-pressures and more likely to be swayed by campaign issues.

Unsurprisingly a great deal of early research into voting behaviour went into documenting the 'working-class', 'Catholic' or 'rural' vote. Indeed, one of the very earliest studies of voting behaviour suggested that 'a person thinks, politically, as he is socially. Social characteristics *determine* political preference'.[11] Butler and Stokes themselves had little doubt that social class was the pre-eminent structural cause of voting behaviour.[12] Quite simply, two-thirds of the working class voted Labour and three-quarters of the middle class voted Conservative. Peter Pulzer's famous statement that 'class is the basis of party politics, all else is embellishment and detail', although intentionally exaggerated, summed up the situation well.[13] Together with the Scandinavian countries, Britain seemed to be the class-based society par excellence.

The partisan alignment

The presence of social alignments offers one plausible explanation of the continuity of political preferences. In addition, Butler and Stokes suggested that many voters developed an enduring sense of identification with or loyalty to a political party. This 'partisan self-image' or 'party identification' was held to be largely the product of childhood socialization.[14] Thereafter, party identification was altered by idiosyncratic changes in life circumstances such as a marriage, or slowly as a result of cumulative political experiences.[15] It could therefore be looked upon as 'exogenous' and therefore as a cause of *both* short-term political attitudes *and* vote. This is illustrated in Figure 2.1 where party identification is shown to have important indirect effects on those variables located between it and the final vote decision, such as policy preferences and evaluations of the party leaders, which also influence vote. However, it may also have a direct effect on the vote that is not mediated by any other variable (indicated by the arrow leading straight from party identification to vote). This is akin to a simple statement of group identity: 'I vote Labour, because *I am* Labour.'

Butler and Stokes suggested that party identifiers tended to seek out information that supported their party. They often selected newspapers because of their partisan endorsements. Moreover, party identification was held to raise a perceptual screen, so that if identifiers did receive information at odds with their partisanship, they tended to filter it out. Party identification therefore acted to conserve prior predispositions and immunize people from political communications.

Butler and Stokes found that the strength of the psychological attachment to party varied across individuals. Some thought of themselves as 'very strong' identifiers, while others felt only 'fairly strong' or 'not very strong' and some – a tiny proportion of the whole – had no allegiances at all. The stronger the attachment to the party, the more likely the individual was to behave in partisan ways: to vote for 'their' party, to approve of its leaders and so on. The weakening of identifications in the early 1970s therefore created an expectation that voters would increasingly form opinions independently of their party and therefore become more volatile.

Political communications in the aligned voter model

It is important to note that Butler and Stokes always suggested that voters' policy preferences, evaluations of the economy and preferences relating to the party leader had some independent influence on voting decisions. Indeed, a great deal of their book is taken up with the analysis of the impact of issues. However, like the authors of *The American Voter* before them, they assumed that the influence of party identification was so pervasive that only rarely would voters form opinions at variance with their party identification.[16] Moreover, if their opinions and party identification were at odds with each other, it was assumed that the operation of group norms would mean that they would stick with their party. Identifiers were therefore very unlikely to change their minds during the short term of an election campaign, since they were 'immunized' to communications. The best that any party could do was to target the small group of 'floating voters' (around 10 per cent of the electorate) that had no identification at all.

In the aligned voter model, political communications are of great importance in the long run. They primarily operate at the interpersonal level as a result of repeated interaction between group members, rather than between party and voter.[17] Such communications are important. It has been calculated, for example, that over four million people actively sought to persuade others to vote Labour in the 1997 election.[18] Parties have even tried to encourage such forms of personal influence. In 1959 the Conservatives produced a 'monthly newsletter about government activities [which] was sent to a select list of 45 000 people in marginal seats; the recipients included doctors, lawyers, clergymen, teachers, publicans, and barbers, all of them likely to talk to large numbers of people'.[19] Similarly, between 1994 and 1997, Labour sought to secure endorsements from business in order to reinforce its reputation for economic competence.[20]

Parties have used their knowledge about the relationship between social characteristics and vote to 'target' groups of voters in the past. The traditional 'canvass' has allowed them to identify their 'core voters', who can generally be relied upon for their support. For many voters the 'vote decision' is whether to vote for 'their' party once again, or not to vote at all. Party workers can provide hesitant voters with arguments to validate and reinforce a decision – made a long time ago – to support that party. They can remind voters of enduring differences between the parties and the consequences of 'letting the others back in'. In the aligned voter model therefore, communications work with the grain of voters' predispositions. Little time is wasted trying to convert partisans of a different political stripe (see Chapter 5).

The rise of issue-voting models

Butler and Stokes's approach to voting behaviour was profoundly influential. Its emphasis on the importance of accumulated political experiences and the conserving effects of party identification seemed to suggest that short-term political issues had relatively little impact on election outcomes. In an electorate characterized by the social and partisan alignments surprise election outcomes were to be unexpected. Yet, the next three elections proved to be surprisingly dramatic. Harold Wilson's Labour government was defeated in 1970, despite having had a healthy lead in the polls at the start of the campaign. Edward Heath's Conservatives were thrown out of office a mere four years later in February 1974 in an election that witnessed a dramatic surge in support for both the Liberals and the two Nationalist parties. Labour was returned to office with a tiny majority in the subsequent October 1974 election. Voters appeared more sensitive to politics than was implied in *Political Change in Britain*. Not surprisingly therefore analysts began to ask whether Butler and Stokes did really 'explain political change in Britain'.[21]

Confidence in the old model dented, analysts turned their attention to more fashionable rational choice models. These assumed that voters are instrumental and deliberative individuals. They do not vote to express their identity, but to influence outcomes: to improve the standard of living of their household, class or society as a whole. Voters choose: thus, vote decisions are best explained in terms of the pursuit of political preferences.[22] Rational choice models also assume that voters are rational in the sense that they 'do not ignore the information they have, do not fabricate information they do not have, and do not choose what they do not want'.[23]

Although the 'aligned voter' and 'issue-voting' models are based on very different assumptions about the world, they share a great deal in common. First, both approaches accept that voting behaviour is rooted in social groupings. The aligned voter model assumes that groups foster norms, while issue-voting models assume that they influence perceptions of interests (see Figure 2.1). Second, issue-voting models suggest that voters develop a 'standing vote' akin to party identification as a response to imperfect information and uncertainty. A standing vote is assumed to be responsive to *current* political preferences and essentially *changeable*. The two approaches therefore rapidly converge albeit from radically different theoretical perspectives. The choice between the two therefore largely depends upon whether one feels comfortable with social-psychological or rational choice notions.[24] In the following sections, we will examine the sorts of preferences that are considered important by both approaches.

Core beliefs and values

In classic democratic theory elections represent a choice between alternative futures. Voters are assumed to support the party whose policies best match their preferences, thus enabling victorious parties to claim a 'mandate'. This simple approach, however, is unrealistic for several reasons. First, voters simply do not have opinions at the level of specificity required of them by classic policy-voting models. Second, they do not have any incentive to learn the detail of party manifestos. Parties therefore help to reduce the costs of acquiring and processing information by producing policy packages that enable voters to judge parties according to their conceptions of the 'good society', such as their general attitudes toward economic and social equality or morality.[25] This is incorporated in Figure 2.1, which suggests that voters judge parties, at least in part, according to their broad agreement with the parties' core beliefs or enduring principles. This fits in well with recent research, which demonstrates that – although opinions on specific issues are often 'wobbly' – positions on issues of enduring conflict are far more stable.[26] The relationship between values and party identification is not well understood at the moment, so the causal arrows run both ways in Figure 2.1.

Policy preferences

There are good theoretical reasons for suggesting that voters rarely cast their vote on the basis of the detailed policies contained in the party manifestos. Voters rarely read these documents and although the contents of the manifestos are discussed at length in the media voters often appear unaware of their contents. However, where voters are directly affected by the policy, or have access to relevant information that enables them to assess its effect on their welfare, they may well be strongly influenced by those preferences. Teachers and parents with children of school age, for example, have a real incentive to keep themselves informed about education policy. Together, they constitute an 'issue public' who are particularly sensitive to educational issues.

Evaluations of performance

Voters also judge parties by their ability to achieve consensual objectives.[27] These include corruption-free government and low levels of crime. However, in recent years there has been a tendency for research to focus on economic objectives such as low inflation, low unemployment and rising standards of living.[28] In general, governments are rewarded for generating 'good times' and punished for generating 'bad times'; that is, their performance is evaluated *retrospectively*. However, voters also evaluate both parties in terms of their *future* competence. In the 1992 election, for example, the Conservatives were rated as having performed poorly in the period 1987–92. However, they won the election, at least in part, because voters thought that the Conservatives would be more competent than the Labour alternative: a case of 'better the devil you know'.[29] Voters are therefore both retrospective and prospective in their orientation.

Although the literature on voting behaviour displays a slight tendency to assume that voters are selfish and look to the standard of living of their household, there is a great deal of evidence that voters judge the performance of the parties in terms of the impact on society in general.[30] Research has also suggested that voters judge governments by their ability to manage the public services.[31] However, governments are not punished if they are not held responsible for outcomes. Most voters blamed the 'Thatcher government' for the 1989–92 recession, thus breaking the link between economic conditions and vote choice. The link between economic circumstances and vote is therefore a contingent one, which depends on arguments about culpability.[32]

Party and leadership images

Voters also judge parties according to generalized attitudes or beliefs about the parties that are usually referred to as 'party images'. Some of these images exist in a 'twilight zone between intellect and emotions'[33] and appear to be based on recent impressions. Others appear to be the result of impressions accumulated by voters over a long period of time. The Conservatives, for example, have traditionally enjoyed a reputation as the party of economic competence. This was partly based on the fact that the Conservatives attracted a great deal of support from 'money people' (lawyers, bankers and financiers and so on). However, it was also based on experience. The Conservatives – unlike Labour – had never been associated with devaluation. Similarly, the Conservatives have generally been perceived as more united than Labour. This was the product of a culture that emphasized loyalty to leaders and the need to express disagreements in such a way as to minimize the damage to the party's standing. It was also based on the fact that no section of the Conservative Party had ever broken away to form another party.

Yet, both these images were revised in the light of experience. In the wake of the ERM crisis in October 1992, evaluations of the Conservatives' economic competence plummeted to new depths. They fell well behind Labour in September 1992 and failed to recover in time for the election in 1997.[34] In 1997, voters perceived the Conservatives as divided as a result of continuous disputes about the conduct of European policy.[35] The nightly reports of Parliamentary revolts, the withdrawal of the whip from rebel MPs, the resignation of John Major, the subsequent leadership election in 1995 and the failure of many candidates to endorse the manifesto line on Europe, created the clear impression of a divided party and thus undermined confidence in the party. Those parties considered 'extreme', 'uncaring', 'incapable of strong government', 'irresponsible' or 'sleazy' are also likely to be punished. Party images are therefore difficult to locate within the voting model outlined in Figure 2.1. Although I locate them very near to the vote decision, some of their effect of 'image' may be credited to party identification.

A final factor influencing voters is assessments of the party leader. This form of 'issue-voting' is relatively easy for voters. While politics is a remote experience for voters, most of them know who the party leaders are and get to 'meet' them almost nightly on their television screens.

They naturally form assessments of both their ability to 'do the job' of prime minister and their personality as an individual. It is also suggested that many people simply think of politics in highly personal terms as selecting a national leader or 'president'. Recent research, however, suggests that the impact of leaders may be overstated.[36] Once one knows a voter's party identification, their basic values and their evaluations of the economy, knowledge of their evaluations of the party leader adds very little to our ability to predict individual votes and does not account for anything other than a minuscule portion of the aggregate vote share. Calculations for the 1997 general election, for example, suggest that favourable evaluations of Tony Blair over John Major resulted in Labour winning a total of just six extra parliamentary seats.[37]

Implications of issue-voting models for political communications

The social characteristics of the electorate are 'givens' that political campaigners cannot alter. Equally, the predispositions of the electorate – their party identifications and ideological positions – must be taken as 'givens' for the purposes of the short formal campaign itself. It follows that political campaigners must focus on those short-term factors influencing the vote (policy preferences, evaluations of national conditions and party leaders) in their campaign. These are a function both of voters' predispositions and the information that is available to them (from direct experience, the media or the political parties).[38] The aligned voter model suggests that voters rely on their party for information and that their preferences are largely predictable from party identification. Rational choice models on the other hand assume a higher degree of autonomy on the part of voters. They have access to information from a variety of reliable sources and may therefore form preferences that contradict their party identification. In some cases, voters will remain loyal to their party, but where the issue is of sufficient importance, they may either vote against 'their' party or reconsider their standing decision. This assumed malleability of party identification leads rational-choice theorists to emphasize the importance of short-term issues and political communications.

Issue-voting models imply that parties do not merely mobilize voters, they can persuade or convert them too. Information from representative surveys can therefore be used to formulate policies that appeal to voters. In early 1997, for example, Labour announced that it would not increase either the basic or the top-rate of income tax in response to survey evidence which suggested that people thought that Labour would massively increase taxation. Survey information can also be used to select campaign themes and produce campaign leaflets in order to provide voters with the 'right' sort of information. Parties can also seek to influence the information provided by other reliable third parties to voters by influencing the news agenda and ensuring that attention focuses on issues favourable to their cause. In the last resort they can engage in 'spin doctoring' in order to ensure that the media accept their interpretations of the news.

The transformation of the electorate?

British politics from 1945 to 1970 was often characterized as a stable two-party system. Between them, the Conservative and Labour parties received approximately 90 per cent of the vote at each general election. Given the operation of the 'first-past-the-post' electoral system, this translated into a virtual duopoly of seats at Westminster. The two major parties appeared to take it in turns to govern as the electoral pendulum swung from Left to Right and then back again.

In the 1970s, however, the stable two-party system came under sustained pressure. Between the 1970 and February 1974 general election support for the Liberals rose dramatically from 7 to 18 per cent and both the Scottish and Welsh Nationalists made spectacular advances in those nations. In the 1980s support for the SDP/Liberal Alliance leapt up in the polls and they won several famous by-elections on enormous swings. Not surprisingly, therefore, attention turned away from aligned voter models to issue-voting models. Indeed, some analysts went as far as to suggest that

> British voters have moved to a more sophisticated basis for voting choice. No longer constrained to the same extent by characteristics largely established during childhood, British voters are now more open to rational argument than they were in the past.[39]

In the following section, I will examine whether voters have indeed become less constrained by their social characteristics and more rational in their behaviour. I begin by examining the evidence for class and partisan dealignment and then go on to examine both the causes and consequences of these phenomena. I then examine the evidence that voters have become 'more volatile', more knowledgeable about politics and more 'rational' than they were in the past. Is it simply the case that, while the aligned model was applicable in the past, issue-voting models are of greater relevance today?

Class dealignment

Butler and Stokes had little doubt that social class was the pre-eminent social basis of the vote in the postwar period. In the three elections for which data is available from the BES (1964–70), an average 63 per cent of voters supported their natural class party (middle class Conservatives and working class Labour). To know someone's class therefore enabled analysts to predict their vote with a fair degree of accuracy. Yet, as Butler and Stokes pointed out, this association appeared to be weakening even in the early 1970s.[40] In the three elections from 1974 to 1979, only 55 per cent voted for their natural class party and in the three elections from 1983 to 1992 this fell still further to 50 per cent. By 1997, it was a mere 46 per cent. This 'class dealignment' is held to have freed 'voters from the bonds of class-voting constraints', so that 'voters were becoming much more like consumers who could make an informed choice between (or among) the political products on offer'.[41]

Partisan dealignment

A progressive weakening of partisanship has accompanied the process of class dealignment. Although the proportion of identifiers in the electorate has hardly fallen, they have become distinctly less enthusiastic about their parties. On average, in the three elections from 1964 to 1970, 43 per cent of identifiers identified 'very strongly' with their party. In the three elections from 1974 to 1979 this fell to 26 per cent and for the three elections from 1983 to 1992 to just 17 per cent.[42] By 1997, a mere 16 per cent identified 'very strongly' with a political party. At the same time, the proportion of 'not very strong' identifiers rose from just 19 per cent in 1964 to 42 per cent in 1997.

Since strength of partisanship is positively associated with 'loyal' behaviour and a tendency to support one's own party, this weakening of partisanship gave rise to the expectation that voters would become more volatile in their behaviour – more likely to 'defect' and hesitant when making their decisions. An increasing proportion of the electorate should be 'up for grabs' and potentially moved by the communications they receive. Before we examine whether this is indeed the case, it is useful to examine the causes of class and partisan dealignment.

The causes of class and partisan dealignment

For some analysts at least, class and partisan dealignment is the result of broader economic and social change. The British economy has altered dramatically since 1945. The old 'staple' industries such as coal, steel and shipbuilding have given way to the new 'high-tech' industries of electronics, computing and information technology. In the process British society has itself been transformed. The old, socially cohesive communities built around the colliery or docks, which propagated consistent partisan messages, have all but vanished. Increased geographical mobility has also eroded the influence of community. The '"pure" social groups are being increasingly broken up and their members exposed to "mixed" political influences'.[43] The expansion of higher education has increased social mobility, blurred class divisions and eroded group norms. The expansion of television has reduced the cost of acquiring information, while increased education has increased voters' ability to process it. This has resulted in a 'cognitive mobilization' of voters. They are now said to be more interested in – and knowledgeable about – politics. They are better able to deal with the complexities of politics and more capable of forming their own opinions without the need for cues from the parties and their leaders.[44] There has therefore been a 'dramatic transformation' in the 'political skills and resources of contemporary electorates'.[45]

Others have suggested that class and partisan dealignment are simply the result of the political failures of the parties. In particular, it is suggested that Labour's failures in office (1964–70 and 1974–79) led to widespread disillusionment with the party, while its adoption of 'extreme' policies alienated a great deal of its traditional working-class support. If this analysis is correct it is changes in the nature of party competition, rather than changing voters, that is largely responsible for the transformation of the British system of political communications.

The consequences of dealignment

The class and party alignments that characterized the 1960s were thought to have one major consequence: stability. The twin processes of class and partisan dealignment were therefore expected to weaken the barriers to short-term change. It was expected that voters would become increasingly volatile in their behaviour and that voters would shift the basis of their decision from their long-term loyalties to short-term, campaign-specific, attitudes and evaluations.[46] However, as the following sections demonstrate, the evidence does not suggest that today's voters are so very different from their counterparts in 1945.

Volatility

Put simply, 'volatility' refers to 'changes in party preference within the electorate'.[47] This is measured in two ways: 'net' and 'gross' volatility.

Table 2.2   Net volatility

	1959–64	1964–66	1966–70	1970–74 Feb	1974 Feb–Oct	1974–79	1979–83	1983–87	1987–92	1992–97
Change in party share of vote	5.9	4.3	6.0	13.3	3.1	8.2	11.9	3.2	5.6	12.3
By-election	13.5	1.8	16.8	13.1	0.5	9.5	11.4	14.0	11.0	19.8

Source: Anthony Heath et al., *Understanding Political Change: the British Voter 1964–1987* (Oxford: Pergamon Press, 1991), p. 17; and Geoffrey Norris and Pippa Evans, *Critical Elections: British Parties and Voters in Long-Term Perspective* (London: Sage, 1999), p. 261.

Net volatility refers to changes in the distribution of vote between pairs of elections. Table 2.2 displays two measures: the sum of the changes in each party's share of the vote divided by two (the so-called 'Pedersen Index') and the mean fall in support for the governing party at by-elections (the 'By-election Index'). The former measure suggests that volatility was relatively low in the 1960s, that it rose dramatically in 1974, fell subsequently and then rose again in 1983. Thereafter it falls again before surging in 1997. Net volatility therefore does not appear to rise steadily as social and cognitive mobilization theories of dealignment appear to predict. Specific elections are indeed characterized by greater volatility, but there is no clear trend. The evidence from the By-election Index tells a very similar story. This suggests that volatility is primarily a function of the specific *political* circumstances rather than the product of social change.[48]

'Gross volatility' refers to the 'total amount of vote switching as revealed by large-scale national sample surveys'.[49] Even if there is little net volatility, there may be a great deal of change at the individual level, since some change is self-cancelling in nature. Table 2.3 displays two measures of gross volatility from the BES series. The first row measures the proportion of the electorate that switches parties between elections. This increases from an average of 17 per cent in the 1960s to 24 per cent in the dramatic circumstances of February 1974. It remains slightly higher in 1979 and 1983, but settles down at 19 per cent for the 1987 and 1992 elections. Although it rises to 24 per cent in the 1997 election, it is again difficult to identify any general tendency toward increased volatility. Such differences that exist are in the order of 2–3 per cent. Class and partisan dealignment do not appear to have had quite as dramatic consequences as many analysts believed that they would.

Table 2.3 Trends in gross volatility

	1959–64	1966–70*	1970–74 (Feb)*	1974 (Oct)–79*	1979–83	1983–87*	1987–92*	1992–97*
Switched parties	18	16	24	22	23	19	19	24
Switched (inc. non-voters)	35	34	42	37	40	37	34	37

Note: Pairs of elections marked with an asterisk are based on data derived wholly or partly from panel data.

Source: David Denver, *Elections and Voting Behaviour in Britain* (London: Harvester Wheatsheaf, 1994), p. 75 and author's own calculations.

Further evidence as to the volatility of the electorate comes from questions that seek to establish how committed voters were to their parties. Table 2.4 displays evidence as to when voters made up their minds and whether they seriously thought about voting for another party. Both series suggest that voters became less certain in their vote in February 1974. There is no clear trend thereafter, though both series peak again in 1997. It appears therefore that there is little evidence of a steady growth in uncertainty as we might expect from class and partisan dealignment. Moreover, it has since been pointed out that the apparent increase in 1974 may be simply the result of a change from an 'open' to a 'closed' question which occurred at that time. The evidence as to increased hesitation is therefore far from decisive.[50] It appears likely that volatility is a function of what parties do rather than change among the electorate.

A more knowledgeable electorate?

An impressive body of research has demonstrated that education is strongly related to both political sophistication and political knowledge.[51] The expansion of education that has occurred since 1945 therefore led many to suggest that voters are more knowledgeable about politics and better able to arrive at their own opinions on the issues of the day. Yet theories of 'cognitive mobilization' are difficult to assess since we lack time series data on political knowledge.[52] American studies have demonstrated improvements in survey methods and questionnaire design can give the impression of increased sophistication.[53] The notion that voters have become more knowledgeable and sophisticated though widespread – and highly plausible – has surprisingly little evidence to support it.

Table 2.4   Late deciders and waverers (1964–1997)

	1964–70 (Avg)	1974 Feb	1974 Oct	1979	1983	1987	1992	1997
Decided during campaign	12	23	22	28	22	21	24	27
Thought about voting for other party	23	25	21	31	25	28	26	31

Source: David Denver, *Elections and Voting Behaviour in Britain* (London: Harvester Wheatsheaf, 1994), p. 75 and author's own calculations.

A more rational and sophisticated electorate?

It is often claimed that voters are more rational and sophisticated than ever before: that they are more capable of strategic (or 'tactical') voting and decide their vote on the basis of issues as debated during the campaign. If this were true, then it might also imply that voters are increasingly open to influence from political communications – whether they originate in the parties or in the media. Simply informing voters about the tactical situation in their constituency might persuade them to cast a tactical vote for their second preference party in order to prevent their least preferred party from winning. Similarly, informing voters about a new policy or highlighting defects in an opponent's record might persuade them to change their behaviour. If voters are increasingly rational then political communications increasingly matter.

Unfortunately, it is easier to assert that voters are more 'rational' than to demonstrate it. Survey evidence about tactical voting is limited since the BES only began asking questions about tactical voting in 1983 and this relatively short period does not cover the most dramatic period of 'dealignment' (1970–74).[54] In 1983 and 1987 a mere 6 per cent claimed to be tactical voters. By 1992 this climbed to 8.3 per cent and by 1997 it crept up further to 9.5 per cent. This steady increase in tactical voting is just what we would expect if voters were increasingly sophisticated. However, this increase may simply be the result of changes in the political context – the result of increasingly unpopular government coupled with greater opportunities to vote tactically.[55] It does not *necessarily* demonstrate that voters have become more sophisticated.

One final consequence of dealignment is said to be that short-term forces loom much larger in voters' decisions and that this leads to the increasing importance of political communications. This proposition is enormously difficult to assess since the early BES studies contained a relatively limited number of questions relating to policy preferences, evaluations of national conditions and so on. In making comparisons, therefore, care is required lest we mistake an increase in the number of variables available for analysis with an actual increase in issue voting. Nevertheless, several analysts *have* demonstrated that an increasing portion of the two-party vote is explicable in terms of voters' attitudes and evaluations.[56] What remains at issue, however, is whether this indicates that voters have changed. It may be that, as parties have moved further apart, they have dragged their voters with them in accordance with the 'aligned voter model' and that it is this – rather than growing voter sophistication – which has increased the statistical association between policies and vote.[57] Ultimately, it is impossible to disentangle the effects of social and political change. Both have clearly been at work, but it appears that the former has dominated the latter.

Conclusions

British society has undoubtedly changed since the war. The economy has undergone considerable change. Television has come to dominate political life in a way that would have been inconceivable in 1945. The idea that voters have changed too is very plausible. They are far less likely to be members of a political party. The intensity of their psychological attachments to parties has undoubtedly declined. Voters are, if anything, slightly more volatile and slightly more hesitant in their support. Voters' attitudes do appear to explain slightly more of the variation in vote than before. Yet none of this evidence can be taken as suggesting that the electorate has been 'transformed' from the habitual, group-oriented creatures of the 'aligned voter' model to the deliberative, rational creatures associated with 'issue-voting' models. Voters may have altered their behaviour simply because the nature of the parties had changed. The rise in support for the Liberals in the 1970s stemmed at least in part from the fact that until 1974 the Liberals had not contested every seat. The decline in support for both the major parties in 1974 stemmed in part from perceptions that they had both 'failed' or were 'too extreme'. Gradual social change may have made it easier to desert the parties, but the correct political circumstances were necessary to motivate voters to change.

It is clear that both the major approaches to voting behaviour offer tantalizing clues as to the forces that influence voting behaviour and the role of political communications in determining that behaviour.

However, neither approach has, to date, provided an entirely plausible account of continuity and change. There is still a great deal that remains mysterious. In particular we need to know a great deal about the micro-mechanics of opinion change, the effect of political communications on long-term predispositions and how they interact with political awareness.[58] We still know relatively little about the formation of 'party images', even though their importance has long been recognized. It therefore appears that the political science of voting behaviour still has a long way to go to catch up with the practice of political campaigners.

3
Power as well as Persuasion: Political Communication and Party Development

Dominic Wring

Introduction

In the run-up to and during the 1997 general election political discourse was dominated by references to the supposed power and influence of the so-called 'spin doctors' and 'image makers'. These terms are often, and quite erroneously, used interchangeably. Those charged with 'doctoring' the 'spin' are primarily concerned with managing so-called 'free' media which is the coverage given politicians by print and broadcast journalists. Working in tandem with this group, the 'image makers' are those marketing experts charged with interpreting popular opinion and developing a strategy to promote their particular party, candidate or leader by the use of 'paid' or 'controlled' communications such as advertising.

By contrast with the 1997 campaign, the 1945 general election was largely devoid of talk about the work of the parties' respective media experts. Nonetheless mass communication did play a role and both Conservative and Labour organizations retained the services of professional publicists. Unlike 1997, however, much of the popular engagement with the electoral process in the 1945 campaign came at grassroots level. Reminiscing fifty years after the election that marked the beginning of his parliamentary career, former prime minister Jim Callaghan observed: 'I was not conscious of any interference from Transport House [party headquarters]. We fought our own election. We were isolated.'[1]

Since the war increased mediation of the democratic process combined with leading politicians' desire to capitalize on this development has transformed the nature of political communication. Once marginal, strategists are now responsible for managing the parties' central campaigns and enjoy a powerful role within their respective hierarchies. Much of the discussion about the consequences of mediated politics has rightly addressed the elusive issue as to the efficacy of professional techniques of persuasion. Most debate has concentrated on these methods' relationship to popular opinion.[2] Yet arguably there has also been an important effect at the level of the political elite.

Party leaderships, eager to adapt and adopt new marketing and media techniques as a means of cultivating voters, have increasingly been using the same methods to manage and police the affairs of their own organizations. Modern political communication is thus inherently concerned with intra-party power relations as well as mass persuasion. This is nowhere more apparent than in the preparation and planning for an election. As Richard Rose observed: 'The activities of campaigning are less concerned with the flow of influence from voters to candidates than they are with the flow within the political parties themselves.'[3]

The opening section of this chapter is concerned with what might be termed 'the communication of politics'. It will assess how election campaigning evolved over the course of the twentieth century and show how changes have been made in response to the enfranchisement of a mass electorate and the challenge of a pervasive mass media. Consideration will also be given to 'the politics of communication', that is the impact that developments in campaigning have had on the internal organization of political parties in Britain. Discussion will focus on the ways in which strategic change have tended to result in the further centralization of power within parliamentary leaderships and their agents.

The communication of politics: the transformed campaign

Each Nuffield study is an important social document that enables researchers to understand and assess how various political phenomena have evolved since the war. The books remain central to the understanding of how election campaigning developed during this period. The 1945 general election, the subject of the first study, is perhaps more important as a landmark political event than as a watershed in communications terms.[4] This is because the campaign, held in the aftermath of such a major conflict, was in many ways atypical by twentieth-century standards. Similarly the elections of 1950, 1951 and 1955, called at short notice and fought by relatively poorly resourced parties, provided few opportunities for strategic innovation.[5] Thus there is a need to look beyond 1945 and the immediate postwar era to start analysing how party campaigning has evolved over time. Changes in organization both before and after this period need to be considered. Several commentators have discussed the transformation of party political communication. A growing consensus appears to endorse the view that there are three principal periods of evolution. The introductory chapter of this volume has labelled them the 'Morrisonian', 'Wilsonian' and 'Mandelsonian' eras. Similarly Farrell[6] and Norris[7] have identified and discussed their own three-stage developmental models of campaigning, while Blumler and Kavanagh note the dawning of the 'third age of political communication'.[8] Adapting a framework popular in commercial marketing, Shama highlighted the parallels between electoral and business strategies.[9] By using this approach together with terminology more relevant to political communication, it is possible to distinguish three key evolutionary periods of electioneering. These are the eras of mass propaganda, media campaigning and political marketing.[10] The essence of this model is that it places greatest emphasis on the nature of the interactions between an organization and its audiences. Critically it is this relationship, rather than any particular media or technological developments, which is central to identifying how election campaigning has developed and changed over time.

The era of mass propaganda

In Britain the era of mass propaganda began in earnest following the introduction of universal suffrage in 1918. Prior to that date campaigns had tended to be dominated by what Ostrogorski called a 'trilogy of action' which consisted of the stump meeting, canvassing and leafleting (see Chapter 5).[11] During the general election year of 1910 the Conservatives managed to distribute 50 million items of literature, the Liberals 41 million and the infant Labour organization a respectable 6 million.[12] But a key event was the Representation of the People Act (RPA), implemented at the end of the Great War, which nearly trebled the electorate, guaranteed working-class men the vote and extended the franchise to some women. This landmark legislation, combined with the development of new mass media forms such as radio, meant that, in future, elections would be fought in a context where mass communications could and would play an important role.

The mass propagandist approach, which was prevalent up to the end of the 1950s, can be characterized by the essentially unidirectional flow of information from politician to voter. The party elites promoted their messages to the populace in the straightforward belief that maximum exposure for a message would heighten its appeal. The era of propaganda did, however, witness some important experimentation in terms of political communication. The interwar period, in particular, saw the major parties' first attempts to use radio from 1924 onwards.[13] Conservative leader Stanley Baldwin proved to be a particularly effective and popular broadcaster. The potential of film also excited the Conservatives and, more belatedly, Labour.[14]

Anticipating the arrival of public opinion polling, several party strategists began talking about the 'psychology of the electorate' during the 1920s. In an influential 1922 article, leading intellectual and Labour strategist Sidney Webb mapped out what he termed 'stratified electioneering'.[15] Seeking to operationalize the concept, Webb outlined how parties might profitably promote themselves to target voters distinguishable by their 'colours', that is their social status, partisanship (or lack of it) or whatever. These, he argued, made it possible to identify specific kinds of elector from the overall 'grey' of mass democracy. Leading party official Harold Croft promoted Webb's idea in his popular *Handbook of Party Organisation* and several organizers sought to operationalize the concept.[16]

The absence of formal market research did not prevent politicians from cultivating links with professionals working in the advertising industry. The Conservatives' intention to use an agency in 1923 was postponed until 1929 when the party's Central Office hired the services of the Holford Bottomley company and another leading firm, S. H. Benson.[17] Benson's, soon to gain fame for their legendary Guinness stout advertising, did not do so well in their first election. The agency helped produce posters and other ephemera based on the chosen theme of 'Safety First'. This campaign could not, however, prevent Labour from taking office. Nevertheless the relationship between Benson's and Central Office developed into an enduring one and lasted for the two further general elections held before the outbreak of war.

Labour for its part was far more circumspect about using advertising agencies and a plan to retain one in 1935 was shelved. As that election proved to be one of the most capital-intensive of all time, political considerations rather than cost seem to have militated against the organization's use of professional expertise. Indeed, the party's pre-election 'Victory for Socialism' campaign raised a creditable £8000. Labour did nonetheless continue with its policy of commissioning highly effective and ingenious copy from design artists like Gerald Spenser Pryse and John Armstrong, creator of the famed 'Now Win the Peace' poster in 1945. In 1924 a highly attractive logo, the 'Liberty' badge, was also approved.[18] One senior party figure, Herbert Morrison, did, however, develop contacts in the marketing industries. Through his publicity work as leader of London County Council from 1934 onwards he managed to build up a formidable group of advisers. Several of the professionals took time off from their agency work and became involved in preparations for Morrison's 1937 re-election campaign.[19] Their expertise was used to good effect and Labour won a further term following a campaign which one trade journal even acclaimed as having 'set the standard' for commercial marketers.

The rise of media campaigning

In the couple of decades following the Second World War two particular changes in the media had a profound impact on political communication in Britain (see Chapter 7). The growth of popular television, most notably between the 1955 and 1959 elections, combined with the pioneering, investigative style of the new Independent Television News (ITN) organization forced the parties to think about how they might exploit the opportunities mass visual broadcasting now afforded them. ITN formed part of the independent network.[20] Crucially this new service was commercially funded by advertising revenues. The marketing industry rapidly expanded in size and influence, giving rise to what cultural commentators termed the 'consumer society'. Political parties would not be immune to the new commercial ways of doing things.

In their study of the 1959 Conservative victory, the Nuffield authors acknowledged the electoral importance of the new commercial media environment when they prominently highlighted Lord Woolton's observation that 'the voter is also the consumer' at the head of an opening chapter.[21] Indeed, it was this election which showcased the emergence of what can usefully be termed the 'media campaign'. Unlike the primarily unidirectional (party to voter) propagandist technique, this approach emphasized the need to solicit feedback through the use of public opinion research in order to better refine and redefine political presentation. Greater attention was paid to the promotion of the party image, particularly through the new medium of television. Professional marketing techniques and personnel began to become integral to the functioning of campaign organizations.

Clearly influenced by his co-authoring of the 1959 Nuffield study and contribution to the following instalment, Richard Rose went on to complete *Influencing Voters*, his seminal study into the emergence of media campaigning in Britain.[22] Central to this analysis was a more managerialist conception of electioneering. Thus reference was made to various constituent parts of a campaign such as the competitors, client, environment, rules and strategy. Scholars like Rose and former Conservative advertising strategist David Hennessy (ennobled as Lord Windlesham) joined David Butler and his fellow Nuffield authors in helping to foster the view that party political communication was a potentially rich and important arena for study and analysis.[23]

The Conservatives' reinvention of themselves as a campaign organization following their landslide defeat in 1945 was painstaking and incremental. By 1948 the Conservative Party Central Office (CCO) had established a Public Opinion Research Department (PORD) devoted to the study of voter attitudes.[24] With help from the Conservatives' newly appointed advertising agents Colman, Prentis & Varley (CPV), the PORD embarked on an assessment of voter attitudes which culminated in a major report called *The Floating Vote*. The document, a wide-ranging survey-based assessment, identified several groups of potential supporters such as young people, women, Liberal supporters and weak partisans (see Chapter 2). But it was the following decade, in the run-up to the 1959 election, that provided a showcase for the new, professionalized methods of communications. CPV played a central role in the long preamble to the campaign. Research and advertising expertise resulted in them producing the celebrated image of nuclear family emblazoned with the slogan 'Life is Better Under the Conservatives: Don't Let Labour Ruin It'.[25] The electoral performance of the Conservatives reinforced the perception that effective political communication could be a determinant of success.

Though initially sceptical about the value of the new media approach, many Labour strategists were wary of committing resources to an advertising process many viewed with hostility. Nevertheless in the intervening years between the 1959 and 1964 elections, the party reorganized its campaigning structures.[26] A key feature of the changes was Labour's preparedness to engage and use marketing expertise in the guise of public relations, opinion research and advertising consultants. The result of the 1964 election once again helped propagate the view that good political communication was an important element of this narrow victory, particularly in a tightly fought contest.

The development of political marketing

The 1966, 1970 and 1974 general elections all saw slight variations and modifications to political communication. The 1979 campaign, however, was qualitatively different. This change was partly brought about by the ground-breaking strategy of the winning party, the Conservatives.[27] The notion that 1979 constituted a watershed election was reinforced by a number of environmental factors. The most notable of these was the perception that there had been a marked rise in voter volatility as suggested by the apparent decline in support for the two major parties over the course of the previous decade. The notion that electoral behaviour might increasingly come to resemble a commercial market in flux appeared to be becoming more than just an analogy. Voters, it was argued, were becoming less fixed in their allegiances and more prone to shop around for the most attractive party offering.[28]

In tandem with the theoretical re-evaluation of voter behaviour came a marked intensification and interest in the use of marketing methods, a trend reinforced during the early 1980s with the rapid growth of the UK's service industries. Central to this development was the growing importance and influence of modern managerialism in all its various guises, including the marketing communications sector of public relations, advertising and market research. The combined impact of these methods and approaches has resulted in the commodification of all aspects of public life. Politics has not been immune. The mediation of the democratic process has also encouraged this trend because changes in broadcast and print journalism have afforded more reportage of key events and thereby enhanced the promotionalism of civic life and current affairs more generally.

The Conservatives' successful campaigns in 1979 and 1983 are often regarded as having ushered in the new era of marketing-driven politics whereby opinion researchers and professional marketeers became increasingly central to strategic deliberations. The partnership between Margaret Thatcher, the advertising agency owned by the two Saatchi brothers and their business colleague Tim Bell made for a formidable team. Thatcher, a keen student of political opinion polling, was widely regarded as a conviction politician. Yet the private regard she showed her marketing advisers was not publicly afforded her parliamentary colleagues. She maintained an interest in the management of the party's communications and saw it as an element of her own appeal.[29]

Scammell reconciles the apparent disparity between Thatcher the conviction politician and her advocacy of marketing by noting how she allowed research to influence the tenor and boundary of policy. Critically, the Thatcherite project used opinion polling but also took advantage of environmental opportunities.[30] Consequently economic circumstances, rising concern over crime, a supportive print media, a divided opposition and other factors were all exploited in a highly strategic manner.

In contrast to the Conservatives the opposition parties were uneasy with the new communications techniques. The cost of using professional methods combined with ideological criticisms to limit the Liberals' and Labour's adoption of marketing techniques and personnel. Nevertheless in the early 1980s the newly founded Social Democratic Party (SDP) did recoup its investment in direct mail by using it to raise funds and recruit members.[31] This approach soon became a key element of Conservative organization. Before the end of the decade Labour too was displaying its commitment to good communications. Hence during the 1987 general election, the party's conscious use of advertising and public relations showcased its belief in image management.

The 1992 general election marked arguably a major turning point in modern campaign history. This is because both of the major parties contending for office had now embraced political marketing as a strategic approach. Labour, having repositioned itself to the right following its polling-saturated Policy Review, fully integrated advertising, market research and public relations into its headquarters' electoral organization. In the aftermath of the 1983 general election defeat Robin Cook had formed a contact 'breakfast' group of sympathetic professionals to help advise on campaign strategy.[32] In 1986 the new Shadow Communications Agency (SCA) deepened the embryonic links between the party and marketing industries. The SCA functioned by allowing Labour supporters working in the business to offer their skills and expertise on a voluntary and anonymous basis. Their charity combined with a lively campaign and creditable performance in the 1987 general election promoted the importance of political marketing throughout the party.[33] By 1992 marketers such as the SCA coordinator Philip Gould and his colleague Deborah Mattinson enjoyed unprecedented positions of influence within the party hierarchy under leader Neil Kinnock. Despite a fourth defeat and the disbanding of the SCA by Kinnock's successor John Smith, marketing personnel and ideas continued to play an important strategic role thereafter.

The Conservatives once again employed the Saatchi agency in preparing for the 1992 campaign. Marketing personnel worked closely with the CCO bureaucracy. They faced several problems: the difficult economic situation and the potentially uncomfortable issue of Margaret Thatcher's resignation 18 months before in November 1990. The personality of John Major, then regarded as a considerable asset, became central to his party's efforts. Major's interest in sport and his perceived qualities of affability and modesty were a key advertising theme along with his profile as a world statesman.[34] The presidential approach was supported by a public relations gimmick, the use of a soap box to address crowds of voters. A response to the allegedly synthetic self-promotion of his Labour opponent, several journalists saw it as an attempt by Major to play down the importance of so-called 'image makers'.[35] Yet arguably image management was precisely what the prime minister was engaged in. The key marginal seats of Bolton and Luton which Major visited in his soap box appearances suggested careful preparations had been made for what were opportunities to manufacture good television pictures rather than to speak directly to voters. The Conservative leader's efforts thus resonated with a mediated political tradition of the 'people's champion' stretching from the Hollywood film *Mr Smith Goes to Washington* through to Boris Yeltsin's famous public denunciation of the 1991 Soviet coup from the top of a tank.

The public goodwill towards the Conservatives evaporated not long into the 1992 parliament. In September that year the government was forced to withdraw the United Kingdom from membership of the European Exchange Rate Mechanism (ERM). The ERM crisis seriously undermined voter confidence in John Major and his party. It never returned. Following John Smith's sudden death in 1994 a marketing-conscious Labour opposition elected Tony Blair to the leadership. Blair had been the candidate most favoured by polls of the electorate. The youthful leader subsequently rewrote his party's Clause Four mission statement and rebranded the party 'New' Labour. Blair kept up the already remorseless pressure on a beleaguered and unpopular government. SCA veterans Philip Gould and Chris Powell together with the latter's BMP DDB Needham agency coordinated the party's marketing efforts. Along with the rest of the bureaucracy, the campaign team relocated to Labour's new Westminster-based headquarters housed within the Millbank building. There strategists coordinated polling and focus group research and discussed tactics.[36] Those in charge were aided by a new rapid rebuttal service, the so-called Excalibur database, donated to the party by Philip Jeffrey, a wealthy supporter. The efforts of Millbank, together with a series of self-inflicted Conservative wounds, combined to deliver Labour a landslide victory.

The politics of communication: the transformed organization

The increased professionalization of political communications has been motivated by party strategists' desire to best promote their case to a mass electorate. The transformation of campaigning may have had some effect on voters but what is more readily demonstrable is the impact these changes have had on the organizations themselves. With the 'marketization' of electioneering over the course of the twentieth century there have been important changes in the internal structures of the party organization.

Conservatives: from gentlemen to players

In 1910 Sir Malcolm Fraser became the first Conservative official to hold a publicity brief. The following year saw the establishment of a party Press Bureau.[37] Enthusiastic support from most of the major privately owned national newspapers made the job straightforward. Fraser's role was to keep sympathetic journalists supplied with useful information, not least about the plans and activities of the Labour and Liberal opposition. The links, even collusion, between CCO and the Fleet Street print media were the subject of some controversy during the 1924 general election when the party was ejected from office. This followed the publication of the so-called 'Zinoviev Letter' in the right-wing *Daily Mail* just before polling day.[38] The paper's story, which alleged the Soviet Union strongly supported Labour's re-election, provoked outrage from a party fearful of guilt by association. Subsequent revelations suggested the letter was a forgery concocted by a conspiracy involving Conservative officials, selected journalists and MI5 agents. Whatever the origins, the incident hinted at the potential power and usefulness of the so-called 'Tory Press'.

Conservative campaigning took a qualitative turn with the appointment of J. C. C. Davidson to the key organizational portfolio of Chairman in the 1920s.[39] A key feature of his tenure was the rejuvenation and use of a more aggressive publicity machine. Davidson was aided by a former secret service agent Joseph Ball, who prepared the party for the 1929 election. Ball went on to be instrumental in forming the National Publicity Bureau (NPB), an ambitious departure from the usual publicity machinery which took in the advice of various strategists. Part of this venture involved the organization of various communications and an ambitious programme of film propaganda that was popular with the public. A Conservative Film Association headed by Sir Albert Clavering supported this incursion into visual political communication.

Following the war a major rethink and reorganization of the party took place. These changes culminated in the party's adoption and popularization of the media type campaign. The young John Profumo began work with CCO as broadcasting officer and visited the United States to observe the election campaign of 1952.[40] In addition Charles

Hill, the so-called 'radio doctor', popularized the party's use of radio by appearing in some PEBs. In the late 1940s the party also recruited the services of the agency CPV and the PORD was set up as part of the reorganization. The publicity team at CCO assiduously incorporated the advice of the marketing professionals while simultaneously working under senior figures in the parliamentary leadership.

Many of the Conservatives who lobbied for the creation of ITV were keen to exploit the public relations opportunities afforded by the new medium in order to promote the party through television.[41] Crucial to these developments were key strategists like R. A. Butler, a keen supporter of the PORD, and Lords Poole and Woolton. Having commercial backgrounds these two peers were especially keen to use established management practices in the organization of campaigning. Their confidence in such techniques appeared to be vindicated by the result of the 1959 general election. In preparing for this campaign a liaison committee had acted as both conduit for information and main decision-making forum for politicians, officials and consultants.[42] Though the party continued to employ an advertising agency throughout the decade, more traditionally minded publicity officials were less than convinced about more modern approaches to presentation. The organization was forced to examine its communications strategy following its defeats in 1964 and 1966.

In 1970 something new was tried and the party retained a group of voluntary advisers. It was an approach directly modelled on that devised by Richard Nixon's aides for his successful presidential campaign of 1968. Ted Heath, the leader, was aided by party official Geoffrey Tucker together with marketing specialists and film-makers including Barry Day and Bryan Forbes.[43] They concentrated on promoting Heath's image and also courting key sections of the public. Women were identified as a particularly important target group. Heath and the Conservatives won the election following a closely fought campaign which once again suggested professional political communication might have played some role in aiding the victors.

Heath only enjoyed a single term as prime minister. Like his patron, Tory Director-General Michael Fraser's nemesis proved to be Margaret Thatcher. Fraser departed his post not long after Thatcher's election as leader in 1975. The vacancy was not filled. Instead, Thatcher sought to forge deeper organizational links with external advisers, most obviously the Saatchi & Saatchi brothers and their colleague Tim Bell. Together with CCO official Gordon Reece, the three advisers became central in the planning of the Conservative campaign victories in 1979 and 1983. Eventually the party chairmanship, a position in the gift of the leader, also went to people more in keeping with the prime minister's thinking such as Cecil Parkinson and Norman Tebbit.

Initially the Saatchi agency's partnership with the Conservatives proved mutually beneficial. Strains developed following Tim Bell's unhappy departure from the company in the mid-1980s. By the time of the 1987 election Chairman Tebbit was taking strategic advice from the Saatchis while the prime minister was simultaneously being privately briefed by other marketing experts such as Bell and John Banks. During the campaign a rogue opinion poll published a week before voting suggested Labour could win the election. The news led to panic at CCO on the so-called 'Wobbly Thursday'. Rival strategists argued with each other over the direction of the campaign. The Conservatives went on to win but the row within the party further highlighted the prominent role now played by marketing and media advisers.

The promotion of John Major to the Conservative leadership initially unified the party. Victory in the 1992 general election consolidated his position. There was, however, a perception that the result had little to do with a negative, fractious campaign. Major's beleaguered administration suffered continual setbacks throughout the 1992–97 parliament. In the circumstances it was not perhaps surprising that he failed to effectively project a favourable image of himself or his government. Opportunities for good communication were limited by a succession of pressing and difficult political problems. The Saatchis continued to advise the party. Yet the political problems the party faced in approaching the 1997 general election made effective planning and preparation difficult.[44] In the event the Conservatives' efforts lacked conviction. Besides the Saatchi executives, politicians such as Deputy Prime Minister Michael Heseltine and Chairman Brian Mawhinney devised and authorized copy for advertising campaigns that did little to promote the party. The heavy electoral defeat that followed has led to a serious re-examination of party goals and organization under a new leader, the former management consultant William Hague.

Labour: from committees to cabals

Following its incarnation as the Labour Representation Committee at the turn of the century, the Labour Party formally fought its first general election six years later in 1906. An ad hoc committee of leading figures led by Ramsay MacDonald oversaw the development of the campaign organization. Similar arrangements were made for the two elections held in 1910. MacDonald worked with a small headquarters team based in the Victoria area of London. Major changes came in 1917 with preparations for an overhaul of structures as part of the ongoing rewrite of the constitution which culminated in the publication of a new statement of aims and values (the so-called 'Clause Four') the following year. Herbert Tracey, a former mill worker, was appointed the first ever official to hold the publicity portfolio. He had trained and worked as a journalist. Reflecting his spiritual beliefs, this Methodist lay preacher had been a correspondent with the *Christian Commonwealth* newspaper. If former military and intelligence personnel dominated appointments to the CCO publicity machine, those from religious backgrounds were prominent within the Labour operation. This difference perhaps embodies something about the two parties' contrasting approaches to political communication during the interwar period.

William Henderson, the son of leading MP Arthur Henderson, held the publicity post after Tracey's departure in 1921. He remained in charge for over twenty years and right up until the end of the Second World War. Henderson's successor as head of publicity Arthur Bax maintained a fairly low profile. Bax's replacement, the journalist and Gaitskell aide John Harris, proved to be quite different. Supported by a new deputy Percy Clark, Harris facilitated a wholesale review of communications following his arrival at headquarters in 1962.[45] The death of his patron Gaitskell did not hinder this work. Indeed, the new leader Harold Wilson keenly supported his efforts. Wilson, himself a noted student of organization, famously chaired the committee whose 1955 report accused Labour of having 'a penny-farthing machine'. On assuming the leadership in 1963 he set about helping to remedy these apparent shortcomings by supporting what amounted to the largest changes in campaigning structures since those introduced in the immediate aftermath of the First World War.

Prior to 1962 Labour had made some attempts to modernize its approach to presentation. During the 1940s and 1950s future ministers like Patrick Gordon-Walker and Tony Benn had come to prominence through their work developing the party's use of radio and television broadcasting opportunities. Benn had hosted a celebrated series of innovative PEBs during the 1959 campaign.[46] Afterwards a group of party sympathizers (rather than the party itself) commissioned market researcher Mark Abrams to undertake a survey of popular political attitudes. The influential work which emerged from this, the book *Must Labour Lose?*, helped raise awareness as to the potential benefits of polling.[47]

By 1964 the party had completed what the Nuffield authors pointedly referred to as the 'modernisation of Labour'.[48] A key feature of this process was the work of Harris, Clark and a new grouping of advisers drawn from commercial advertising, market research and public relations' backgrounds. These included aides like David Kingsley and Michael Barnes whose original offers of help had been refused in 1959. Their work on the successful 'Let's Go' campaign helped return a Labour government and reinforced the view that good communications were an integral part of electoral success.

The Labour victory was followed by a more resounding success in the 1966 election. The campaign was organized by the same strategists.[49] The formidable partnership forged between them and the new prime minister led to some of them joining Wilson's controversial 'kitchen cabinet'. The charge of presidentialism levelled at the Labour premier for his maintenance of such an entourage drew considerable criticism. These attacks reached a crescendo following Labour's defeat in 1970.[50] This, combined with the ensuing debate over Labour's programme, resulted in a growing desire on the part of activists to reassert their rights and powers within the party's federal structures, most obviously at the Annual Conference.

Organizational issues became the subject of intense factional debate within the party and this inevitably influenced the development of strategy. Percy Clark, now Director of Publicity, continued to work closely with Wilson and key campaign advisers. Wilson's retirement in 1976 marked a significant turning-point in the party's strategic development. A committed student of public opinion polling, the prime minister had supported an ambitious market research programme from pollsters MORI prior to the two general elections in 1974.[51] The busy policy agenda of Wilson's successor Jim Callaghan, combined with the need to manage a precarious Commons' majority, left comparatively little time for strategic matters. He remained distant from a headquarters now presided over by General Secretary Ron Hayward, a tribune of the party's grassroots left and an official wary of professional consultants. Following the 1979 election defeat, marketing advisers such as Tim Delaney and Edward Booth-Clibborn expressed dissatisfaction about their effective isolation from the central decision-making structures within the campaign organization.[52]

It is ironic that the most traumatic Labour campaign of modern times, in 1983, was also the first in which the party formally retained the services of an advertising agency. The relative distance of the firm, Johnny Wright and Partners, from the party's decision-making structures limited their effectiveness.[53] Nor did they have continuous access to Labour's own market research evidence. These organizational problems were closely linked to political factors and, in particular, to ongoing factional divisions within the party. They were in turn exacerbated by Michael Foot's personal preference for not playing a central role in the management of strategy.

Foot's enthusiasm for the practical rather than managerial side of campaigning created a vacuum. Harold Wilson had been the link person at the centre of an uneasy alliance that he had in effect created. This had arisen because Labour's National Executive Committee (NEC) system, traditionally responsible for campaigns, had been in effect supplemented by a network of strategic advisers. The latter often worked with individuals, notably the leader, rather than through official structures. Though Foot did support the use of marketing expertise, his relatively low-key organizational role made effective decision-making difficult. The problem was exacerbated by the lack of a core group of leader aides and party officials able to execute committee decisions and liaise with outside advisers. The resulting campaign was thus paralysed before it started.[54]

The experience of the 1983 campaign defeat greatly influenced new leader Neil Kinnock. He made the rejuvenation of campaign organization a major priority. His leadership would see the party's embrace of political marketing techniques. More profoundly for this social democratic organization, managerialist thinking also began to inform its approach to electioneering. Kinnock's reform of the party came in two major phases. During the run-up to the 1987 campaign, the first stage saw the reintegration of professional expertise into party structures now overseen by a new Campaign Strategy Committee.[55] To ensure decisions were implemented, the headquarters at Walworth Road were completely reorganized in 1985. These changes amounted to the most complete overhaul since 1918. A new four-person Directorate was installed to assist the recently appointed General-Secretary Larry Whitty. The only outsider to join this team, Peter Mandelson, took over a publicity portfolio now redesignated as Director of Campaigns and Communications.[56]

Soon after Mandelson took charge he commissioned advertising consultant Philip Gould to investigate how the party's political communications might be improved. Following a critical report, Gould set up the SCA to help develop campaigns.[57] The SCA was central to party preparations for the 1987 general election. As such it was little different to the informal advisory panels that had helped Morrison in the 1930s and Wilson in the 1960s and 1970s. The SCA also played a critical strategic role following the 1987 defeat. It had a central role in organizing and presenting market research findings to Labour's Policy Review. As its title suggests, the Review was a wide-ranging process that cumulatively served to firmly reposition the party towards the right.

Following the Review, and the disappointment of the 1992 election defeat, Labour continued to use marketing and advertising expertise. Initially key strategists under Kinnock, like Mandelson and Gould, were isolated under the new leadership of John Smith. However, the new leader consolidated the modernization process in his brief tenure between 1992 and 1994 by reforming the party's candidate selection procedures. Like his successor Smith was adept at using the media to mobilize opinion within a greatly changed organization. During this period much was made of the party's 'spin' doctors' ability to manipulate debates. The election of Tony Blair as leader in 1994 and Labour's subsequent victory in 1997 did little to diminish the considerable speculation as to these actors' supposed power to subvert and control every facet of the organization and its business.

Other parties

The comparative poverty and small size of the other British parties has meant that the Conservatives and Labour are responsible for most of the major innovations in political communication. There have, nevertheless, been times when the less funded and staffed organizations have made significant breakthroughs in campaign terms. During the 1929 general election the Liberals, for instance, broke with precedent when they began advertising in the press. The following decade the party once again set a precedent by becoming the first to hire an advertising executive to manage its publicity campaigns. The official in question, William Allison, joined Liberal headquarters direct from the leading agency J. Walter Thompson in 1937.[58] More recently the party challenged conventional wisdom when, during the 1974 general elections, it took advertising in national newspapers. Politicians had hitherto assumed this was illegal. By their actions, the Liberals forced a change that led to the larger parties spending huge amounts on print advertising in the 1980s. That decade saw the Liberals' then allies in the newly formed SDP experiment with professional direct marketing techniques. Through the use of personalized mail shots the SDP was able to build its membership base and raise funds. During the 1985 by-election in the huge rural seat of Brecon and Radnor, the Liberal/SDP Alliance demonstrated its mastery of direct marketing and niche targeting in an ultimately successful campaign.[59]

In recent years there has been a rise in minor party and independent parliamentary candidates. Most rely on traditional grassroots work, the occasional PEB and new media forms to put across their message. Others, however, have attempted to emulate the approach of the larger parties. During its relatively successful European election campaign of 1989, the Greens employed advertising experts to help create a memorable PEB. In the 1992 general election the Natural Law Party became, in spending terms, the fourth largest competitor when it funded a major, if ineffectual, print and outdoor advertising campaign. During the subsequent campaign of 1997 the Referendum Party led by the billionaire businessman Sir James Goldsmith outspent all but the two largest parties. Before its demise the Referendum organization brought one notable innovation to British politics: the campaign video, copies of which were sent to millions of householders.

Conclusions

Three key stages in the development and transformation of British political communication have been identified. In discussing what have been termed mass propaganda, media campaigning and political marketing the emphasis has been on the changing relationship between the party and electorate rather than on any media or technological innovations. The growing use of market research as a feedback mechanism is central to understanding how political communication has developed over the course of the twentieth century. That said, there is sometimes a tendency on the part of the politicians and media to inflate their own importance as innovators or actors. Consequently it is important to recognize that while there have been major changes in the way campaigns are now conducted, there are some significant continuities in practice and theorizing. Visual media such as film and posters began to play an influential electoral role during the interwar period. In the same era, strategists started to talk about the importance of 'image', advertising and the psychology of the electorate. Interest in these and other phenomena intensified following the Second World War with the arrival of the so-called 'consumer society'. More recently the terms 'image maker' and 'spin doctor', both obvious manifestations of a managerial approach, have come to dominate modern political discourse. Arguably the 1992 general election was something of an electoral watershed because both major parties subscribed to a marketing-driven strategy.

Political communication, most obviously in the form of campaigning, is concerned with more than just electioneering. It forms the civic link between the people and their representatives. Marketing and media methods have transformed the relationship in various ways. Most crucially the views of key sections of uncommitted voters, as determined by public and private opinion polling research, now play an influential role in the respective parties' preparation for a campaign. Furthermore effective political communication is not only about persuading the mass of public opinion but also seeks to mobilize and manage dissent inside the organization. The increased mediation and marketization of politics has further centralized power within leaderships to the detriment of rivals within the party. Any dissent from party orthodoxy is criticized as risking party unity. This belief therefore stifles debate and may result in increased tension within the party organization. Indeed it is this change, rather than any improvement in voter persuasion, that may be the most significant outcome of the increased professionalization of political communication.

4
The Rise of Campaign Professionalism

Martin Harrop

Introduction

Contributing a chapter on the rise of the campaign professional raises two problems. The first difficulty is that it is far from clear whether 'campaign professionals' really exist in British elections. In the candidate-centred elections of the United States, firms of political consultants help candidates secure election in exchange for a fee. The staff of such companies are campaign professionals in the strict sense of selling their expertise about elections specifically. However, the British experience is rather different. British elections are still party-based and much campaigning expertise is located within parties, for example in the post of Director of Communications or in the leader's personal office. Such party employees may be 'professional' in the derivative sense of doing good work (their proficiency in Labour's 1997 campaign can hardly be doubted) but they work for the party as employees, not as contractors or volunteers. In Britain, independent professionals such as polling and advertising executives are of course called on by parties but they are commissioned precisely because they possess *non*-political skills unavailable or in short supply within the party: for instance, copy-writing, media-buying, public relations, journalism and opinion research. Such skills are needed in elections but they do not belong there primarily. In theory, therefore, the 'campaign professionals' who participate in British campaigns are political amateurs, working outside their normal line of business. They are often 'amateurs' in an additional sense: rarely do they turn a profit from their work. Parties are demanding and slow-paying clients and the Labour Party has in any case preferred, at least until recently, to rely on volunteers from the advertising world – of which there has always been a ready supply. In short, Britain's 'campaign professionals' (a phrase we will continue to use to describe external contractors to parties) are gentlemen players of the electoral game. They enjoy the challenge of applying their professional skills in a fresh, competitive and high-profile arena – but they always retain their day job. In Weber's terms, campaign professionals may live *for* politics but they are unlikely to live *off* politics.[1]

A second difficulty with the theme of the 'rise of the campaign professional' is that it is doubtful whether the authority of the independent contractor in campaigns is growing. To be sure, the common perception is that the influence of the campaign professional is like the Aids virus: new, dangerous and spreading everywhere. However, that stereotype is false and, worse, it obscures understanding. The myth fails to distinguish between party employees (such as Peter Mandelson) and independent professionals (such as Saatchi); to the extent that the competence of the former is growing, the significance of the latter group is declining. The myth also exaggerates the extent of recent change in the role of contractors, ignoring the fact that campaign professionals were on the scene as early as the 1950s, establishing career paths which were followed but not created by their high-profile successors. The myth also misleads in treating campaign professionals as a single group. Take the two areas on which this chapter concentrates: polling and advertising. I aim to show that the authority of opinion pollsters peaked in the 1970s and that in the 1980s their influence was partly supplanted by advertising agencies, particularly Saatchi. In the 1990s, the influence of advertising agencies itself declined and the question now is whether the campaign professional will in future be limited to implementing party-defined communications objectives, as with Labour in 1997. Certainly, in understanding how the political influence of the campaign professional has waxed and waned, we must recognize that the crucial variables are political, not technical. What matters is whether, how much and how well parties use the tools of the communications trade which are on offer. Politics is primary and, in consequence, developments in the role of the outside professional tend to be large and periodic rather than small and regular.

Exemplars

Before we begin our historical account it is helpful to consider two early exemplars of the breed: Geoffrey Tucker and Mark Abrams. Both were influential figures in the decisive phase of innovation in the late 1950s, though in contrasting ways which helped to shape how their respective parties subsequently engaged with communications professionals. A brief review of these two careers will also scotch any non-historical claims that the roles played more recently by the likes of Tim Bell and Robert Worcester were wholly new.

Geoffrey Tucker, a copy-writer by training, was involved for thirty years in Conservative campaigning, beginning in 1957 as the executive responsible for the Conservative account at the Colman, Prentis & Varley (CPV) advertising agency. Tucker moved easily between the political and advertising worlds. He was a Conservative candidate in 1959 and worked as the party's Publicity Director from 1968 to 1970. During his tenure at Conservative Central Office (CCO) he recruited several advertising men who were to form the core of the party's publicity professionals into the 1980s.[2] After leaving the party organization, Tucker continued his involvement with Conservative campaigns, declining to work for Mrs Thatcher but maintaining links with William Whitelaw. As late as 1987, he was to be found acting as a link between Downing Street and Young & Rubicam, the agency he had joined after CPV. As one seasoned observer comments, 'although Tucker never achieved the public acclaim of Tim Bell in the Thatcher era, arguably he was as influential as any advertising expert has been in a Conservative campaign'.[3] In fact, Tim Bell himself joined CPV in 1959 and his career continued to track Tucker's. Bell was second-generation; Tucker was the model.

While the Conservatives have always valued advertising experience above polling skills, Labour has reversed the priorities. Research has always been an acceptable word in the party's vocabulary and this approval has frequently extended to polling, even during the long decades when employing an advertising agency would have meant supping with the devil. In addition, as Gould, Herd and Powell observe, 'within the communications industry, Labour's support is strongest in research and planning'.[4] Labour was in fact the first British party to engage with polling when it commissioned Mark Abrams to conduct a small survey in 1956.[5] Abrams was an appropriate choice: he could locate his work within the British tradition of ameliorative social surveys rather than the American tradition of private-sector market research.[6] Even so, Abrams's initial work was soon stymied by the party's old guard and his influential 1959 survey with Richard Rose, *Must Labour Lose?*, was not funded directly by the party.[7] However, the party's attitudes developed rapidly in the early 1960s. By 1962 Abrams was back at work on extensive surveys of 'uncommitted voters in uncommitted constituencies'. His findings formed part of the general modernization of the party which contributed to Labour's return to office in 1964. Abrams continued to conduct some surveys for Labour until 1970 when Robert Worcester's MORI, essentially a market research agency albeit with a sympathy for public sector clients, began a 17-year association with the party. Robert Worcester, like Tim Bell on the Conservative side, achieved a higher profile than his predecessor but again Abrams, like Tucker, was the real innovator. Indeed, Abrams's consistent emphasis on the need for Labour to respond to the changing demands of a modern society meant that he probably influenced Labour's overall thinking more than Worcester did.

The careers of Tucker and Abrams illustrate what proved to be enduring contrasts between the parties: the Conservative's sympathy for advert- ising agencies as opposed to Labour's emphasis on opinion research and the Conservative's distinctive capacity to attract personnel from the communications industry to work directly as party employees, where they have proved to be a considerable force for change. But as we will see in the next section, the careers of these early campaign professionals also showed some common features. First, each was summoned when the party concerned was anxious about its electoral prospects; fear has always been the mother of campaign innovation and complacency as much as incompetence has been its enemy. Second – and here we come to a feature which has not endured from these early days – both our exemplars completed their work before the campaign proper got under way. Unlike their modern equivalents Tucker and Abrams were *pre-* campaign professionals. Their contemporary counterparts are not necessarily more influential but they do at least participate in the final frenetic weeks of the campaign.

1945–55

It is tempting to examine election communication in the postwar period in before-and-after terms, with the innovative 1959–64 period serving as the pivot. Certainly, 1959 and 1964 were breakthrough elec- tions but, as we will see, even the earliest postwar campaigns exhibited some 'modern' features, including a major role for the leaders and the mass media. There is therefore value in looking at the early postwar elections in some detail, if only to overcome our natural tendency to compare current elections against a stereotyped image of the past.

Certainly, the elections from 1945 to 1955 now appear to come from another era: no private opinion polls, no campaign press advertising, no television, no daily press conferences, no instant rebuttal units, no websites. A few illustrations from 1950 summon up the character of these early contests: Clement Attlee's reply of 'no' when asked on the eve of the campaign whether he had anything to say about the election; 20 000 people turning up at Ninian Park on a cold wet evening to hear a speech from Winston Churchill; and Mrs Attlee famously driving her husband round the country in the family car from one speaking engagement to the next, with just a detective and a journalist in the back (see Chapter 1). For stressed-out campaigners half a century later, though not necessarily for all the participants at the time, campaign time in these early contests seemed to run charmingly slow.[8]

However, we should beware of oversimplifying the nature of campaign communication in these postwar elections. The party faithful did conduct their elaborate canvassing, the local candidates did address public meetings in village halls and the paid agent did keep a beady eye on expenses. But alongside these traditional activities another, more significant national contest was unfolding. At least as much as today, and in some respects more so, the national campaign was dominated by the party leaders and the mass media. This national campaign consisted of exchanges between the leader of each party occurring through radio broadcasts and public speeches. These debates were then reported and interpreted in the partisan national press. The leaders read reports of each other's speeches and responded as they saw fit. The absence of an elaborate entourage did not indicate a lack of leadership for the leaders were their own spin doctors. Of course, other politicians had their say, not least in the radio broadcasts – 'Miss Hornby Smith came next, making the women's contribution to the Conservative appeal' – but at least as much as today the tone seems to have been set by the leaders themselves.[9]

In two respects, the mass media were *more* significant in the pre-1959 elections than in modern campaigns. First, the circulation of national daily papers was larger. In 1950, circulation amounted to 49 per cent of the electorate compared to just 30 per cent in 1997; of course, readership was much larger than circulation then as now.[10] Second, party broadcasts on radio were far more important than their contemporary equivalents, whether on television, radio or both combined. Radio broadcasts were longer and more frequent: in 1945, one broadcast of 20 to 30 minutes was delivered every night of the campaign except Sundays. In addition, such broadcasts reached a much larger share of the electorate. The average audience in 1945 was 45 per cent of the population and Churchill's four broadcasts averaged 49 per cent, figures only exceeded by the most popular variety shows. Such reach is inconceivable today after half a century of decline in the significance of party broadcasts and the growth of channels. And of course in the early post-war period the election on radio *was* the broadcasts. Until 1959 the BBC refrained from any news coverage of the campaign at all. No wonder H. G. Nicholas could comment in *The British General Election of 1950* that 'it is increasingly through the broadcasts, with their vast audiences and intimate appeal, that the major battles for the votes of the electorate are fought'.[11] The postwar campaigns were truly media elections, in which the party leaders reached live and direct into the country's front rooms. How modern leaders must envy the ability of their predecessors to reach so many undistracted voters so directly through the media.

Yet although party leaders and the media were central to these baseline elections, such modern features did not lead to the immediate emergence of campaign professionals. The specialists were available: advertising agencies and opinion polls had been established in Britain in the interwar period. Nor was such expertise completely alien to the electoral process. Between the wars the Conservatives had imaginatively exploited cinema newsreels and had commissioned advertising agencies to design leaflets and organize expensive poster campaigns (see Chapter 3). But immediately after the war the political will to exploit professional communications expertise did not exist. The atmosphere was one of rationing, not marketing. More importantly, no impetus to use campaign professionals came from the parties or their leaders. Labour had never shown much interest while for the Conservatives the 1945 campaign was a step back: 'the highly sophisticated party propaganda machine that had served the party so well in the 1930s was allowed to run down, with the result that the 1945 election saw little in the way of financial investment in propaganda compared to the previous three elections'.[12] So even these first postwar elections should not be taken as a representing a fixed model of 'old' campaigning; election communication has never been static but has always undergone phases of progress and decay.

In the aftermath of their 1945 defeat, the Conservatives did begin to relearn their communication skills. As with several later innovations, the mechanism for change proved to be appointing outsiders with commercial experience to party posts. Lord Woolton, window-dresser supreme, became party chairman in 1946. He set about teaching the party that 'the voter is also the consumer' long before consumer models of voting entered political science. The Conservatives began to run poster campaigns and press advertisements, with CPV engaged to place the adverts. So even before the 1959 watershed, the campaign professionals were beginning to be called upon again by the Conservatives.

1957–64

In the run-up to the elections of 1959 and 1964, campaign professionals achieved a much higher profile as both parties launched extensive advertising campaigns, the Conservatives in 1959 and Labour, partly in response, in 1964. These watershed developments owed more to political initiative than to technological innovations such as the coming of television. Certainly, 1959 was the first television election: the expansion of set ownership, the introduction of a commercial channel, the onset of election news and a near doubling in the number of party election broadcasts all added up to a major shift in the terrain. Yet the 'campaign' professionals played no part in television coverage for the simple reason that they were absent from the campaign itself; their role was restricted to press and poster advertising in the build-up. Drawing on analogies with product advertising, the justification was that 'party image' (as hot a phrase in 1959 as in 1997) must be built up over the long term. More practically, parties were dissuaded by legal advice from advertising in the press and on posters during the campaign. This limitation continued to apply until a legal judgement before the 1974 elections made clear that the costs incurred need not be charged to the strictly-limited expenses of candidates in individual constituencies. The spur to innovation in the late 1950s was, as ever, political rather than technological: the parties' fear of defeat if they did not present a modern face to the electorate. This mind-set allowed newly appointed officials, supported by sympathetic leaders, to innovate. It is this combination of circumstances – a supportive leader and innovative officials seeking to recover from a difficult political position – which has been the classic recipe for developments in electoral communication.

The innovative advertising which the Conservatives ran in the build-up to the 1959 election was a decisive breakthrough in the involvement of campaign professionals. CPV was intimately engaged with a campaign which was unprecedented in both length and cost. When the advertising began in June 1957, the Conservatives were seven points behind Labour in the Gallup poll and less than one in three respondents approved of the government's record or of Harold Macmillan's performance.[13] With victory anything but assured, CCO was under pressure to 'do something'. Under its new chairman Lord Poole, the party responded with a long-term advertising campaign, the success of which was based in part on an exceptionally close relationship with CPV. Executives from the two sides formed a single, informal publicity group which developed a shared perspective on electoral communication, based on three assumptions: (1) the need for a style of communication which was simple and direct; (2) the opportunity provided by social change to detach affluent workers – and their wives – from Labour; and (3) the value of advertising over the long term. Whether these assumptions were correct is neither here nor there; certainly, today's professionals would not want to confine their advertising to the pre-campaign period. But what really mattered was the success of the publicity group in both achieving and acting on an agreed outlook. Then as now, the relationship between parties and their campaign professionals is a crucial factor in determining the quality of the professionals' contribution.

Typically for Conservative propaganda, the 1957–59 campaign was advertising-led rather than research-based. From CPV's perspective, one of Lord Poole's best traits was that he did not believe in over-testing advertisements. His preferred method of comprehending voters was not to commission elaborate surveys but rather to observe shoppers in Watford supermarkets on Saturday afternoons. Although the Conservative campaign may have been sharpened by an intuitive appreciation of its target groups, its success owed rather more to timing and flexibility. The theme was eventually modified to 'Life's Better With The Conservatives, Don't Let Labour Ruin It', a classic slogan which captured the mood of economic optimism that spread across the country in the warm summer of 1959. It is interesting to note that even this most strategic of campaigns showed the willingness to adapt and respond which is now accepted as a distinctive feature of electoral, as opposed to mainstream commercial, advertising.

The Conservative innovations of the late 1950s were not lost on the Labour Party 'modernizers' who gained the initiative after the party's third successive defeat in 1959. It was becoming clear that press and poster advertising, designed by professionals, could supplant the mass distribution of leaflets traditionally produced in-house by the central party. However, any developments in Labour's communications had to work round that ever-present block on the road to innovation, the party's National Executive Committee (NEC). So rather than sign a straightforward contract with an agency, in 1962 the party's new Publicity Director formed an unofficial team of market researchers, advertising and public relations executives. Again, we should note that the explanation for Labour's innovation in the early 1960s came on the demand side, from the party, rather than on the supply side, from the professions. Volunteers from advertising had in fact come forward in 1959 but had been rebuffed. Due to a shortage of money and to the party's continuing reluctance to spend what resources it did have beyond its own boundaries, the volunteer group has remained the characteristic device by which Labour has linked with campaign professionals.

Despite its unofficial standing, Labour's team organized an influential press and poster advertising campaign starting in May 1963, well over a year before the 1964 election. The theme was 'Let's Go With Labour'. With Abrams as a prominent member, the campaign was based more carefully on research than the Conservative effort of the late 1950s had been. Even the fear that the slogan might imply diarrhoea to Northern voters was investigated. Butler and King judge that 'from [May 1963], survey research was exploited in a manner quite unprecedented in this country.'[14] Even more than with the Conservatives, though, there was little follow-through into the campaign proper. Rather than pick up systematically on the themes established in the advertising, the politicians continued to go their own way. Butler and King are clear in their judgement:

> ...there was in fact no Labour campaign, no central directive or plan. Harold Wilson decided tactics from day to day, essentially on his own... It was as though Labour had reverted to the methods of its earlier, pre-scientific era. Instead of the party's campaign appearing as the logical extension of its pre-campaign activities, it seemed hardly related to them.[15]

The integrated campaign, in which the same message is sent through different channels and advertising adapts to the flow of events, remained a long way off. The 1957–64 period established the relevance of campaign professionals to elections but their role remained ancillary. They were scouts rather generals.

1965–97

In 1965, when the Conservatives encouraged Humphrey Taylor to set up the Opinion Research Centre with the promise of polling work, Britain's two major parties had each engaged at some stage in the postwar period with a professional advertising and research focus. With breakthrough achieved, one might expect the story from then on to be a simple tale of ever greater professionalism, as the Conservatives learned to incorporate research findings into their marketing efforts, Labour came to grips with a world in which advertising played an integral part and both parties took advantage of the increasing freedom from 1974 to advertise during the campaign proper. Yet as is often the case with British political parties, progress proved to be distinctly irregular. The integration of the campaign professional into the work of parties has proved to be as halting and unsteady as a drunkard's walk. When the leader is sympathetic, top officials are supportive and the party is united, the professionals generally perform. But the nature of politics is that these conditions are rarely satisfied together. In practice, given the fluid and non-institutional relationship between parties and professionals, much has depended on personal relationships. Professional advisers with the leader's ear have been able to move towards the strategic role which enables parties to speak with a single voice during the din of the final campaign. The classic example here is the role of Saatchi in the Conservative Party at least during parts of the 1979–92 period. But an alternative, and perhaps more logical, method of achieving an integrated campaign is to impose control over communication from within the party itself. The model here is the Labour Party in its post-1983 recovery phase and particularly in the near-flawless campaign of 1997. In 1997, for the first time, Labour's advertisers and researchers became what arguably they should always have been: suppliers of technical services to a client which knew its own mind. Paradoxically, as the party itself (or at least the campaign unit and the leader's office) became more professional, so the scope for the independent contractor diminished. The campaign professional had become a commodity.

Rather than treating the post-1964 period as a single era, we can capture more of the moving picture by dividing the final third of the century into three broad phases: the 1970s – the decade of the pollster (and MORI specifically); the 1980s – the decade of the advertising agency (and Saatchi specifically); and the 1990s – the decade of the political party (and Labour specifically).

The pollster's decade

The pollster's tale is especially worth telling for the insights it offers into the changing priorities of election communication. In the 1960s, parties commissioned ever more sophisticated survey designs, even extending to expensive panels in which the same respondents were re-interviewed. The Conservative panel, beginning in 1965 and lasting a full ten years, was undoubtedly the most elaborate survey research undertaken by any political party in Britain, before or since. The design of the study echoed Butler and Stokes's *Political Change in Britain;* academic psephology generally seemed to add a little extra legitimacy to pollsters' efforts in this decade. Despite the Conservative's late start, their spending on polls averaged £30 000 a year between 1966 and 1970. In the 1970 campaign, the party commissioned three daily samples each with 500 respondents, with results available the day after fieldwork.[16] By now, Labour had fallen behind in its use of polling but it was beginning its long relationship with MORI. As a result, February 1974 was the first campaign in which both parties invested in daily campaign polls, a pattern repeated in October of that year. The pollster had become the accepted guru.

By 1979, though, the pollster's magic lamp was already beginning to dim. New leaders – Margaret Thatcher and James Callaghan – were sympathetic but neither were obsessive poll-watchers. Labour, in particular, was beginning its descent into a decade of introspection during which internal politics, not opinion polls, would dominate. As Kavanagh notes, 'no pollster for Labour has been part of the key strategy group around the leader since Robert Worcester in 1974; thereafter, he was rarely part of the inner core of campaign decision-making'.[17] The increased availability of public polls meant politicians began to question the added value of private surveys; parties were also somewhat discomfited to discover 'their' pollster popping up on the media, delivering opinions for free. In any case, British politicians (typically arts graduates or even in the 1970s non-graduates) and pollsters (typically social science graduates) had never been natural bedfellows. Politicians prefer qualitative findings, a few main points and an emphasis on implications. By contrast, pollsters are naturally quantitative: they believe that the more findings they deliver, the better value they are providing; and they tend to caution in advising politicians about what to do. As one Conservative official said, to be informed by a pollster that Ted Heath appeared aloof on television was to be presented with a problem, not a solution. By the end of the 1970s, Nigel Lawson's early comment on the limitations of polls was turning into a powerful critique: 'perhaps the biggest myth about survey research is that it tells you what to do.'[18]

A marriage of convenience is soon torn apart by a fresh face. In the political world, the 1980s witnessed growing recognition, and then acceptance, of the value of qualitative research on public opinion. This work typically took the form of focus groups but also covered depth interviews with individual electors. Both techniques were well-established in the advertising world where agencies typically employed 'planners' (researchers and/or strategists) to underpin their creative effort. Indeed, individual interviews had been used to test the advertising copy used in some of the early postwar campaigns. In practice, qualitative research tended to emphasize 'soft' topics: party image, tone, emotional resonance and the links (if any) between the political and the personal. Where the pollster aimed merely to measure isolated attitudes, the advertising agency sought to grasp how attitudes fit together in an overall package. Where pollsters sought to describe public opinion, advertising agencies aimed to mould it. Of course, the parties by no means dispensed with traditional polling in the 1980s; indeed, they sometimes commissioned special analyses of published surveys to identify trends in particular regions or subtypes of seat. However, polling was now used in conjunction with qualitative work.

To some extent, this transition from quantitative to qualitative research may have reflected long-term changes in perceptions of electoral behaviour as 'voters began to choose'.[19] Much more directly, the re-orientation signalled a move in control over opinion research from pollsters (influenced by academic and political science models) to advertising agencies (influenced by commercial and particularly marketing perspectives). While some qualitative work was conducted by specialist researchers working in traditional polling companies, most was controlled directly by advertising agencies themselves. In particular, the shift to qualitative research reflected the rising authority of Saatchi & Saatchi in the business of electoral communication. New magicians had arrived and, what's more, their lamp told politicians what to do.

The agency's decade

If the 1970s was the decade of the pollster, the 1980s was the era of the advertiser. The significance of this rebalancing of professional power was far more than a matter of research methods. Saatchi penetrated into areas of Conservative electoral communication previously off-limits to outsiders and its achievement was to do so in a manner which encouraged more coherent campaigns. Saatchi offered a more strategic approach than pollsters had or could. But again, we should note that the Conservatives sought out the Saatchi treatment and submitted willingly to it. The initial decision to appoint the agency, without an extensive beauty parade, was taken in the full knowledge that Saatchi was 'an aggressive, publicity-conscious, energetic and creative agency'.[20] From the start, the firm was charged not just with preparing paid advertising but also with producing election broadcasts and developing an overall communications strategy. The crucial figure in producing this ambitious brief was Gordon Reece, appointed to the position of Director of Publicity in 1978 and a former television producer who had worked on election broadcasts in 1970 when Geoffrey Tucker was in post at CCO. Reece remained close to Mrs Thatcher and Saatchi's impact was heightened by the money made available for advertising through Lord McAlpine's renowned fund-raising. As Saatchi's ads raised party morale, so more money came in, permitting more advertising. In these ways the party provided all the conditions needed for its agency to shine: a sympathetic leader, a clear brief, a professional Publicity Director, straightforward lines of accountability and money. Above all, perhaps, what communicators need is a proposition to sell and Mrs Thatcher both had one and was one. As in Tucker's day, personnel movements solidified the links between party and agency: for instance, Michael Dobbs took leave from Saatchi to assist Norman Tebbit as chairman of the party. In locating Saatchi's success in its political context, we should also remember the help offered by the Labour Party: it provided multiple targets for the agency to attack.

By and large, Saatchi did deliver the more coherent communications which the party sought. In addition to integrating qualitative research into its communications (which any agency would have done), it drew up strategic themes such as those emphasized for the 1983 campaign: continuity, leadership, realism, aggression, wrong-footing the opposition and remaining true to the party's strengths. The agency also took over production of Party Election Broadcasts (PEBs) from the self-interested bands of politicians which had previously controlled them; the style of the programmes changed though their impact remained limited. Saatchi also vastly extended the use of press advertising within election campaigns, adopting a flexible response to shifts in the agenda. Clearly, the game had moved on since 1959 when CPV completed its work before the campaign even started. In effect, Saatchi was taking on the political consultancy role long familiar in the United States.

Two examples illustrate Saatchi's reach into the Conservative Party. The first is the prominent role which the agency played in the successful relaunch of the party's appeal at its annual conference in 1986, a role which both Saatchi and neutral observers described as 'unprecedented'.[21] Saatchi market-tested the conference theme of 'The Next Move Forward', advertised the slogan beforehand, briefed the press extensively and agreed with ministers how their speeches to conference would fit into the framework. The agency even wrote sections of speeches for some ministers. In effect, the 1986 conference became a launch-pad for the successful 1987 re-election campaign. The second example of Saatchi's influence is the build-up to the 1992 election, when the agency visited each minister in charge of a department to discuss the implications of opinion research for campaign strategy. In meetings lasting 90 minutes or so, ministers were advised to seek to dent Labour's credibility on its strong issues.[22] Although Saatchi may be remembered most for its tactical flexibility in the heat of battle, these examples show the agency fulfilling the strategic side of its brief.

Yet it would be simplistic to assume that Saatchi was the driving force in the Conservative campaigns of the 1980s. Like any other agency, Saatchi sought to understand and then communicate the message; it could not, nor did it seek to, create the proposition itself. Further, it would be naive to conclude that just because Saatchi wrote a strategy document, therefore there was a communications strategy, still less that Saatchi decided what it was. Such documents are never self-implementing; often they gather dust on the top shelf. Nor is there any evidence that specific forms of communication produced by Saatchi, such as press and poster advertising or party election broadcasts, affected voting behaviour, even if they did boost morale within the party. Significantly, Saatchi's extravagant purchase of white space in newspapers has never been repeated. And we should not assume that the relationship between agency and party was always harmonious; if anything, trust seemed to dissipate as the decade proceeded. As early as 1983, we learn of 'a determination in Central Office to keep the agency on a tighter rein and subject it to more financial constraint'.[23] By 1987, authority in CCO had fragmented, Tim Bell had left the agency and Mrs Thatcher was placing more faith in research conducted by Geoffrey Tucker's former agency, Young & Rubicam. The situation recovered in 1992, aided by early planning, but by 1997 Saatchi itself had split and M & C Saatchi, a successor agency, could do little more than warn the party of impending doom.[24] An era had ended and the new model of party/ agency relationships it spawned probably ended with it. Saatchi's lamp had burned brightly but its fuel was soon spent.

The party's decade

After the pollster had been eclipsed, and the Saatchi meteor had flashed by, where were the new gurus to be found? The answer was in that most unpropitious of environments: the Labour Party. From 1987 on, the party's campaigns demonstrated a level of communication expertise unparalleled in its history. In the process, the party drew on, but also contained, the outside professional, delivering a new, party-led model of party/professional relationships. The magicians had moved back inside the party and they found a base for their tricks in and around their leader's office.

Labour's communications breakthrough could be so dramatic precisely because its skills had atrophied. After the innovations of 1964, endemic problems – conflict between the leader and the NEC, continuing suspicion of modern methods combined with a naive faith in the power of slogans, lack of clear briefing to volunteer communications teams,

Harold Wilson's preference for tactics over strategy, and a concern with secrecy which meant most people in the party were never permitted to see survey results – served to frustrate the communications professionals. The party's volunteer-based Publicity Advisory Committee found itself politicking over what work it was permitted to do rather than getting on and doing it. In contrast to Gordon Reece at CCO, Labour's officials notably failed to communicate with their communicators. As Tim Delaney despondently concluded after the 1979 campaign, 'without a more professional approach in the Labour Party to problems of political communication, one party will be talking through Saatchi & Saatchi to the people and the other will basically be talking to itself'.[25]

We should note one exception to this rather grim litany: October 1974. In this campaign, the publicity team was brought into the party's deliberations and efforts were made to elaborate in press conferences, television broadcasts and even the leader's speeches the theme of a competent team with long-term plans. Martin Harrison judged that 'Labour's television broadcasts were far better integrated with the party's broader campaign themes than in recent elections'.[26] But October 1974 was no mould-breaker. Indeed, Labour's next two campaigns in 1979 and 1983 were showpieces of incompetence.

In 1987, and culminating in its historic triumph in 1997, Labour developed communication campaigns as strongly professional as the Conservatives' had been with Saatchi but generated within, and controlled by, the party's new elite (see Chapter 3). Judged by electors' ratings, Labour 'won' each of the last three campaigns. The essential actors in Labour's three 'victories' were not professional outsiders but rather reforming leaders, Neil Kinnock and Tony Blair (though not John Smith), supported by a younger generation of staff in the leader's expanded personal office, for instance Charles Clarke and Patricia Hewitt. Peter Mandelson, Director of Campaigns and Communications (1985–90) and Chair of the General Election Planning Group (1995–97) maintained close links with the leader and his office. Philip Gould, master of the focus group, occupied a variable position, working both within the party and as an adviser to it, but he had been a committed Labour strategist from his youth. He was a party man through and through.[27] Given that reforming leaders could dominate or at least circumvent the NEC, though not without the occasional grumble from the old guard, the party operatives could exercise strategic authority over the campaign more easily than Saatchi could within the Conservative Party. Such control was symbolized in 1997 by the decision to establish a media and communication centre at Millbank, separate from party headquarters.

So the 1990s witnessed the triumph of a new party-led model of campaigning. What could be more logical, we might ask, than for a political party to formulate its own campaign themes and to present these in political forums itself, relying on outsiders for technical help with more peripheral media such as press and posters? Subcontracting the development of a communications plan to an outside agency, as the Conservatives had done with Saatchi, suddenly began to look like a sign of weakness rather than strength. The 1980s notion of a communications strategy developed by hired hands had acquired a dangerous and successful competitor.

In formulating its communication plans for recent elections, Labour certainly learned from Saatchi's successes of the 1980s. However, it did not copy the device of entrusting its marketing to an outside firm. The party lacked both money and a history of successful contractual relationships with advertising agencies. In 1987 and 1992, the party used its traditional method of relying on volunteers, quickly discarding its 1983 experiment with a paid advertising agency.[28] In the 1980s, the emphasis on volunteers from the communications world was perhaps a forced choice, given the party's lack of credibility: what firm would want to be linked with Labour? For 1987, Mandelson organized the volunteers into a Shadow Communications Agency in which staff from Boase, Massimi, Pollitt (BMP), which had handled the 'Save the GLC' campaign, played a leading role. A similar structure was employed in 1992. In the even more controlled campaign of 1997, Labour employed both an advertising agency (BMP again, after a break) and a polling firm (NOP) on a commercial basis. However, the contrast between BMP's role for Labour in 1997 and Saatchi's for the Conservatives in the 1980s was clear: 'few people were aware of the name of the BMP agency, let alone that it was working for Labour. It maintained a low profile and there was no doubt about its subordinate status in Millbank Tower.'[29] The agency's chief executive put it this way: 'In 1985 we were showing Peter Mandelson how to do it because he was new to the job but by 1997 he knew how to do it in his sleep.'[30] The moment had taken a long time to arrive but the Labour Party had finally become just another client.

Conclusion

If our review of campaign professionals in British elections has shown one thing, it is that their role is more subtle and varied than is commonly assumed. Polling companies and advertising agencies have risen and fallen at different times and have varied in their significance across the two major parties. It would certainly be an act of violence against history to postulate, as some observers seem to do, a steady increase in the power of campaign professionals in response to the increasing complexity of communication. Rather, changes in communications have been punctuated rather than uniform and have tended to redistribute influence within parties as well as between different kinds of contractor (see Chapter 3). Our discussion of the Labour Party in particular lends support to Bowler and Farrell's conclusion from their cross-national study: 'changes in campaigning methods reveal not so much party decline as party adaptation; indeed, one could go so far as to suggest that, if anything, this is a phenomenon of a strengthening party apparatus at the centre.'[31]

It is certainly clear that in Britain the key variables are political rather than technical. Political parties are the initiators (1) in deciding whether to seek assistance from campaign professionals in the first place, and (2) in providing or failing to provide the conditions needed for the professionals to make an effective contribution. Even when the relationship between the party and its professionals is constructive, based on a shared understanding of the task at hand (and ideally on shared political sympathies as well), communication professionals are ultimately the junior partner. They can condense, reinforce and help to articulate the party's core message but they can never create it. Where there is no message, there is little that they can do. Ultimately, the party leader must define the message and provide political support for the communications technicians who help to transmit it to the electorate.

Because politics is the driver, speculating about future trends in the relationship between parties and campaign professionals is no easy task. As we have seen, past progress has been spasmodic and the simplest, if least useful, prediction is that this combination of normal campaigns and occasional decisive innovations will continue. We should also remember the lesson of Labour in 1983 and the Conservatives in 1997: campaigns can get worse as well as better. However, we can be sure that communications agencies will continue to be called on to supply technical services such as buying advertising space and designing, writing and testing copy. We can also expect parties to continue to use the services of polling companies though perhaps with a renewed focus on Abrams's 'uncommitted voters in uncommitted constituencies'. In the future media buyers may purchase space on web pages and researchers may conduct their interviews over the Internet but these are technical, and therefore secondary, developments.

The main issue is whether Labour's new model communications strategy – in which the party itself becomes the integrating force, calling on outside advisers to help implement rather than form the strategy – becomes the new norm. Although Labour itself is likely to retain its winning formula, it seems unlikely that the party will advance this model much further in the first decade of the new century. With the hunger for victory dulled by its very achievement, and experienced figures preoccupied by problems of government, the likelihood is that the party's campaign communications will tread water. Although the ruthless focus on results shown by Labour's new model campaigners between 1987 and 1997 was politically necessary, the failure to institutionalize new campaign skills within traditional party structures may yet prove to be a weakness. Divisions between the leader and the party, always a vulnerable area, have proved in the past to be a particular difficulty when the party has been in office. While it is difficult to imagine Labour's campaign communications sinking back to the depths of the 1980s, it would still require a cheque drawn against the future, and in particular against its next leader, to assume that the party will remain the standard-bearer of Panebianco's 'electoral-professional' party.[32]

But in truth the communications ball rests with the Conservatives rather than Labour. Throughout the postwar period, defeat has proved to be a powerful tonic for reform and the Conservative debacle in 1997 therefore presented the party with a window of opportunity. The question is whether the Conservatives can or will copy Labour's method of developing a communications strategy in house, thus allowing the search for additional innovation in Britain's competitive party system to enter new territory, or whether the party will continue with its traditional reliance on advertising agencies. In either case, past form suggests the party would have been well advised to begin its reconstruction by appointing outside professionals to senior positions within the party hierarchy. Fresh blood, drawn from the communications industry itself, has been the tonic for innovation in the past and has laid the basis for constructive engagement with independent professionals. Further, the Conservatives had additional incentive to recruit in this way because it has not been a policy which Labour has practised; the relative permeability of the Conservative organization can be a strength. Of course, improved communication is not itself a project for government. But as long as the Conservatives remain in opposition, the voters will ruthlessly test the party's claim to have rebuilt its competence against its ability to communicate effectively and coherently in a general election campaign. There is little else against which the management ability of opposition parties can be judged.

5
The Fall and Rise of Constituency Campaigning

David Denver and Gordon Hands

Introduction

Modern British general election campaigns take place at two main levels. Firstly, in every constituency there is a local campaign. Volunteers working for the parties canvass the electorate, distribute leaflets and put up posters, while the candidates seek to meet the electorate by going on walkabouts, visiting clubs and pubs in different parts of the constituency and so on. In addition, of course, there is a national campaign, directed by party headquarters, which centres on the activities of the party leaders, the daily press conferences in London, election broadcasts and the like. The development of election campaigning over the past century has involved, broadly speaking, a switch in focus on the part of the political parties from the constituency campaigns to the national campaign. But the two general elections of the 1990s seem to have gone some way to reverse that trend. There has, apparently, been something of a resurgence of local campaigning, with significantly greater resources being poured into the constituencies by all of the major parties, and this has been matched by a renewed interest in this aspect of electoral politics on the part of academics.

Campaigning and communication

All election campaigning involves communicating with the electorate, and this communication has one overriding purpose – to maximize the number of votes cast for the party concerned. In order to achieve this effect, campaign communications at both local and national level have four main aims. The first and simplest is *informing* voters – about when the election will take place, where the polling stations are, who the candidate is, what the party's policies or achievements are and so on. Closely allied to this is the task of *persuading* voters to support the party. This is undertaken in a variety of ways, including distributing leaflets and personal encounters between candidates and voters at the local level, and party election broadcasts, advertising campaigns and so on at the national level. Thirdly, campaigns also involve *reinforcing* the support of favourably inclined voters. Some people support one party regularly and they usually do not need to be persuaded to vote for it at a particular election. Rather, the task of the campaign is to ensure that they are not tempted to defect – by appealing to their loyalty, providing evidence that their support is valued and the like (see Chapter 2). Finally, campaigns also seek to *mobilize* voters. Informing, persuading and reinforcing are all aspects of mobilization, but in the sense in which we mean it here mobilizing activities go well beyond transmitting information to include the organizational arrangements made to ensure that supporters actually turn out and vote on polling day. The changing weight attributed to national and constituency campaigns can perhaps best be understood as a response to the changes in the means available for informing, persuading, reinforcing and mobilizing voters.

The rise of the national campaign

Throughout most of the nineteenth century these activities were carried out almost entirely at constituency level. General elections were not particularly 'general' – elections were held at different dates in different constituencies, many candidates were only loosely connected to national parties and there was little that could be described as a national campaign. From the late nineteenth century onwards, however, national campaigning became more important and there was a relative decline in local campaigning. This was due to a number of factors. Legislation in the 1880s imposed much more effective controls on what until then had been the traditional methods of campaigning – bribery, treating, payments to election workers and unlimited expenditure. In addition, the Reform Act of 1884 greatly increased the size of constituency electorates, thus making it more difficult for local volunteers to communicate with the voters. A further large extension of the franchise took place in 1918 as a consequence of which the average constituency electorate more than doubled to around 35 000. With this size of electorate, face-to-face communication between candidates and voters became very difficult. But it was the appearance of cheap, mass circulation, national newspapers around the turn of the century that was most important in causing the first marked shift of emphasis from local to national campaigning. The way to reach the newly enlarged electorates was via the popular press (and after the First World War via radio and the cinema). It appeared that informing, persuading and reinforcing an electorate running into many millions was most effectively done through the national mass media.

These developments reached a peak with the arrival of television in the 1950s (see Chapter 7). By the end of the decade, television ownership was almost universal and political coverage was extensive. By means of television the parties could easily communicate informing, persuading and reinforcing messages to a truly mass audience. Moreover, because British television (like most of the press) is nationally organized its focus during elections is on the national campaign. Campaign coverage is overwhelmingly concentrated on national-level events, such as the daily party press conferences, and is highly London-centred. Even regional election programmes tend to cover national stories or concentrate on visits to localities by leading national figures.[1] From the 1960s onwards television has been a major player in election campaigns and it quickly became the major (and most trusted) source of political information for most voters. The parties devoted great efforts to improving their coverage, organizing the leaders' campaign activities to fit in with nightly television news broadcasts, for example, and employing professional media experts. Television interviews with party leaders became major campaign events. All of this appeared to sound the death-knell for local campaigning.

The downgrading of local campaigning – at least by academics – over the postwar period is illustrated in the highly influential series of 'Nuffield Studies' of British general elections. In the study of the 1951 election fully 99 out of 289 pages were devoted to constituency campaigning; by the 1992 election 'the local battle' merited only 16 pages out of 380.[2]

Local campaigning as mobilization

Despite the increasing concentration on the national campaign, local constituency campaigning remained a familiar feature of British elections. Local campaigns in the 1950s generally took a standard form, involving public meetings addressed by the candidate (frequently in drab and dingy halls, or else at factory gates), the circulation of an election address from the candidate, the distribution of leaflets and displays of window and other posters. These were the traditional local-level activities intended to inform, persuade and reinforce voters but, as we have suggested, it was now clear that these objectives could be more effectively met by the national campaign communicated to the electorate by television. Increasingly, therefore, local campaigning focused on the one activity that could best (or only) be done locally – mobilizing voters to go to the polls. Although much campaigning is national, it is in local constituencies that voting takes place and it is constituency results that determine the outcomes of elections.

While persuasive campaigns focus on voters with weak party loyalties or none at all and attempt to use communications to sway their vote, mobilizing campaigns focus on known supporters and concentrate on building an effective organization to ensure that as many as possible of them vote. In all parties the central mobilizing technique is canvassing. In its classic form, canvassing is carried out by teams of volunteers calling on voters in their homes and attempting to ascertain their intentions in the forthcoming election. Usually there is no attempt to solicit support or persuade opponents – 'arguing on the doorstep' is explicitly discouraged in party handbooks. Rather the purpose is simply to compile a list of potential supporters which is as full and accurate as possible. The relevant names, with electoral registration numbers, are transferred to specially prepared sheets. On polling day 'number takers' take up a position outside polling stations and record the registration numbers of electors as they go in to vote (with representatives of the different parties frequently helping one another out by swapping numbers). From time to time the numbers are relayed back to a committee room where those who have voted in the relevant ward or polling district are crossed off the prepared lists. Teams of volunteers then go off to 'knock up' or 'fetch out' those who haven't voted, often offering a lift to the polling station. In a well-run campaign, this continues until well into the evening to ensure that as many as possible of those on the list have been prevailed upon to vote.

This organizational effort is usually directed by the election agent. The appointment of an agent is a legal requirement in British elections – he or she being responsible for all expenditures and ensuring that other aspects of electoral law are complied with – and the agent is almost always also the person in charge of campaign organization. Although the 'canvass-and-knock-up' campaign requires a fairly complex organization – usually involving dividing up the constituency into manageable areas overseen by 'sub-agents', ensuring that polling stations are covered by number takers, that workers and cars are directed to key areas and so on – it is in principle a relatively straightforward operation.

It requires a lot of volunteer workers, but as a technique for ensuring that as many supporters as possible go to the polls it is difficult to see how it could be improved upon. From the 1950s, although a variety of other activities were undertaken, effective local campaigning was essentially about building a machine to mobilize voters on election day.

Throughout most of the postwar period, this view of local campaigning as essentially a mobilizing operation was the dominant theme in the material produced by the parties to train volunteers in running campaigns. It is also a view that is consistent with the picture of an 'aligned' electorate that emerged from early studies of voting in Britain. These studies (for example, Butler and Stokes's *Political Change in Britain*) found that most voters had a standing commitment to a party, frequently based on class.[3] When an election came along there was little chance that a candidate or a party could override the voter's standing commitment. The main thing that a campaign could affect, therefore, was whether someone voted or not, and elections could be won or lost depending on the effectiveness with which parties could get their supporters to the polls (see Chapter 2). Very few voters would be available for conversion during a campaign, so it made little sense to put a great effort into persuasive campaigning. The most efficient form of local campaigning was simply to identify supporters and make sure that they voted. The more extreme versions of this model of campaigning even held that potential opponents should be avoided altogether in case they were stirred into voting for one of the rival parties.

Party professionals concerned with local campaigning remained convinced that a strong local mobilizing effort could bring electoral rewards but, throughout the postwar period, academics, other commentators and some politicians suggested that even with this restricted role local campaigns achieved little. The dominant view came to be that constituency campaigns are old-fashioned rituals that parties indulge in out of habit. As early as the 1951 election David Butler suggested that 'the quality of the candidate and his organisation matter remarkably little',[4] and during the 1992 campaign Ivor Crewe bluntly asserted that 'constituency organisation counts for next to nothing'.[5] This view of the effect of local campaigning was developed in the Nuffield Studies during the 1950s and was largely based on the fact that the 'swing' between elections tended to be uniform across constituencies. It was argued that if swing was more or less constant regardless of party effort, then constituency campaigns could not be having any significant impact. Even though swings have become markedly less uniform over the past thirty years, the hold of the original Nuffield view has been tenacious. There was a small dissenting literature (for example Bochel and Denver; Holt and Turner),[6] but the orthodoxy remained that modern election campaigns are so dominated by the national mass media and the national party leaders that what happens on the ground in the constituencies is of little or no consequence.

The revival of local campaigning

By the late 1980s then, in the eyes of most commentators, constituency-level campaigning had more or less been consigned to the grave. During the 1990s, however, the corpse began to show signs of life. There was renewed interest both in the parties themselves and on the part of academic analysts. These two developments are clearly interconnected, although the direction of causation is unclear.

The traditional view of the significance of local campaigning came under sustained criticism as academics developed a renewed interest in the subject. There were three main reasons for the growth in interest. The first has already been mentioned – the decline of uniform swing. The standard deviation of two-party swing averaged only 2.6 between 1959 and October 1974, but rose to an average of 4.4 from 1979 to 1992.[7] In other words, from 1979 there was greater variability in changes in party support between elections across constituencies. No longer, it seemed, were local candidates entirely at the mercy of the national swing. The basis of the orthodox view was thus undermined and it was at least possible that variations in swing resulted from variations in local campaign effectiveness. Secondly, from the 1970s onwards there was powerful evidence that the electorate was becoming increasingly dealigned.[8] There was a decrease in the extent to which party support was aligned with class and, perhaps more importantly, a decrease in the strength of party identification among voters. The consistent and almost automatic support for one party or another, which had been the norm in the 1950s, became less common. In the words of Ivor Crewe, more voters were 'up for grabs' – and local campaigns might 'grab' them (see Chapter 2).[9] Thirdly, academics began to find answers to the problem that had bedevilled previous research in this area, namely how to devise a measure of the intensity and organizational effectiveness of local campaigns that could be applied across a large number of constituencies. Johnston and Pattie argued that campaign spending was a useful surrogate indicator of the strength of a campaign and, on this basis, produced evidence that campaigning had a significant effect on election results, especially improving the performance of non-incumbent candidates.[10] Whiteley and Seyd used their nationwide surveys of Labour and Conservative party members to derive an indirect measure of the intensity of campaign activity and found that this too suggested that local campaigning had an effect on constituency results (although in our view their findings in relation to Labour are more persuasive than are those for the Conservatives).[11] Finally, in studies of campaigning at the 1992 and 1997 general elections, we ourselves constructed a direct measure of the strength of local campaigning on the basis of surveys of election agents. We found clear evidence that in 1992 Labour and Liberal Democrat campaigning improved their performance and, in spite of Labour's landslide victory, there was evidence that all three parties' campaigns were effective in 1997.[12]

The parties' renewed interest in local campaigning began with by-elections. Although they had always been seen as important events in the life of a parliament, media interest in by-elections grew rapidly from the 1960s. The parties came to realize that a good by-election performance could bring them massive publicity and give a major boost to their fortunes. They began to pour massive resources into by-election campaigns and spectacular results were achieved, especially by the famed by-election machine of the Liberals and their successors.[13] It was not until the 1990s, however, that local campaigning in general elections began to be treated with the same seriousness. In part this was due to an awareness of the results of the 'revisionist' research. It was also a consequence of technological changes – especially the spread of computers – that made some aspects of local campaigning significantly easier and more effective. At the same time there was a general professionalization of campaigning which was evident in all parties and which involved borrowing and adapting techniques developed in the United States. Perhaps also by the late 1980s the party campaign organizers were seeing diminishing possibilities of improving the effectiveness of national media campaigns, while continuing to be aware of the potential of the local campaign in the crucial area of mobilization. It is in the nature of election contests – at least where the main contenders are anything like equally matched – that each side is looking for a relatively small edge or comparative advantage over its main opponent. This, together with the emerging results of revisionist research, would be sufficient to explain the parties' renewed interest in what went on in the constituencies. Even if the evidence is not conclusive, campaign organizers are unlikely to give up the possibility that effective managing of constituency campaigns might give them that edge.

Revisionist research on local campaigns

The continuing academic research on constituency campaigning has focused on three main areas. Firstly, it has sought to describe and assess the significance of the technological changes briefly referred to above. Secondly, it has explored the ways in which the party organizations at national level have reassessed the significance of the local campaign and revised their national campaigning strategies to incorporate the local campaign into a combined overall effort. Thirdly, it has attempted to establish whether well-run local campaigns have a pay-off, in the sense of significantly increasing the party's vote. We discuss each of these areas of interest in turn, referring mainly to our own research on the 1992 and 1997 elections for corroborating evidence.

New technology

The nature of local campaigning has changed a good deal since the 1950s. One early casualty of the advent of television, especially in urban areas, was the public election meeting. These were once a standard feature of all campaigns, but by 1997 only 13 per cent of Liberal Democrat campaigns, 20 per cent of Labour and 30 per cent of Conservative campaigns included more than one public meeting.[14] This form of face-to-face communication with electors is largely now confined to some rural areas, where it can be an effective way of meeting voters in scattered small communities.

Perhaps the most obvious changes in the nature of constituency campaigning, however, are those associated with the introduction of new technology, in particular information and communications technology of various kinds. There have been three important developments. Firstly, personal computers are ideally suited to taking the drudgery out of many of the more routine aspects of the traditional canvass and knocking-up campaign. Electronic versions of electoral registers can be obtained from Electoral Registration Officers, and these can be used to prepare the necessary lists of voters, to maintain records of individuals canvassed and responses received, and to prepare knocking-up lists for use in mobilizing voters on polling day. Though we do not have comparable figures for earlier elections, the figures in Table 5.1 give details of the use of PCs by the local constituency organizations of the major parties in 1992 and 1997. Computer use was already widespread by 1992, but it increased further in 1997 – more than three-quarters of all campaigns were using PCs, and the figure was virtually 100 per cent in marginal seats. The figures in the second row of the table reflect the

Table 5.1 The use of computers in local campaigns in 1992 and 1997

	Con		Lab		Lib Dem	
	1992	*1997*	*1992*	*1997*	*1992*	*1997*
% used PCs	79 (93)	88 (96)	77 (97)	90 (99)	68 (84)	77 (100)
% (of all) used party software	45 (77)	75 (86)	48 (84)	70 (94)	15 (42)	50 (79)
Mean number of PCs (of users)	1.6 (1.6)	1.8 (1.9)	2.9 (4.3)	3.4 (4.8)	2.4 (3.6)	3.6 (4.5)

Note: The figures in brackets are for marginal seats only – marginal seats for a party are those in which it won with a majority of 10 per cent or less of the vote, or was less than 10 per cent behind the winning party. The numbers on which the percentages in this and the following table are based are as follows (numbers for marginals in brackets): for 1992, Conservative 265 (57), Labour 356 (73), Liberal Democrat 383 (19); for 1997, Conservative 434 (121), Labour 455 (94), Liberal Democrat 411 (14).

efforts made by the parties' headquarters to assist and encourage their constituency organizations. Between 1992 and 1997 there were very sharp increases in the proportions of constituency campaigns using their national party's specially-designed software. Finally, where computers were used, there was an increase in the number of machines available. The Conservatives lagged somewhat, but by 1997 Labour and the Liberal Democrats, on average, used over four PCs per constituency in their marginal seats.

In addition to keeping canvass records for knocking up, computers have numerous other applications in campaigns. Our respondents reported using them for correspondence and printing address labels for election addresses, for example. In addition, they can be used to produce leaflets at local level. Leafleting has always been an important part of the conventional constituency campaign, alongside canvassing, but in the past leaflets usually had to be produced by professional printing firms and were relatively expensive. As a consequence, local parties usually bought standard leaflets printed in large numbers for their regional or national headquarters. Modern computers and laser printers have led to two important improvements. First, the local parties themselves can now produce highly professional leaflets relatively quickly and cheaply, and so they can deal with locally relevant issues. Second, computer databases allow leaflets or customized letters to be targeted on specific individuals. Direct mail of this kind is such a recent innovation at the constituency level that we did not ask about it in our 1992 study. In 1997, however, we found that computers were used for this purpose by

56 per cent of all Conservative campaigns, 50 per cent of Labour and 30 per cent of Liberal Democrat campaigns.

A third major change in local campaigning arising from technological development is the increased use of telephone canvassing, a campaigning technique imported from the United States. Telephone canvassing has a number of advantages over traditional 'doorstep' canvassing. It can be done in bad weather and by people who would be unable or unwilling to meet voters face-to-face, and it enables the parties to contact voters who live in remote areas or are otherwise difficult to reach in person. Perhaps most importantly, telephone canvassing can be done from anywhere in the country and parties can set up central or regional telephone 'banks' from which teams of volunteers can ring voters. What has made this method of canvassing feasible is the explosive growth in ownership of telephones in Britain. This stood at only 42 per cent of households in 1972, but had reached 91 per cent by 1994.[15] The first use of telephone canvassing on a significant scale was in the 1992 election. The legal implications of telephone canvassing – whether and how it should be counted as an election expense against the amount allowed – remain unclear, but there is no doubt that its use has rapidly increased. Table 5.2 shows the proportions of party campaigns undertaking telephone canvassing. The Liberal Democrats have been slower to adopt this technique, but it is clearly increasingly common in the other parties with about a quarter of all their campaigns claiming to have done 'a substantial amount' of telephone canvassing in 1997, and substantially more in marginal constituencies. The last row of the table shows the proportions who were aware of telephone canvassing of their constituency having been organized at regional or national level in 1997. (We did not ask a similar question in 1992 since nationally organized efforts of this kind were then in their infancy, and the parties were very wary of the legal implications.)

Table 5.2 Telephone canvassing in 1992 and 1997

	Con		Lab		Lib Dem	
	1992	*1997*	*1992*	*1997*	*1992*	*1997*
% did a 'substantial amount'	15 (26)	25 (40)	8 (1)	26 (62)	1 (5)	1 (7)
% did 'a little'	54 (40)	42 (44)	38 (62)	35 (29)	11 (24)	26 (64)
% telephone canvassing from outside constituency	–	8 (22)	–	16 (50)	–	9 (0)

Note: The figures in brackets are for marginal seats only. (See also note to Table 5.1.)

The spread of telephone canvassing has encouraged other important changes. Firstly, parties no longer wait until an election is in the offing before they start to gather information about voters' preferences. Rather, the operation begins months or years before an election is due. Secondly, more detailed information is now sought from voters. In addition to their current voting intention, those staffing the telephones will typically now also ask voters about their past voting record, opinions on issues, current concerns and evaluations of the party leaders. A range of demographic details – age, sex, occupation and so on – will be collected. Subsequently, voters can be sent targeted direct mail specifically tuned to their situation and, if necessary, arrangements made for party workers in the locality to pay a visit. This clearly reintroduces elements of persuasive communication into canvassing, and also involves some feedback from voters to parties. In preparing for the 1997 election, to emphasize the change from traditional canvassing, the Labour Party renamed the process 'voter identification'.

The national party organizations and constituency campaigns

Although these technological developments have been very important in changing the nature and potentially improving the effectiveness of campaigns at the local level, what has been crucial to the revivification of local campaigning has been the recognition by national party organizers that this was an area in which the overall effectiveness of campaigning could be improved. From the 1950s onwards, the emphasis of party headquarters was very much on the national campaign, and they devoted much time, effort and money to bolstering all aspects of the battle at the national level. Faced with diminishing returns in that direction – as all parties consulted media experts and adopted similar strategies and techniques – the professionals have been looking to find other ways in which they could gain an organizational edge over their rivals. The long-neglected and much-derided local campaign effort came to be seen as an area in which superior organization could be brought to bear and pay dividends. What has in effect emerged is a new relationship between the national and local campaigns, in which national party professionals seek to manage local campaigns in crucial respects.

One aspect of this, common to all parties, is the 'targeting' of resources and effort into key seats. The parties have always attempted to make special efforts in their marginal seats, but up to the 1990s local campaigns in the marginal seats remained *local* campaigns – organized and run by constituency parties or associations with some help and guidance from the centre. In more recent elections, however, targeting has reached new peaks of sophistication – with individual voters as well as constituencies being targeted by both Labour and the Conservatives – and this has transformed the relationship between the local and national levels in running local campaigns. This process has not gone as far, and the change has not been as rapid, in the Conservative and Liberal Democrat parties (partly because their local associations are constitutionally independent of the central party organization) but a brief account of Labour's campaign strategy in 1997 illustrates this new approach in its most developed form so far.

Elsewhere we have referred to Labour's campaign in 1997 as a 'triumph of targeting' and this encapsulates what is involved here.[16] The basis of Labour's strategy – codenamed 'Operation Victory' – was the ruthless targeting of national and local resources on 90 key seats. These resources were as much organizational as anything. Thus the national organization sought to ensure that candidates were selected early in these seats, that a campaign organization was in place with either a trained agent or alternatively a special organizer 'parachuted' in from Millbank. As noted above, canvassing was now renamed 'voter identification', and the central element of the strategy was a mass telephone voter identification campaign in the key seats during the 18 months before the election. Telephone banks were established in regional and local offices across the country and workers from all constituencies (with a centrally written script) were used to contact key seat voters. On the basis of the telephone interview, voters were divided into one of a number of categories depending on whether they were reliable Labour supporters, had a weak Labour preference, were potential switchers and so on. Reliable Labour supporters received little more attention and firm opponents were subsequently ignored while potential switchers, first-time voters and weak Labour supporters were then the subjects of a direct mail campaign and further telephone calls. During the 'short' campaign before the election, candidates and party workers were directed to individual voters whom they should contact personally, and finally there was a massive 'get-out-the-vote' operation on polling day, based on the detailed canvass returns. This whole operation was tightly managed from the centre by a key seats unit in Millbank. To a large extent in the target seats the initiative in local campaigning had ceased to lie with the local candidate and the agent.

The effect of targeting on the strength of local campaigning in the 1997 general election is illustrated in Table 5.3, which compares scores on our overall index of campaigning in target and non-target seats for each party. On this measure, in all three cases – and unsurprisingly – campaigns

Table 5.3   The strength of campaigns in target and non-target seats, 1997

	Con	Lab	Lib Dem
Target seats	0.758	1.218	1.288
N	(64)	(65)	(29)
Non-target seats	0.144	0.234	–0.745
N	(370)	(390)	(382)

Note: Campaign strength is measured by a standardized index incorporating seven dimensions of campaigning. For details see David Denver and Gordon Hands, *Modern Constituency Electioneering*, ch. 8.

in target seats were considerably stronger than those in non-targets. The strongest campaigns of all were by the Liberal Democrats in their relatively small number of targets closely followed by Labour in their targets, with Conservative targets lagging some way behind.

The effects of constituency campaigning

The evidence we have presented so far suggests that there was a rejuvenation of constituency campaigning over the past two general elections. This still leaves unanswered the question of whether it makes any difference to constituency election results. If the traditional view of academics – that it doesn't – is right, then the parties are unlikely to continue to give it a high priority as they did in 1992 and 1997. This is not the place to consider the evidence in detail and, indeed, the evidence is not straightforward,[17] but we summarize below the main conclusions from our studies of the 1992 and 1997 general elections.

Table 5.4 shows correlations between our index of campaign strength and measures of party performance in 1992 and 1997. Our preferred measure of party performance would be the change in a party's share of the electorate since the previous election but, unfortunately, we cannot use this measure for 1997 due to the extensive boundary revisions that were implemented between 1992 and 1997. We concentrate, therefore, on two other measures – change in share of the vote obtained (change from the notional share in 1992 in many instances) and actual share in 1997, controlling for share in 1992. These results, which were broadly confirmed by multiple regression analysis controlling for other variables, certainly provide some support for the revisionist view.

The first two rows show simple bivariate correlations and they suggest that in both 1992 and 1997 Labour and Liberal Democrat campaigns had an appreciable effect – vote share rose more in those seats where stronger campaigns were fought. Somewhat perplexingly, however, the

Table 5.4   Campaign intensity and party performance in 1992 and 1997

	Con	Lab	LibDem
Change in share of vote 1987–92	–0.201	0.408	0.263
Change in share of vote 1992–97	–0.342	0.411	0.316
% share of vote 1992 (controlling for share 1987)	–0.062*	0.437	0.405
% share of vote 1997 (controlling for share 1992)	0.418	0.432	0.410

Note: The first two rows are bivariate and the second two partial correlation coefficients.
* = not significant. Ns are as in Table 5.1.

coefficients for the Conservative campaigns are negative – the better they campaigned the more their vote share decreased. We have explored this 'peculiar case' elsewhere and suggest that it is perhaps something to do with the fact that Conservative supporters are likely to turn out and vote regardless of the strength of the local campaign.[18] The third and fourth rows show partial correlations between the campaigning index and share of vote in the relevant election while controlling for vote share in the previous election. Again these figures show a clear positive campaigning effect for Labour and the Liberal Democrats, but in this case the figure for the Conservatives in 1992 is not significant while that for 1997 suggests a small positive effect. Once we take account of the fact that the Conservative vote declined most in their strongest areas, local campaigning made for a better performance.

The fact that there was a clear local campaign effect in 1997 is in some ways surprising as we might have expected that any campaigning effect would have been washed away in the tidal wave flowing in Labour's direction. In an explicit criticism of Labour's key seats strategy, Ken Livingstone and other MPs noted in an early day motion shortly after the election that while the swing to Labour in its target seats averaged 11.8 per cent, it was 14.3 per cent in the 54 non-target seats which were won.[19] But using raw figures in this way is misleading. It takes no account of regional variations, for example, or the campaign effort made by other parties. We do the latter in Table 5.5, which shows the relationships between campaign intensity and party performance in 1997 in seats in which we had responses from all three major parties. The bivariate correlations show that in these seats, not only was stronger Conservative campaigning associated with a poorer Conservative performance but it also had no significant effect on the Labour share of

Table 5.5   Campaign intensity and party performance (cases with three responses), 1997

	Con index	Lab index	Lib Dem index
Change in share of vote 1992–97			
Con	–0.265	–0.142	–0.105*
Lab	0.059*	0.420	–0.264
Lib Dem	0.170	–0.242	0.327
% share of vote in 1997 (controlling for share 1992)			
Con	0.168	–0.147	0.150
Lab	0.059*	0.438	–0.399
Lib Dem	0.135*	–0.231	0.395

Note: The first two rows are bivariate and the second two partial correlation coefficients. Figures are for constituencies from which responses were received from all three parties (N = 198). * = not significant.

the vote and was associated with relatively better results for the Liberal Democrats. On the other hand, for both Labour and the Liberal Democrats stronger campaigns resulted in better performances by themselves and poorer results for the other two parties. The alternative measure using partial correlations tells broadly the same story although, as before, it suggests that Conservative campaigning did have an impact once the previous strength of the party is taken into account.

As noted above, this is not the place to attempt any more detailed assessment of this evidence. It does suggest, however, that in both 1992 and 1997, notwithstanding the landslide result in the latter election, there is clear evidence that local campaigning can work. A good local campaign produces a better election result than would otherwise be the case. This should be enough to encourage national party organizers to continue their efforts to manage campaigns at the local level.

Future trends

If anything, the British electorate is likely to become even more dealigned, more influenced by short-term factors and, as a consequence, more open to persuasion and mobilization. Local campaigning – even though it is increasingly organized from the centre – is now recognized to be an effective means of achieving these ends. We should, therefore, expect to see the developments in local campaigning which occurred in the 1990s continuing for the foreseeable future (assuming that there is no change in the electoral system).

Firstly, there will be even more sophisticated use of PCs. Their use is now all but universal in marginal and key seats but will spread to almost all local campaigns. Secondly, telephone canvassing will become more common. Indeed, the sight of canvassers going from door to door armed with canvass cards and other material may soon be a rarity in British elections. Thirdly, with the aid of computers and telephone interviews with voters, targeting will become more sophisticated, focusing on key individuals in key seats (as with Labour in 1997). Local campaigns will, therefore, be directed at a small minority of the electorate. Fourthly, because there is an electoral payoff, the professionalization of campaigning will extend further to local campaigns. Although for a variety of reasons the number of full-time agents has declined, parties will ensure that in key constituencies there is a full-time professional campaign organizer in place well before elections to prepare for and direct the local campaign. Fifthly, campaigning will be more or less continuous. It used to be that local parties started from scratch when an election was called but the new approach involves an enormous amount of work well in advance of the election. Finally, local campaigns in key seats are likely to be seen as too important to be left to volunteers in the constituencies. In the past, party headquarters simply provided back-up to local campaigns; in the future they are likely to want to manage and control them in order to ensure their effectiveness.

The paradox in all of this is that the resurgence of local constituency campaigning involves more central control. Local campaigns will no longer be the preserve of 'amateur' local party activists but integrated into the overall campaign strategy designed, monitored and managed by professionals at party headquarters.

6
The National Daily Press

Colin Seymore-Ure

Introduction

Even a commentator steeped in tabloid journalism would have to be overexcited to claim that the political role of the press has been 'transformed' over the last half-century, especially compared with that of broadcasting. Compared with broadcasting, too, the changes with which this chapter is concerned are less clearly marked with milestones, such as the broadcasters' decision to report the 1959 general election campaign in news bulletins (see Chapter 7). Nor have the changes gone in one direction: press partisanship, for instance, has waxed and waned. In general the changes in the press reflect its longer history: its interwoven relations with political parties; its enduring tensions with government; and the tradition that the press, unlike broadcasting, is almost never an explicit area of government policy.

Politics and the press: the broadcasting context

The very intrusion of broadcasting, however, means that it would be impossible to write about politics and the press without some preliminary reference to broadcasting. Television has been an enveloping mist, indefinite but omnipresent. The claim that 'Television *is* the campaign', shocking in the early 1970s, is a reminder that broadcasting has become part of the environment within which politics is carried on, while the press remains principally a medium applied *to* politics.

Until 1959 the press had almost no competition in reporting politics. Thereafter, broadcasting increasingly and literally got in the way. The point can be simply illustrated with the example of press conferences.

As Prime Minister, Edward Heath held three experimental televised conferences in the early 1970s, and they were a flop. One reason was that the newspaper journalists did not want to waste their questions in a session that would be broadcast before their papers hit the streets. The introduction of press conferences at the parties' headquarters during election campaigns, in contrast, had been a great success in 1959 because they suited newspapers. 'It is a wry comment on electioneering and on the national press', remarked Butler and Rose, 'that parties with a membership of millions could do so much to create an appearance of nationwide activity simply by using the wits and industry of half-a-dozen people for a few hours each morning'.[1] The conferences were extremely successful both in capturing the news agenda and in helping the Labour campaign outshine that of the other parties. Although Labour started the conferences chiefly with the press in mind, they also had obvious attractions for the broadcasters, and in subsequent elections the conferences became an election staple increasingly geared to broadcasters' needs.

Broadcasting thus not only became a competitor to the press in reporting and analysis: it also created new forums of political communication, which the press needed to cover. Party leaders' broadcast interviews were reported in the press next day and their performances were marked up or down, like footballers and actors. Columnists evaluated future leaders in terms of their television appeal. Weekend papers set the agenda for Sunday current affairs programmes, which in turn might affect Monday morning's papers. Print journalists routinely took part in broadcast discussion programmes, since broadcasters themselves were not allowed to editorialize. Television also influenced politicians' behaviour in traditional news forums, such as the House of Commons and the hustings; indeed it contributed to the hustings' decline. Beyond that, broadcasting had an effect – again, indefinite – on the press as a business. Bit by bit, for instance, television ate into the national advertising cake, taking eventually about one-third of it. The national press managed to cling onto a fairly constant share, some 15 per cent (the big losers were magazines and the provincial press). Without television advertising, papers might have been cheaper or larger, and a few more titles might have survived. It remains unclear how far television affected reading habits – even concentration spans – and thence the propensity to look for detailed political content in a newspaper. But by the late 1960s, television had certainly replaced the press as the main medium through which people got their news.

Changes in the structure of the press

National daily newspaper reading is an obstinate habit. Television and the leisure opportunities brought by prosperity to some extent fuelled rather than undermined it. Table 6.1 shows circulation figures for national daily and Sunday newspapers for selected years. The peak was 1957, before the expansion of television had begun to bite. In the forty years after that, the decline was 20 to 25 per cent. On average, each copy was read by more than two people, and many people (one in four in the 1960s) read more than one paper, so overall readership remained high. The majority of adults saw a national daily every day.

Sunday papers, on the other hand, lost about half their readership in the same period. It is incredible to think that the *News of the World* sold nearly eight and a half million copies each week in the early 1950s. The few provincial Sundays held their own. But the provincial dailies, both morning and evening, struggled: the combined circulation of the roughly one hundred titles fell from about 60 to 40 per cent of the national dailies'. At the end of the century as in 1945, a citizen's view of the political world, seen through the press, was refreshed on a 24-hour cycle, was national more than local (except in Scotland) and, allowing

Table 6.1 National newspaper circulation, 1945–99

Year	National daily[a]	National Sunday
	(millions)	
1945	12.35	19.76
1949	16.45	29.32
1953	16.07	30.20
1957	16.71	29.08
1961	15.69	23.33
1965	15.59	23.98
1969	14.80	24.37
1973	14.55	22.10
1977	13.95	18.95
1981	15.39	17.82
1985	14.73	17.83
1989	14.55	17.50
1993	13.23	15.77
1997	13.18	14.95
1999	12.90	13.96

[a] Excludes *Daily Worker/Morning Star*.

Sources: Audit Bureau of Circulations, Press Council; Colin Seymour-Ure, *The British Press and Broadcasting Since 1945*, 2nd edn (Oxford: Blackwell, 1996).

for some regional editions, was much the same everywhere. This is what the British expect; yet it does not happen in France, Germany, North America, Australasia and many other parts of the world. In all those places, equivalents to Scottish and Welsh nationalism (or even the Liberal strength in the South West), for instance, would probably have been represented in strong regional newspapers.

The number of different newspaper titles actually increased (see Table 6.2). In 1945 there were eight – nine if the small and restricted Communist *Daily Worker* is included. This number omits the *Guardian*, which had a small circulation, retained the name Manchester in its title and was based in Manchester until 1960. The *Financial Times*, too, did not then count as a normal national newspaper, since its contents were highly specialized with no sport and arts, for instance.

In 1999 there were nine titles, the result of several goings and comings. Competition for advertising revenue forced the loss-making Liberal *News Chronicle* out of business in 1960. The *Daily Herald*, similarly uncompetitive, limped on until 1964, when it was relaunched as a mini-broadsheet *Sun*, hoping to bring Harold Wilson's brand of techno-socialism to a younger and more affluent working-class readership. Such readers remained elusive. The title was sold to Rupert Murdoch in 1969, in one of the most damaging commercial decisions of the post-1945 press. Murdoch immediately turned the paper into a close copy of the *Daily Mirror* (which hitherto had no effective competitor), keeping many of its old readers and overhauling the *Mirror*'s circulation within eight years. Meanwhile Lord Rothermere closed the tabloid *Daily Sketch*, a quavering voice for the conservative working class.

Until Mrs Thatcher's industrial relations legislation in the early 1980s, it was unpractical to try and launch a new national daily from scratch. Total advertising revenue was inadequate to make even the existing titles profitable, and union power – fascinatingly strong – made it unfeasible to cut production costs by removing restrictive practices. Between the launch of the *Daily Sketch* in 1908 and of the *Star* in 1978, not a single new national daily was founded.[2] The *Star* worked, because the owners of the *Daily* and *Sunday Express* had spare printing capacity in Manchester and saw that a downmarket tabloid with a small staff would reduce the overall costs of the group, even if the title itself made a loss.

The next completely new title was Eddy Shah's tabloid *Today* (1986), which used new technology (in effect, early word-processing) and non-union labour. It was closely followed by the *Independent* (1986), launched with capital raised in the city and the ambition of having no shareholder owning more than 10 per cent. The goal was political independence,

Table 6.2 National daily newspapers: circulation (thousands)

Newspaper (launch date)	1945	1950	1955	1960	1965	1970	1975	1980	1985	1990	1995	1999
'Broadsheets'												
Daily Telegraph (1855)	822	976	1055	1200	1337	1409	1331	1433	1202	1076	1060	1045
The Times (1785)	195	245	222	260	254	388	319	316	478	420	647	741
Financial Times (1888)	(35)	(57)	(80)	122	146	170	181	196	234	290	294	385
(Manchester) Guardian (1821)	(80)	(140)	(156)	212	270	304	319	379	487	424	400	399
The Independent (1986)	–	–	–	–	–	–	–	–	–	411	294	223
Total	1017	1230	1277	1794	2007	2271	2150	2324	2401	2621	2695	2793
(%)	(8)	(7)	(8)	(11)	(13)	(15)	(15)	(16)	(16)	(18)	(20)	(22)
(including Financial Times and Manchester Guardian)	(1132)	(1427)	(1513)									
'Middle market'												
Daily Express (1900)	3239	4116	4036	4270	3987	3563	2822	2194	1902	1585	1279	1096
Daily Mail (1896)	1752	2225	2068	2825	2464	1890	1726	1948	1815	1708	1788	2350
Daily Herald/Sun (1912)	2000	2017	1759	1418	1273	–	–	–	–	–	–	–

Table 6.2 (continued)

Newspaper (launch date)	1945	1950	1955	1960	1965	1970	1975	1980	1985	1990	1995	1999
News Chronicle (1930)	1454	1534	1253	–	–	–	–	–	–	–	–	–
Today (1986)	–	–	–	–	–	–	–	–	–	540	566	–
Total	8445	9046	9116	8513	7724	5453	4548	4142	3717	3833	3633	3446
(%)	(68)	(60)	(57)	(53)	(49)	(37)	(32)	(28)	(25)	(27)	(27)	(49)
'Mass market' tabloids												
Daily Mirror (1903)	2000	4567	4725	4649	5019	4570	3968	3625	3033	3083	2518	2313
Daily Sketch/Graphic (1908)	883	717	950	1075	844	785	–	–	–	–	–	–
Sun (1970)	–	–	–	–	–	1615	3446	3741	4125	3855	4080	3730
Daily Star (1978)	–	–	–	–	–	–	–	1034	1455	833	738	615
Total	2883	5344	5675	5724	5863	6970	7414	8400	8613	7771	7336	6658
(%)	(23)	(32)	(35)	(37)	(38)	(47)	(53)	(56)	(58)	(55)	(54)	(52)
Total	12345	16520	16068	16031	15594	14694	14112	14886	14731	14225	13664	12897

Guardian and *Financial Times* not counted as national dailies until 1960. *Financial Times* figures in the 1990s include more than 120 000 copies overseas. *Daily Express* was renamed *The Express* in the 1990s. *Today* was closed in November 1995.

Sources: Audit Bureau of Circulations, Press Council Annual reports; individual newspapers. Some figures are part-year averages.

both editorial and proprietorial. Both these launches were bolstered by Murdoch's astonishing *coup de théâtre*. Overnight in January 1986 he moved production of his newspapers from the Fleet Street area east to Wapping, sacking staff, defying pickets and protected by waves of police (thanks to recent trade union legislation).[3] He had fooled the unions into thinking the new premises were for a new publication.

In the wake of Murdoch's success, a few other new titles bobbed briefly before sinking: *News on Sunday* (1987), *The Post* (1988), *Sunday Today* (1986–87), the *Sunday Correspondent* (1988–89). Yet even with reduced production costs, there were arguably still 'too many' titles for the available advertising. *Today* was closed by Murdoch, who had salvaged it, in 1995, and several other titles remained at risk.

There is a presumption in democratic politics that more titles are better than fewer. But for Britain this presumption needs heavily qualifying both in terms of circulation and of ownership. Circulation is polarized between broadsheets and tabloids.[4] In 1945, as can be seen from Table 6.2, there was a flourishing 'middle market' group of 'popular broadsheets'. These, indeed, included all the mass circulation papers except the *Daily Mirror*, and they were read by two-thirds of the nation. The tabloid *Daily Mirror* and *Daily Sketch* were read by one quarter, and the 'quality broadsheets' satisfied the remaining 8 per cent.

Steadily over the next thirty years the middle market shrank. Two of the four papers ceased publication (the Liberal *News Chronicle* and the Labour *Daily Herald*), and the circulation of the Conservative *Daily Express* and *Daily Mail* leaked away. The quality broadsheets increased in number and circulation, and the tabloid *Sun* forged ahead. By the mid-1990s the downmarket tabloids accounted for some 55 per cent of circulation, the broadsheets for 20 per cent and the remaining middle market for about 25 per cent. During the same period, the *Daily Mail* (1971) and *Daily Express* (1977) adopted a tabloid format.

To oversimplify only a little, in 1945 one person in five read a tabloid paper: in 1995, one person in five did not. The old middle market broadsheets had what might be called broadsheet tastes and news values – but expressed in a 'popular' style. Their new tabloid format was a further move in the mass-market direction. There was a greater difference between the style and content of the *Daily Mail* and *Daily Telegraph* of 1995, say, than between those two papers fifty years earlier. The 'tabloidization' of the press has continued apace (see Chapter 10).

The other important feature lurking behind such terms as 'quality' and 'mass market' is social class. The huge differences in circulation between the broadsheet papers and the tabloids (including the former middle market titles) developed with the growth of the popular press in the first half of the twentieth century. Newspaper finances depended upon large advertising revenue. Broadsheet readers had more money, so those papers could make the same amount from a smaller circulation. Labour's *Daily Herald*, a serious, highly political, working-class paper, lost money with a circulation of one and a quarter million in 1964, while the *Financial Times*, with an upper middle-class readership, coined it with a circulation one-eighth as large. The *Daily Herald* and the *News Chronicle* went broke because there was not enough advertising revenue to support them at the cover price readers were prepared to pay.

In their heyday, the middle market papers were comparatively classless, in the particular sense that the readership of the *Daily Express* and *Daily Mail* in the 1960s, for instance, roughly reflected the class distribution of the population as a whole. The later broadsheet/tabloid polarization thus partly polarized readers, not only style and content. Having said that, it was true that upper- and middle-class readers (ABC1 in social researchers' terms) always had a greater effective choice of papers than did working-class readers (C2DE). A middle-class household frequently subscribed both to *The Times* and the *Daily Express*, or some similar combination. But a *Daily Mirror* reader was more likely just to stick with the *Mirror*. At its peak circulation, in about 1965, half the adult population and thus a large majority of the working class read (as distinct from buying) the *Daily Mirror* every day. No middle-class paper enjoyed anything like such domination.

The political implications of these features are discussed below. But first the key patterns of press ownership must be distinguished. The largely unchanging number of newspaper titles during the second half-century conceals much buying and selling. One reason was the very difficulty of starting from nothing: better, if you wanted to be a press magnate, to buy your way in. Altogether there were about forty changes of ownership during that period among the national dailies and Sundays. Only the *Daily Mail* and the *Guardian* remained in the same hands throughout. The Mirror group papers changed four times (1970, 1984, 1991, 1999), and the *Independent* titles (1994, 1998), *The Times* (1966, 1981) and the *Express* titles (1977, 1985) all changed twice.

Politicians found themselves dealing with a changing cast of owners, and with newspaper groups not individual titles. The trends of ownership were towards more concentration, more internationalization and more conglomerates. In 1945 the 11 national dailies (on the inclusive definition) belonged to 11 separate owners; at the end of the century, four out of ten belonged to two owners (see Table 6.3). In 1945 the

Table 6.3 National daily newspapers: ownership 1945–99

Newspaper	Controlling owner in 1945	Launch/Change of ownership	Controlling owner in 1999 (date of purchase)
Daily Express	Lord Beaverbrook	Trafalgar House, 1977	United Newspapers, 1985
Daily Herald/ Sun	Odhams/TUC	Mirror Group, 1961	Murdoch, 1969
Daily Mail	Lord Rothermere		Lord Rothermere
Daily Mirror	Various	Reed, 1970; Maxwell, 1984; Mirror Group, 1991	Trinity Holdings, 1999
Daily Sketch/ Graphic	Lord Kemsley	Lord Rothermere, 1952 (closed 1971)	–
Daily Star	–	Trafalgar House, 1978	United Newspapers, 1985
Daily Telegraph	Lord Camrose/ Berry Family		Black, 1985
Financial Times	Eyre Trust		Pearson, 1957
(Manchester) Guardian	Scott Trust		Scott Trust
Independent	–	Various, 1986; Mirror Group, 1994	O'Reilly, 1998
News Chronicle	Cadbury Family	(Closed 1960)	–
The Times	Col. J. Astor	Thomson, 1966	Murdoch, 1981
Today	–	Shah, 1986; Lonrho, 1986; Murdoch, 1987 (closed 1995)	–

three largest groups owned three dailies, with 61 per cent of total circulation; at the other end, the three largest groups (a different three) owned five dailies with 66 per cent of circulation. By 1993 all the Sunday papers belonged to one or another daily paper; fifty years earlier, one quarter of them were independent. Concentration in fact reached its peak in the later 1960s, when three groups owned half the national daily and Sunday titles, with 85 per cent of total circulation. Thereafter, circulation share decreased, but for a while in the 1990s seven national dailies were in the hands of three companies.

In 1945 all the press groups were mainly owned by British capital and their principal business was newspapers; by the century's end, almost all belonged to international organizations in which newspapers might be a minor (and in a few cases, such as Express Newspapers, lately acquired) part. Some groups, such as Rupert Murdoch's, were largely media businesses. Others were highly diverse: Pearson (*Financial Times*), for example, had properties ranging from merchant banking to Royal Doulton china. Lord Hollick's MAI, which bought control of the Express titles after getting involved with ITV in 1990, had been created from financial and insurance services. Murdoch was born Australian and naturalized American; Conrad Black (*Daily* and *Sunday Telegraph*) was Canadian; Tony O'Reilly (*Independent*) was Irish.

Above all, newspapers entered joint ownership with terrestrial and satellite television, radio, cable and other electronic services. This was possible as a matter of policy from the start of ITV in 1955, to protect papers from the possible effects of ITV on their advertising revenue. It became immensely more important as the range of television services expanded, and – especially – after the 1990 Broadcasting Act allowed for concentration of TV franchise ownership and more flexible cross-ownership with newspapers. Groups' overseas interests, of course, frequently included electronic media too.

These ownership trends gave an extra twist to the political role of the press. From one end of the century to the other, they reported and interpreted politics and (if they wished) weighed in as participants. Until they became involved with electronic media and these media themselves became an inescapable subject of government policy, newspapers benefited from a pretence that governments did not have policies about the press. A 'free press' was understood to mean freedom from explicit government control (except during wartime). But electronic media were an important and growing sector of the economy. Once involved with them, newspapers too found themselves therefore increasingly affected by regulatory policy, so that they had a more direct interest than ever before in the outcome of elections. The role of detached observer was still possible in theory, but in practice it might lack credibility.

General political implications

The changes in the structure of the press did not in themselves make much difference to the press and politics. For the entire half-century, for instance, newspapers took what might be called a Westminster view of politics. The most obvious illustration was the attention paid to general elections. With the exception latterly of the World Cup, probably no event received so much concentrated coverage for an entire month or more at a time. Papers may have become sceptical about the raw power of parliamentarians as the decades passed, but they never wavered in their commitment to general elections as an expression of popular legitimacy. In 1997 as in 1945, editorialists paid readers the compliment of assuming that casting a vote was – and ought to be – the outcome of a rational process of evaluating principles, evidence and argument. Even the *Sunday Sport*, a soft porn magazine dressed up like a newspaper, had 'leading articles' in the 1992 general election.

Between general elections, the Westminster view was reflected in the use of Parliament as a reference point for deciding the news agenda, both on a day-to-day basis and for longer-term issues (such as decolonization, social policy, the future of Europe, etc.). MPs and peers enjoyed preferential access for their opinions. The press arguably lagged behind in its awareness of the political leverage of interest groups. Groups prodded the body politic wherever it would squeak; yet the routines of political reporting (as of most news) depended on recognizable and predictable events, offices and institutions – legislature, city councils, bureaucracies, courts – into which most interest groups did not tidily fit. Even trade union coverage was the strict preserve of specialist labour and industrial correspondents, not political correspondents.

As this last example indicates, the dominance of the Westminster view, and its gradual decline, were reflected in the machinery of political journalism. In 1945 newspapers' political staffs were focused on Parliament. The broadsheets still had teams reporting debates (*The Times* had a staff of 14). But the reporter with most pay and status, sometimes staying in the job for decades, was the Lobby Correspondent. He enjoyed privileged access to MPs and ministers at the House of Commons. He might see the prime minister from time to time (prime ministers varied in their accessibility: Churchill almost not at all, Wilson quite often). He would see the prime minister's press secretary twice a day for a collective briefing and would talk to him privately whenever he wished. No paper was allowed more than one Lobby correspondent, and the Sunday, provincial evening and overseas papers were excluded altogether. The lobby was therefore a group of perhaps 35 trusties, who would keep confidences – and who, as a result, were given confidences.

This system began to disintegrate, on the newspaper side, in the early 1960s. Staff grew more numerous. Papers were allowed 'alternates' and then multiple membership. Turnover of membership increased. Broadcasters muscled in, especially during the Thatcher era. By the late 1990s the Lobby list numbered more than 230. The collective briefings, always an object of resentment and suspicion to the excluded, became public knowledge – and controversial. The *Independent*, the *Guardian* and *The Scotsman* made great play of boycotting them in the later 1980s. TV made the Downing Street press secretary a public figure, after

Mrs Thatcher's Bernard Ingham had been in the job a few years. (He served for her entire incumbency, less the first six months.)

The disintegration can be summed up in three developments. On the press side, first, papers increasingly broadened their conception of politics as their resources grew. In the mid-1960s, an era of frustrated Wilsonian ambition after 13 Conservative years, specialist correspondents proliferated in most of the policy areas across Whitehall. Lobby correspondents stuck to Westminster, but now Whitehall was effectively encroached too. The coverage of economic and social policy, for example, increased immensely both in scale and sophistication. In the 1990s, a further increase in space and resources saw the institution of entire supplements in such fields. In the general news and feature pages, political columnists sprang up in unprecedented numbers. These innovations slurred the tones of the traditional leader page. Papers now had editorial voices, not a single, anonymous editorial voice. Altogether, the total political news operation of the broadsheets in the 1990s dwarfed the output of even twenty years earlier. Newspaper pagination is a crude but indicative measure. In 1947, *The Times* had a daily average of ten pages, the *Daily Mirror* nine and the middle market papers five. By the mid-1970s, *The Times* had 26, the *Mirror* and *Sun* 28 and the *Mail* 34. In 1999 the broadsheets averaged about 50, the *Mirror* and *Sun* 60 and the *Mail* 80 to 90 – not counting their various supplements.

The second development was a corollary and arguably overdue reduction of press interest in the chamber of the House of Commons. This was encapsulated in the decision of *The Times* in the mid-1990s to abandon its daily page summarizing parliamentary debates. This did not of course mean the abandonment of Parliament itself. Rather, coverage concentrated proportionately more on the work, for example, of parliamentary investigative select committees. These paralleled the interests of each Whitehall ministry, and they had won increasing prestige in the twenty years since Mrs Thatcher took office. Their policy influence was intangible. But they grilled civil servants and sometimes ministers, and – above all, one may claim – they brought into the open the aims and expertise of a wide variety of interest groups and lobbyists.

The third point about the disintegration of lobby journalism is simply that it reflected changes in the working of central government and politics across the decades. The role of the prime minister in government was different in the 1990s from the 1940s, for instance. There was no 'Prime Minister's Department', but the Downing Street machine was bigger and more influential. The Press Office, chiefly as a result of television, became necessarily more active in seeking to manage the news. Clement Attlee's press secretary spurned that title: he served the whole government, and as 'Press Relations Adviser'. Bernard Ingham and Alastair Campbell were both happy to be press secretaries. They were key members of the prime minister's entourage. Strictly speaking, they too served the whole government, but in reality their overriding loyalty was to the prime minister. A more presidential prime minister required press coverage less focused on, and organized round, his or her parliamentary roles. So press reporting adjusted to that fact.[5]

Press partisanship

A Westminster view of politics meant a concentration not only on Parliament but also on political parties. Between parties and newspapers there is a natural affinity: the same social forces that find expression in a party tend to find expression also through the press. Parties organize to represent people and principles, to find common ground and to fight campaigns. Newspapers are a good instrument of organization, information and campaign propaganda. In the nineteenth century, partisan individuals and groups often owned newspapers – and did not care whether they made a profit. Even in a television age, the fledgling Social Democratic Party ran its own magazine in the early 1980s, and there was a residual electronic echo in the distribution by Sir James Goldsmith's Referendum Party of a staggering five million videos to unsuspecting households during the 1997 general election campaign.

Referendums, indeed, show the affinity of newspapers and parties or other campaigning organizations very well. In the 1975 referendum on Common Market membership, both major party leaderships (apart from a few cabinet ministers 'licensed' to disagree) and the entire national press, excepting the *Daily* and *Sunday Express*, were behind the 'Yes' campaign. The 'No' campaign organization, lacking its own papers, had almost no opportunity for publicity on its own terms. It had to rely on opposing newspapers' fairness – and on the level playing field provided by the broadcasters. Moreover, in the absence of candidates running for office, 'the campaign' was a national event – taking place in, and dependent on, the news media even more than a general election does.

By 1945 only the *Daily Herald* still belonged to a political party – and, even then, only indirectly. The TUC owned 49 per cent of the shares and the printer, Odhams, owned 51 per cent. Odhams' boss, Lord Southwood, had commercial control, but he was content to leave policy to the TUC. The *Daily Herald* held a big rally at the Albert Hall during the 1945 campaign, and every year the editor had to give an account of himself to a closed session of the Labour Party Conference.

The Labour leadership could command the *Herald*. In this it was unique. All other partisan papers in 1945, and ever after, had to be persuaded or cajoled: hence the reflexive regularity with which new owners were offered peerages. In the late 1960s, when Labour depended almost exclusively on the *Daily Mirror* and its sister Sunday papers for press support, the Mirror group contained at least five life peers. Murdoch could have had a peerage for the asking. Conrad Black, as the century was ending, accepted one – but was baulked by Canadian government rules.[6]

Many owners needed little cajolery. The press is a thoroughly capitalist business. Rewards can be great but risks are high; great fortunes are made and lost in a lifetime; entrepreneurs can stamp their personality on the product. The imagery of the 'baron' is apt. Typically, therefore, owners' instincts favoured the Conservative Party during most of the period from 1945. The Conservatives usually had little need for formal control over the press. The Nuffield study of the 1950 election suggested that the hallmark of an 'official' party paper was that all its 'themes and leader subjects seemed to be raised first in speeches or party declarations'.[7] Such a comment might equally have been made of the *Daily Telegraph* or *Daily Mail* at any election until the mid-1970s (and after, in the former case). The characteristics that in the 1955 campaign made the *Herald* seem if anything 'a little duller and more orthodox' than ever to the Nuffield author would certainly have fitted the *Telegraph* while it remained in the ownership of Lord Hartwell, up to 1985.[8] Boring as they were, these must have seemed veritable virtues to the party leaders.

Press partisanship after 1945 could therefore be measured scarcely at all by party ownership. A better measure is the number of partisan titles. This is shown in Tables 6.4 and 6.5 (detail in Table 6.4; summaries in Table 6.5). The Conservative dominance is obvious. In 1945 it was not bad, in the sense that there were equal numbers of Conservative and anti-Conservative papers, if the *Manchester Guardian* is included. But the death of the Liberal *News Chronicle* (1960) and Labour's *Daily Herald* (1964) were body blows. The successor *Sun* eased Labour's pain, but its replacement by the stridently Conservative Murdoch *Sun*, plus the foundation of the *Daily Star* in 1978, made things even worse. In 1964 twice as many papers supported the Conservatives as Labour, and from then onwards the proportion was never less, until the turnaround in 1997. The extreme was 1983, the nadir of Labour's fortunes in general, when only the *Daily Mirror* supported Labour outright and the ratio was seven to one.

The first qualification to these comments is that after 1964 more papers were willing to blur their commitment. The strength of the partisan tradition is seen in the fact that across the complete run of 15 elections from 1945 to 1997, individual papers refused to commit themselves at all only six times – and three of these were in 1987 and 1992. Among compromisers, the chief was the *Guardian*, which is required by the terms of its trust ownership to support, in effect, a pragmatic liberal radicalism. This made the paper change its electoral support nine times between 1945 and 1997. The other chief waverer was *The Times*. This had a tradition of non-commitment, which it abandoned in 1950. Its instincts were, and remained, Conservative, but it flirted with the Liberals during the Wilson era, and in 1997 it campaigned as a Eurosceptic and cheerfully endorsed candidates from six different parties.

The strength of the partisan tradition, in a different way, accounts for perhaps the most astonishing fact about individual partisanship. Across the entire half-century, there were only two unqualified U-turns from one party to another. Both were by the *Sun* – from Labour to Conservative in February 1974, and from Conservative to Labour in 1997. That made two U-turns out of a possible 150 or so (if every daily paper, that is, had changed at every election).

These election commitments are snapshots, of course, since elections force papers to crystallize their general opinions. In between, only the most 'official' papers have not qualified their support from time to time. Every Conservative prime minister will have felt to a greater or lesser degree that with friends like the press, who needs enemies? Labour leaders and prime ministers, too, did not always see eye to eye with the *Daily Mirror* (and the *Guardian*) on such matters as party organization, Europe and Defence. To reduce the point to its simplest, a paper's commitment to a party, when that party is in office, is always likely to clash with a potentially stronger journalistic commitment to the principle of independence from government.

The extraordinary continuity of electoral commitment does, however, put the 1997 election in perspective. For this time Labour had six supporters – three times as many as the average since 1945 and twice its former maximum (three, in 1964). In addition to the *Sun*'s dramatic conversion, the *Independent*, *Daily Star* and *Financial Times* all came off the various fences they had sat on in 1992. Having said that, those shifts seem more likely to be a *de*-alignment, arguably, than a *re*-alignment. New Labour was unproven in 1997, and papers' endorsements gave the

Table 6.4 Newspaper partisanship at general elections, 1945–97

| | Circulation (m) and party support | | | | | | | | | | | | | | |
	1945	1950	1951	1955	1959	1964	1966	1970	Feb. 1974	Oct. 1974	1979	1983	1987	1992	1997
Daily Express	3.30 Con	4.10 Con	4.17 Con	4.04 Con	4.05 Con	4.20 Con	3.99 Con	3.67 Con	3.29 Con	3.26 Con	2.46 Con	1.94 Con	1.70 Con	1.52 Con	1.21 Con
Daily Herald/Sun[a]	1.85 Lab	2.03 Lab	2.00 Lab	1.76 Lab	1.47 Lab	1.30 Lab	1.27 Lab	–	–	–	–	–	–	–	–
Daily Mail	1.70 Con	2.22 Con	2.27 Con	2.07 Con	2.07 Con	2.40 Con	2.46 Con	1.94 Con	1.73 Con	1.76 Con	1.97 Con	1.83 Con	1.76 Con	1.67 Con	2.13 Con
Daily Mirror	2.40 Lab	4.60 Lab	4.51 Lab	4.73 Lab	4.50 Lab	5.08 Lab	5.02 Lab	4.85 Lab	4.29 Lab	4.26 Lab	3.78 Lab	3.27 Lab	3.12 Lab	2.90 Lab	2.39 Lab
Daily Sketch/Graphic[b]	0.90 Con	0.78 Con	0.79 Con	0.95 Con	1.16 Con	0.85 Con	0.84 Con	0.84 Con	–	–	–	–	–	–	–
Daily Telegraph	0.81 Con	0.98 Con	1.00 Con	1.06 Con	1.18 Con	1.32 Con	1.34 Con	1.39 Con	1.42 Con	1.42 Con	1.36 Con	1.28 Con	1.15 Con	1.03 Con	1.13 Con
(Manchester) Guardian	0.08 Lib	0.14 Lib/Con	0.14 Lib/Con	0.16 Lib/Con	0.18 Lab/Lib	0.28 Lab	0.27 Lab/Lib	0.30 Lab/Lib	0.35 Con/Lab/Lib balance	0.36 More Lib influence	0.28 Lab	0.42 Not Con landslide	0.49 Lab	0.43 Lab more Lib Dems	0.40 Lab
News Chronicle	1.55 Lib	1.53 Lib	1.51 Lib	1.25 Lib	1.21 Lib	–	–	–	–	–	–	–	–	–	–

The Times	0.20 None	0.26 Con	0.23 Con	0.22 Con	0.25 Con	0.26 Con	0.25 More Lib	0.41 Con/Lib	0.35 Con/Lib	0.35 Con/Lib	Not Published Con	0.32 Con	0.44 Con	0.39 Con	0.77 Euro sceptic
Financial Times[c]	–	–	–	–	–	0.15 Con	0.15 Uncommitted	0.17 Uncommitted	0.20 Con	0.20 Con	0.21 Con	0.25 Con	0.28 Con	0.29 Not Con majority	0.30 Lab
Sun	–	–	–	–	–	–	–	1.51 Lab	2.97 Con	3.15 Coalition	3.94 Con	4.16 Con	3.99 Con	3.57 Con	3.93 Lab
Daily Star	–	–	–	–	–	–	–	–	–	–	0.88 Uncommitted	1.31 Con	1.29 Con	0.81 Uncommitted	0.66 Lab
Independent	–	–	–	–	–	–	–	–	–	–	–	–	0.29 Uncommitted	0.39 Uncommitted	0.26 Lab
Today	–	–	–	–	–	–	–	–	–	–	–	–	0.31 Coalition	0.53 Con	–
Total circulation	12.79	16.64	16.62	16.24	16.07	15.84	15.59	15.08	14.60	14.76	14.88	14.78	14.82	13.53	13.18

[a] The Sun replaced the *Daily Herald* in 1964. It was bought and relaunched by Rupert Murdoch in 1969.

[b] Named *Daily Graphic* 1946–52.

[c] Not counted as a general interest paper before 1964.

Sources: Royal Commission on the Press, 1974–7; Nuffield College election studies by D. E. Butler and co-authors. Circulation figures are for the periods covered by the elections.

Table 6.5 Newspaper partisanship 1945–97: summary

	1945	1950	1951	1955	1959	1964	1966	1970	1974	1974	1979	1983	1987	1992	1997
No. of papers supporting															
Conservative:															
wholly	4	5	5	5	5	6	4	4	5	4	5	6	7	5	3
in part	–	–	1	1	–	–	–	1	2	2	–	1	–	–	–
Labour:															
wholly	2	2	2	2	2	3	2	2	2	1	2	1	2	1	6
in part	–	–	–	–	–	–	1	1	1	1	–	1	–	2	–
Liberal:															
wholly	2	2	1	1	1	–	–	–	–	–	–	–	1	–	–
in part	–	–	1	1	1	–	2	2	2	3	–	1	1	2	–
Uncommitted	1	–	–	–	–	–	1	1	–	–	–	–	–	–	–

Total circulation	12.79	16.64	16.62	16.24	16.07	15.84	15.59	15.08	14.60	14.76	14.88	14.78	14.82	13.53	13.18
Total votes cast (mill.)	24.08	28.77	28.59	26.76	27.86	27.66	27.26	28.34	31.34	29.19	31.22	30.67	32.54	33.61	31.29
Conservative:															
% circulation[a]	52	50	52	52	54	57	55	57	71	69	67	78	74	64	33
% votes	40	43	48	50	49	43	42	46	38	36	44	42	42	42	31
Labour:															
% circulation[a]	35	50	39	40	38	42	42	43	32	50	27	22	26	27	62
% votes	48	46	49	46	44	44	48	43	37	39	37	28	31	34	43
Liberal:															
% circulation[a]	13	10	10	9	9	–	3	5	5	26	–	–	2	5	–
% votes	9	9	2	3	6	11	8	7	19	18	14	25	23	18	17

[a]Includes papers with divided support. Percentage may therefore add to more than 100. In 1974 there were general elections in both February and October.

Sources: Derived from Colin Seymour-Ure, *The British Press and Broadcasting Since 1945*, Table 8.2; Royal Commission on Press, 1974–7; Nuffield College election studies by D. E. Butler and co-authors. Circulation figures are for the periods covered by the elections.

impression of general sympathy more than of a hard-and-fast commitment to a not at all hard and fast manifesto. The 1997 election may prove to have marked a new changeability in press partisanship rather than a long-term editorial shift to the left.

Measured by circulation, the press party balance looks different, largely because of the tabloid/broadsheet contrasts. Labour in 1997 had a disproportionate share: 62 per cent of circulation and 44 per cent of the vote. This was the position enjoyed by the Conservatives at every previous election. Labour's landslide in 1945 was won with roughly half the votes but one-third of circulation. Double counting papers with divided support, the disproportion was rarely very great until 1964; indeed circulation split half and half in 1950. But from 1964 onwards, the discrepancy became huge. The extreme case was 1983, when the Conservatives had 78 per cent of circulation and 42 per cent of votes. Double counting makes Labour's position look better than otherwise, and several times the party appeared to enjoy a 'fair share' only if its figures were not set beside the Conservatives'. While the *News Chronicle* survived, the Liberals had disproportionately large press support. Thereafter they had practically none because of the failure of any tabloid to give even partial support.

These figures necessarily oversimplify. Not least, at any time from the mid-1970s, it would have needed only the *Sun* to transfer its loyalty to Labour for the circulation imbalance to have shifted against the Conservatives (although the number of Conservative titles would have remained greater). In 1987, for instance, that shift would have given Labour 53 per cent of circulation and 31 per cent of votes, compared with 46 per cent of circulation and 42 per cent of votes for the Conservatives.

Apart from that kind of consideration, the circulation figures alone say nothing about readers' partisanship and the nature of editorial content. Although surveys have usually found that politics ranks low on the scale of readers' interests, papers do generally have a plurality of readers supporting the same party as their paper. Only in the super loyal – the old *Daily Herald* and *Daily Telegraph* – has the dominance been very large. In 1963 Butler and Stokes, in their pioneering study of the British voter, found that half their sample could not even name the party support of their paper correctly (except for the *Herald* and *Telegraph*, where the figure was about three-quarters).[9] Not until 1983 did the majority of *Sun* readers realize that their paper was Conservative. In 1987 15 per cent of *Telegraph* readers did not identify their paper as Conservative, and a mortifying 13 per cent of *Guardian* readers did think the *Guardian* was Conservative.[10]

The degree of readers' party support obviously varied with their voting preferences. With the 1970s these appeared to become more volatile, and there was major turbulence in the 1980s as a result of the rise and fall of the Social Democratic Party – which won nearly as many votes as Labour in 1983 without any categorical press support. The correspondence between a paper's partisanship and its readers' thus became even less consistent in the second half of the period since 1945 than in the first. Nonetheless, a persistent worry for Labour was that far too many of its natural constituency in the working class were reading the 'wrong' papers. In 1963 more than one-fifth of Labour supporters were reading a Conservative paper, compared with just one-tenth of Conservatives exposed to a Labour paper. Later, and until the great switch of 1997, the imbalance was much worse. With the largely working-class *Sun* supporting the Conservatives, probably a majority of working-class Labour was reading the 'wrong' paper.

How far papers contributed to voting preferences, however, regardless of their volatility, remained extremely difficult to establish, and the question is outside the scope of this chapter (see Chapter 9). After the narrow Conservative victory in 1992 the *Sun* crowed, 'IT'S THE SUN WOT WON IT' (11 April 1992). This was an unusually vivid illustration at least of how seriously papers take their partisanship. If they have failed to influence readers, it is not for want of trying.

For thirty years after 1945 the trend of coverage was away from deliberate, full-blooded bias. A study of the four general elections from 1966 to 1974 showed that papers still consistently gave more space to the party they supported editorially.[11] But by then papers had virtually abandoned traditional election scares and stunts, such as Labour's 'Whose Finger on the Trigger?' campaign aiming to discredit Winston Churchill as a warmonger in 1951. By 1966 the *Mirror* was making a virtue out of 'First the Inquest – Then the Verdict', delaying its (predictable) commitment and producing balanced coverage. From 1955 it became common for papers to feature articles contributed by leaders from each of the parties.

The expansion in the size of newspapers in the late 1950s gave much more space, too, for sophisticated analysis of the electoral process, especially in the broadsheets. Manifestos and policies were subjected to detailed and expert scrutiny. Concepts such as 'swing', 'marginal' and 'image' became widely understood and did not fit easily into partisan polemic. Nor, increasingly, did opinion polls. Until the 1960s these had been rare and were treated as copyrighted 'exclusives' by their sponsoring papers. Thereafter they were milked for publicity and other papers – and broadcasters – were encouraged to quote them. Papers found themselves lumbered with polls showing a clear lead for a party they opposed, as happened to the *Daily Telegraph* in the landslide Labour election of 1966, to the *Mirror* in 1983 and to the Conservative press at large in 1992.

Even when papers were clearly committed, journalistic values might trump partisanship. For instance newspapers disliked 'quiet' campaigns: they wanted clear 'issues', which neatly divided the parties, were 'fresh' and were 'real' (that is, important by the newspaper's own standards). Yet it sometimes suited a party to have a 'quiet' campaign ('business as usual' for the Conservatives in 1955 and 1959; 'Crisis? What crisis?' for Callaghan in 1979), or to play down an issue (such as Europe, which neither big party wished to play up in 1997). Again, non-election stories could get mixed up with the campaign. Workplace justice famously injected an industrial relations 'noose trial' row into the 1966 campaign. A party election broadcast by Labour about the NHS ('Jennifer's Ear') provoked controversy that knocked both parties off course for nearly a week in 1992.[12] Conservatives in 1997 were dogged by 'sleaze' stories of only peripheral concern to the campaign. The tabloid papers, moreover, became more and more like daily magazines, in which politics took second place to, or would be shaped to fit, the reductionist priorities of celebrity and showbiz. As television fastened its grip, press partisanship of the type that demonized, say, Nye Bevan became arguably less convincing, since readers might regularly observe the vaunted demon on the box.

The divisions between the startlingly radical Conservative Party of the Thatcher era and the post-Wilson/Callaghan Labour Party set press partisanship back in the other direction again. It is neatly symbolized in the fact that by the time of the 1987 election the weight of coverage in the Conservative press favoured Labour – but much of it was knocking copy.[13] This feature was characteristic of the tabloid tendency in the 1980s and beyond. Yet how was a paper like the *Sun* to address complex stories such as the Maastricht Treaty or European monetary union? The answer was to do so partly by traditional tabloid methods. Parties were personified in their leaders – Major and Kinnock/Blair (with barely a mention for the Liberal Democrats). The range of coverage was narrow. The language was reductive: campaigners made 'gaffes' and dropped 'clangers'. What was distinctive compared with the popular journalism of the 1940s, however, was a reversal of historic print priorities. Then pictures were in the service of words; now words were in the service of pictures. As a result, the forms of political argument changed. Evidence ceased to be statistical or verbal – the stuff of White Papers and think tanks. Instead it was graphic and symbolic.

In 1992 these features were combined in the *Sun* in a unique and humorous blend of fact and fantasy, pictures and text, in a weeklong 'Nightmare on Kinnock Street' campaign. A double page spread polled famous dead voters, quoting them verbatim through a clairvoyant and enabling Marx and Stalin to confirm they would have been voting Labour. A grotesque but genially overweight 'flabbogram' lady posed like a Page Three nymphet, opposite a story claiming that a spoilsport Labour government would ban such harmless frivolities as pin-ups ('fat chance of fun'). Most striking was an election-day front page consisting almost entirely of a picture of Kinnock's head in a light-bulb on a blue background, with a headline saying 'IF KINNOCK WINS TODAY WILL THE LAST PERSON TO LEAVE BRITAIN PLEASE TURN OUT THE LIGHTS'. The message was obvious: save yourself from having to emigrate by extinguishing Labour at the ballot box with a flick of the pencil, just as you extinguish a light-bulb with a flick of the switch.[14]

Such stories did not deal in everyday untruths: the paper protected itself by devices like the clairvoyant and the complaisant fat lady. But they traded in assertions, protected by humour and thus not easy to counter except humorously, and they backed them up with visual symbols rather than the sort of evidence found in the broadsheets and, to a lesser extent, in the middle market tabloids. In 1997 the *Sun* had a different editor and campaigned for a party out of office. Its methods were different, but only in degree.

Conclusion: changing press and changing politics

General elections are milestones, and the *Sun*'s innovative 1992 campaign is a good case with which to end. It probably exemplifies more dramatically than anything else the changes in the way the press deals with politics. But even the *Sun*'s campaign does not really justify the language of transformation. The striking feature of the press was surely its continuity across the half-century after 1945. Changes were gradual – repeated hiccups, not one big belch – and they are correspondingly awkward to analyse succinctly. Newspapers turned out not to be like canals, sludged into uselessness by railways. Rival media – notably television and the motor car (which is indeed a mass medium) – and all the material detritus of everyday life and leisure did not destroy the general-interest national daily newspaper. Nor did the British political system change in its fundamentals. Papers became more like magazines, with a more personalized and informal attitude to politics. Parties lost much of their historic mass base; they became, at least for the present, less ideological, and some of their policy roles were poached by pressure groups. Governments became more energetic about news management. Yet all these were changes of degree. In 2000 as in 1945, press, parties and governments still tangled in a rough and tumble which, like that of children, was part love, part hate, and in which each recognized its dependence on the other.

7
Political Broadcasting in Britain: System, Ethos and Change

Peter Goddard

Introduction

Political broadcasting in Britain has developed slowly over the last 75 years, but enormous changes to the political environment have followed in its wake. Before the Second World War, political broadcasting was uncommon and broadcasting authorities were acutely cautious of it. When politicians did give radio talks or Parliament was reported, it was in a manner which was formal and correct. Its impact on popular engagement with politics was small. Since the 1960s, television political coverage has been much less cautious. There has been very much more of it, a great deal of which has proven lively, probing and irreverent. The major events of Parliaments and electoral campaigns have been played out before the viewing audience or even staged solely for their benefit. Television has come to represent the single most important means by which parties communicate with voters and voters gain an understanding of politics, offering a reach and potential impact greater than any other form of communication.

Party communications are therefore now organized around television. Campaigning has been adapted to its particular representational strengths; television privileges the visual and the personal, so its primacy has led to campaigns increasingly organized around positive visuals and images of the leading participants, arguably at the expense of policy information and reasoned debate.[1] Television now provides the public face of the party – displaying the efficiency of the organization, the flair of the leading actors, the dynamic image of the leader. To that end, parties routinely employ techniques and personnel from parts of the television industry – advertising and marketing, video production, television news – in an attempt to provide positive images and to both place and spin stories. The rise of political marketing techniques has accompanied a growing belief that the reality of the political process is far less important to voting behaviour than voters' perceptions of it. Television has been at the forefront of parties' attempts to control the way in which they are perceived. These perceptions concern not only what is explicit, but more abstract impressions of parties' trustworthiness and reliability.[2] The primacy of television in this process has caused techniques of media management to become central to parties' promotional activities – arising, of course, from the complication that such activities are inevitably mediated by the interpretations of broadcasters. Ironically, the party broadcast, the sole television opportunity for parties to put their case to viewers without journalistic mediation, is the least trusted and the least persuasive in consequence.[3] As parties have become more convinced of the power of image, these techniques of television campaigning have been carried into government. Indeed, their use has become one of the defining aspects of the Blair government.

Political communications throughout the Western democracies are widely thought to have been 'transformed' as a result of the rise of television. Yet throughout the world, television broadcasting has, for the most part, been organized at a national level with considerable national variation. The precise character of such transformations in any given territory therefore depends on – indeed, is *determined by* – the structure, regulatory framework and ethos of its television system, at least as much as it is by the particular nature of its constitution and political system. Political communications in Britain, therefore, reflect a very British state of affairs.

In their analysis of British election coverage between 1966 and 1992, Blumler and Gurevitch draw attention to the system-specific nature of political broadcasting and emphasize the lack of attention given to the incremental development of such a system.[4] It follows that an understanding of the role that broadcasting systems play in determining the nature of political communications requires an examination of the broadcasting systems themselves and their development over time. Yet political communications research has usually concerned itself with the outcomes – techniques of political campaigning and persuasive communication – which arise from them. This chapter attempts to redress the balance by providing some background information about the development of political broadcasting in Britain. In so doing, it reaches back to the earliest years of the BBC to place the evolution of the ideas and practices that underlie it in a historical perspective.

Broadly speaking, the history of British political broadcasting falls into two distinct periods divided by the watershed election of 1959 (see Chapter 1). In the early period, radio and later television gradually established their public role, ethos and correct status in relation to party politics. Politicians were wary of broadcasting and rarely saw it as much more than a necessary evil. In the later period, television has become firmly established as one of the principal axes of British political life. Most of those involved in the relationship – broadcasters, politicians and even the electorate – understand, almost innately, both the British broadcasting system and the rules of the game. As a result, a key feature of political broadcasting since the 1960s has been a de facto struggle for dominance between the politicians and the broadcasters.

The organization of this chapter reflects this division. The first section is arranged chronologically and traces the gradual development of the public service broadcasting system and its coverage of politics up to 1959. In this period the public service system developed without a great deal of engagement with the politicians. In the period since 1959, the dynamics of the broadcasting system have largely been reversed. The second section is organized thematically and examines some key issues in modern-day political broadcasting. The system is now well established, but politicians' and broadcasters' engagement with it has been subject to a process of perpetual modification and increasing sophistication.

British political broadcasting to 1959: the developing system

Since the earliest days of radio, Britain has had a public service broadcasting system. The public service ethos and accompanying regulatory system arose out of the proposals of two government commissions: the Sykes Committee (1923) and the Crawford Committee (1925). The justification for the regulation of broadcasting was provided by the scarcity of available wavebands, together with fears about the persuasive potential of broadcasting and a presumption that the public interest would be better served by public, rather than private, provision. The allocation of wavebands, reported the Sykes Committee, 'should be subject to the safeguards necessary to protect the public interest in the future' because broadcasting carried with it 'such a potential power over public opinion and the life of the nation'.[5] A system was chosen therefore which incorporated a range of 'safeguards' intended to ensure that British broadcasting operated in 'the public interest'. Broadcasting was to be in the hands of a public corporation, the BBC – a monopoly broadcaster regulated, but not controlled, by the state. A charter, granted through the Post Office, laid down the standards under which it would operate. Commercial broadcasting or the conveying of any commercial or political advantage was forbidden. The BBC's Governors were charged with overseeing its operation in practice.

Apart from giving guidance on standards, the charter merely established mechanisms for the control of broadcasting. Equally important for the development of public service broadcasting was John (later Lord) Reith, the BBC's first Director-General, who was charged with applying and interpreting these 'safeguards' in practice. Reith saw public service as 'a cultural, moral, and educative force for the improvement of knowledge, taste and manners',[6] terms, which appear excessively high-minded by modern standards but which reflected the prevailing morality of the time.[7] Reith also recognized the huge democratic potential of broadcasting if it could provide an impartial, universally available source for information and debate on social and political matters. He wrote of 'a new and mighty weight of public opinion' that might emerge as a consequence.[8] In practice, however, the BBC was slow to take on this role and, despite Reith's vision, matters of public controversy, including politics and public policy, caused particular difficulties. Concerned above all with maintaining impartiality, the Postmaster General and the Governors proved cautious in their interpretation of the charter.

As a result, talks and discussions involving politicians could be mounted only with considerable care and forethought. Among the earliest, however, were ministerial and electoral broadcasts, the forerunners of the modern party broadcast. The three main parties were each allowed a radio broadcast during the 1924 election campaign, and again in 1929 by which time a third of households owned a radio.[9] There were nine broadcasts altogether in 1931 and, by 1935, radio was almost universal and an accepted campaign tool despite the constraints – partly self-imposed – under which the BBC operated. Already broadcasting was thought to have consequences for the character of political campaigning. As early as 1929, the *Manchester Guardian* foresaw 'a profound change' in the 'the whole technique of elections'.[10] In 1931, the 'etheric presence' of party leaders reportedly threatened to overshadow local candidates.[11] By 1935, politicians were becoming more skilled in the use of radio, even if listeners seemed less inclined to listen to party broadcasts than 'normal' programming. This was also the first election in which broadcasts were allocated by the parties themselves according to their relative strengths at previous elections, Reith having declined to adjudicate on the issue.[12] This 1935 model for the allocation of party broadcasts has continued with little modification.[13]

The war changed the BBC's role considerably. The Reithian 'public interest', hitherto concerned with serving the educational and cultural needs of the people, was supplanted by a wartime requirement to sustain morale and carry news to an information-hungry populace. The BBC was quickly forced to shed its paternalism in favour of a more inclusive popular service – a process made easier, perhaps, by Reith's departure from the Corporation in 1938. Prewar anxieties about 'controversy' became redundant as the BBC took on a central role in a national struggle, to which party politics took second place. In effect, the over-zealous prewar interpretations of the BBC's charter were replaced with a more practical approach which could sustain the spirit of public service broadcasting while matching the spirit of the times. Such changes were lasting and, although it was many years before the BBC could be said to be genuinely independent of the state, the loosening of its shackles in wartime was significant. Paradoxically, however, another wartime development had the effect of further constraining the BBC in its coverage of political matters. The Fourteen-Day Rule conceived in 1944 was a 'self-denying ordinance' preventing the discussion of any issue to be debated in Parliament in the coming fortnight. It suited both the government and the cautious BBC, offering a ready excuse for the avoidance of controversy. But it severely constrained the producers of news, talks and features, who came to resent it bitterly.[14]

At the 1945 election, radio's role was an escalation of that in the prewar years. There were even more party broadcasts – ten each by Labour and the Conservatives. They attracted large audiences and were again blamed for undermining interest in local contests, although their principal contribution may have been negative: Churchill's allegation that Labour would introduce a 'gestapo' is credited with enabling voters to identify him once again as a partisan rather than as a national figure.[15]

Television's first significant excursion into the field of politics came in the first election night programme, reporting the results of the 1950 election. Initially television had concentrated mainly on entertainment and was thought to be unsuited to politics or news. Even as it embarked tentatively upon political coverage, it was subject to the same safety-first approach as radio, as well as a lack of interest from the parties themselves.[16] Michael Cockerell neatly sums up its coverage of the 1950 election:

[BBC television] prided itself on pre-empting any charge of unfairness or partisanship during the campaign by avoiding any mention at all of the election. It was only after the polls had closed that the BBC dared to refer to the fact that there had been a campaign at all.[17]

In fact, until 1959, the BBC consciously instituted 'close periods' on radio and television during election campaigns, in which, besides party broadcasts, anything that might be deemed remotely politically controversial was dropped from the schedule. This was an indication not only of the corporation's innate caution but also of its belief that broadcasting could be particularly influential: 'The aim', wrote its Director-General, was 'not to ensure balance but to obtain exclusion. Voters can be influenced even by the most balanced broadcast.'[18] This attitude clearly illustrates the importance of the regulatory system and its interpretation in determining the role which broadcasting could play in political communications in Britain. Moreover, such a statement was made in full knowledge of the much greater political impact achieved as early as 1948 by the lightly regulated, commercial television networks in the USA.[19]

Television was not yet national, however. It was available only in London and the Midlands in 1950, and was extended to the metropolitan North just before the 1951 election. But with a third of the population able to watch and the parties finally appreciating its electioneering potential, 1955 has been described as 'the first television election'.[20] Strictly speaking, it wasn't. Again television's involvement was confined to party broadcasts and a results programme. Precisely because of the absence of other coverage, however, the party broadcasts took on a huge significance. Parties and public alike appeared to believe that television could deliver electoral success at a stroke, partly as a result of its success in covering the Coronation of Elizabeth II.[21] Television party election broadcasts (PEBs) had begun in 1951. In 1955, the Conservatives and Labour had three each and the Liberals one, lasting for up to half an hour.[22] Eden organized his campaign around the broadcasts, reshowing them at public meetings, and even hired the first television consultant, Ronald Gillett, to introduce the flair and innovation gained from wide experience in American television.[23] Far-sighted younger MPs, including John Profumo and Anthony Wedgwood Benn, recognized not only that mastery of television was essential for politicians but that it would soon become the principal campaigning tool, replacing public meetings and doorstep canvassing. Although the broadcasts were mostly chaotic, senior politicians received a crash-course in the mechanics of television and the need to be telegenic – a lesson taken to heart by Harold Wilson.[24] For viewers, television made politicians available in close-up and may have enabled the electorate to imagine for the first time that they could evaluate them as personalities rather than as mere partisan politicians.

That of 1955 was the last election of its kind. Those that followed were genuinely 'television elections'. By 1959, television had ceased to be the cautious and timid creature it had previously been when confronted by the whiff of politics. In those four and a half years, it underwent a series of liberating changes that enabled it to become, before long, a dominant factor in the campaign. Already, in 1953, a system of televised party broadcasts in non-election periods, extending the existing arrangements for radio, had begun.[25] In 1954, excerpts from the Conservative Party Conference were televised, and the following year the annual blanket coverage of 'the conference season' commenced.[26] The most important breakthroughs, however, were associated with the establishment of Independent Television (ITV) and the end of the BBC's monopoly.

For all their brashness and novelty, the ITV companies were also public service broadcasters. The Television Act 1954 bound the ITV companies to duties of impartiality similar to those in the BBC's charter. Like the BBC's Governors, ITV also had its own regulatory body – the Independent Television Authority (ITA). But competition provided alternative approaches to political broadcasting from companies more prepared to take risks and created, in the process, a situation where the BBC's traditionally compliant interpretation of its political role was exposed and the Corporation itself was forced to change.

News broadcasting underwent a profound change. ITV dismissed the BBC's fear that in-vision newsreaders could compromise impartiality by becoming public personalities. Instead it created 'newscasting' as a lively, engaging and, at times, critical 'performance' – an approach which the BBC later followed, albeit in a more sober fashion.[27] The next casualty was the notorious Fourteen-Day Rule. The ITV companies found themselves in the invidious position of being committed to this huge constraint on topical broadcasting because of an undertaking given by the BBC 11 years earlier. Although the rule had the support of many senior politicians, including both Attlee and Churchill, this may have owed less to a belief in its intrinsic value than to a patrician distrust of broadcasting. Privately, however, even the Postmaster General himself opposed it, and the Rule was the subject of separate lobbying by the BBC and the ITA.[28] The key issue was the primacy of Parliament as a debating forum and fears that its status could be threatened if broadcasting were used to appeal directly to the public. Ironically, subsequent developments in political broadcasting offer some justification to these fears, as television and radio have indeed become the prime sites for political pronouncements and topical debate. However, far from being a threat to democracy, this development has arguably produced a better-informed electorate and been exploited above all by the politicians themselves.

However, debates over the wisdom of the Fourteen-Day Rule were soon overtaken by events. The Suez crisis, beginning in July 1956, overwhelmed the British political establishment and challenged many of the established tenets of political broadcasting. Eden and his colleagues attempted to employ ministerial broadcasts to manage public disquiet about his government's belligerence over Suez. This placed the BBC, as the broadcaster responsible for sanctioning such broadcasts, in an unprecedented situation. Previously, it had been inclined to equate the national interest with the opinion of the government of the day, but political opposition to Eden's position became so fierce that the BBC feared that repeated acquiescence to government requests to broadcast would compromise its duty of impartiality. Through its Governors, it was forced to make autonomous political decisions under immense government pressure. Broadly, its decisions favoured the government, but when Gaitskell demanded a right of reply, following a broadcast by Eden in October on the eve of the invasion, the BBC defied the government and granted it. Gaitskell used the broadcast to demand Eden's resignation.[29]

These events had far-reaching consequences for political broadcasting. Here began the tradition of politicians using television to explain policy, to attempt to rally the nation and even to demand an opponent's resignation. Eden's final broadcast was the first direct from No. 10. In a situation where the government's actions conflicted with charter requirements for impartiality, the Suez crisis placed a stress on the BBC–government relationship that would change it forever. After years of caution and deference to the mandate of senior politicians, the BBC was unsure how to react, finding precedent and the guidance of the Governors to be insufficient. Meanwhile, ITV – with neither such a culture of deference nor such political sensitivity – had fewer qualms and this further increased the pressure on the BBC. The Suez crisis represented the moment when the BBC could no longer argue that impartiality could be served by the 'exclusion' of politics. As a result, broadcasting began instead to achieve a measure of political independence.

Another consequence of Suez was to render the Fourteen-Day Rule untenable. As Sir Robert Fraser, ITA Director-General, wrote: 'The truth of the matter is surely that when the country is confronted with an issue of great magnitude the broadcasting organizations are under a moral obligation to contribute towards a public understanding of it.'[30] In the circumstances, the Rule became impossible to police. ITN's editor wrote: 'Every interview we did...every report...was a breach of the Fourteen-Day Rule. The issues of Suez went too deeply into the lives of the public to be inhibited by such formalities.'[31] The rule was suspended in December 1956, although it continues to exist – in suspension – to this day.[32]

Early in 1958, Granada, the northern ITV contractor, took an even more significant step by initiating the first election coverage. This had been thought impossible for two reasons – regulatory obligations to maintain impartiality, and the Representation of the People Act (RPA).[33] The BBC had interpreted its charter obligations to remain impartial as prohibiting references to any candidate or party in an election period, lest it be accused of endorsing them – hence the 'close period'.[34] Section 63 of the 1949 RPA determined that the costs of 'presenting to the electorate the candidate or his views' were chargeable to candidates' election expenses. The press, but not broadcasting, was excluded. Broadcasters feared that a strict interpretation of the RPA would embrace the production costs of any television coverage (although it was generally agreed that national political figures were exempt providing reference was not made to their constituency). At a by-election in Rochdale, backed by supportive legal opinion and the ITA, Granada mounted two programmes giving unprecedented coverage – with the candidates discussing the issues of the election both among themselves and with three journalists.[35] In another first, ITN reported the by-election in its news bulletins. There was no storm of protest, nor even a legal challenge; instead, it was a breakthrough: '[T]he televoter is born...Rochdale has changed the nature of democratic politics...Television is established as the new hub of the hustings', wrote Kenneth Allsop with little exaggeration.[36] An NOP poll also suggested that the programmes helped voters to decide.[37] Rochdale introduced elections to television news and established the enduring principle that, where all candidates in a constituency agreed, they could be shown or interviewed.[38] Granada and ITN were able to establish balance through 'stopwatching', recording to the second the coverage allocated to each candidate. The BBC immediately followed suit, with coverage of the following month's by-election at Kelvingrove appearing regularly in news bulletins.[39]

So the effect, perhaps unforeseen, of ITV's creation was to alter forever the relationship between politics and broadcasting which had been developed so painstakingly through the attitudes of the BBC. Without the burden of historical convention, the ITV companies produced fresh interpretations of their legal obligations and challenged the orthodoxy of deference. But this was no one-way process. Politicians were also learning to master the medium beyond the controlled conditions of the party broadcast. Harold Macmillan's emergence as prime minister, shortly after Suez, exemplified this. 'Supermac' was the earliest prime minister to cultivate a television image and to take television and its techniques seriously.[40] He quickly learned that the oratory of the hustings was useless for such an intimate medium: 'What you have to remember is that on television you are talking to two people – that is quite different from talking to two thousand people. It is a conversation, not a speech.'[41] Television gave Macmillan the opportunity to foster an image of 'unflappability', to give (carefully prepared) 'instant' reactions to news events. Such statements would later be called 'sound bites' – memorable and pithy phrases that capture perfectly the intended sentiment but, by their brevity, also serve the needs of television news equally well. His description of the resignation of his three Treasury ministers as 'these little local difficulties' was a particularly memorable example.[42]

Macmillan also took part in the first prime ministerial television interviews – which are now such a familiar occurrence. In February 1958, the BBC and ITN both requested interviews with him. Macmillan and his advisers saw them as opportunities to capitalize on the growing popular support fostered by his appearances on television news and readily agreed. The BBC interview was tame and deferential, but ITN's proved more challenging and characteristic of ITV's fresh approach to political broadcasting. Robin Day questioned Macmillan 'as vigorously as in Parliament'[43] and asked him directly whether he was going to sack Selwyn Lloyd, the foreign secretary. Macmillan, unflappable as ever, brushed it aside with a polite response but such a question broke new ground for television and politics: 'the most vigorous cross-examination a Prime Minister has been subjected to in public'.[44] Another account noted that the qualities of television itself exacerbated the inquisitorial nature of the encounter, wondering whether 'the Prime Minister should have been asked what he thought of his foreign secretary before a camera that showed every flicker of the eyelid'.[45] Macmillan, however, was astute enough to realize the value of the interview not only as a source of positive publicity but as contributing to a carefully crafted public image which could best be promoted via television. It amounted to his 'breakthrough as a "television personality"'.[46] Macmillan used television expertly in other ways. His 1959 visit to Moscow was most notable for his affectation of a white Russian hat as a means to capture popular attention in news coverage at home. Just before the election, a fireside discussion with President Eisenhower at No. 10 was elaborately staged for live television. Such techniques demonstrated the value of television to build political image and relay positive visuals. They measurably increased public perception of him as a statesman,[47] even though the appearance with Eisenhower was criticized as 'the first of the campaign broadcasts' after Macmillan dissolved Parliament the following week.[48]

The 1959 general election

By 1959, the main factors that had constrained broadcast coverage had been eliminated. Television was ready to play a leading role in the election – 'arguably the single most important moment in the history of political broadcasting'.[49] Broadcasters and politicians alike were still finding their feet, so, by later standards, there was a tentative and experimental quality to the television coverage. But its significance was undeniable: many of the patterns of electoral coverage and television electioneering that have since become routine were first instituted in 1959. Even at the time, changes to campaigning practices for the benefit of television were noted. News programmes offered nightly coverage of campaign developments and, although the scarcity of film cameras with sound severely restricted the coverage of speeches, they were allocated so that the parties were covered with scrupulous fairness.[50] Where sound recording was impossible, lesser campaign events were covered using voiceover and silent film. One consequence of this was further to increase the prominence of party leaders.[51] Both the BBC and ITN claimed that their coverage would be based on news values alone, although the ease with which they could cite figures demonstrating balance between parties suggests that they paid very close attention to the stopwatch.[52]

For the first time, parties had to earn broadcast coverage – a significant shift in the balance of power with broadcasters. Broadcasters encouraged the parties to organize campaign events so that film could be available for the nightly bulletins. The parties themselves began the practice of mounting daily morning press conferences in an attempt to control the day's news agenda.[53] Butler and Rose noted that major speeches were often delivered earlier than hitherto and that parties exploited the opportunities provided by regular news broadcasts for 'quick retorts (which enabled a public argument to be carried through several exchanges in a single day)'; the idea of 'rapid rebuttal' is older than many would believe. Butler and Rose also foresaw the effects of television on campaign discourse: 'some remarks may have been made with an ear for their quotability in the bulletins'. But they stressed that 'all parties still had to perfect the art of "making news" – concocting quotable sayings in less than fifty words'.[54]

Nonetheless, a number of now-familiar aspects of campaign news coverage were absent. Broadcasters remained concerned about the precise interpretation of the RPA, so constituency reports avoided discussing candidates, no mention was made of opinion polls (for fear of influencing voters) and a rather narrow range of issues was covered.[55] Moreover, in spite of the Macmillan interviews, neither channel yet had the courage to interview politicians directly in a campaign period.[56]

The party broadcasts continued of course – more than before and better planned.[57] And the election also featured in current affairs programming. The BBC's regular series largely avoided the election, although this was not the case from 1964 onwards.[58] Instead, it ran a set of special, regionally based television election programmes, *Hustings*, in which candidates were questioned before an invited audience selected according to party allegiance.[59] Some of the ITV companies were more adventurous. Granada again led the way. In its programmes, journalists debated the campaign's progress, post mortems followed the party broadcasts and each candidate in the region was invited to appear in *Marathon*. This was a unique experiment – an extension of Granada's challenge to the RPA at Rochdale – with candidates offered one minute to address their electors and one minute to reply to their opponents. Despite criticism that it was potentially illegal, it passed off smoothly. Only two-thirds of candidates appeared, however. Fifty-four refused, with the result that other candidates in their constituencies were also barred.[60] *Marathon* was enormously significant in establishing what television could do but was not deemed a success. Despite its democratic credentials, Granada felt that it made for 'artless earnest programmes' that 'very few people watched'.[61]

Finally, there were the election night programmes, whose form has changed little since 1959. The BBC's featured a vast, technically complex, nationwide effort with results announced minute by minute, instant statistical analysis (including Bob McKenzie with the first 'swingometer') and immediate reactions from politicians and commentators in the studio.

ITV's was only a little less ambitious. Between them, they drew an unprecedented audience of 22 million viewers.[62] Although neither as television-dominated nor as technically proficient as subsequent elections, 1959 unequivocally marked the moment when television emerged as the central factor in political campaigning. It was fitting, therefore, that Gaitskell chose a television interview on election night to concede defeat.[63]

The basic structure of British broadcasting is laid down by the regulatory system – the BBC charter, the various Broadcasting Acts, the BBC Governors and the ITC.[64] Yet the liberalization of political broadcasting that took place in the 1950s demonstrates that the law is not the only factor determining its output. The main developments in this period concerned changes not to the regulations themselves but to the way in which the regulatory system was interpreted. The public service ideal places conflicting obligations on broadcasters. The BBC had traditionally placed its obligation to be impartial above its duty to provide public information – partly because of a strong Reithian imperative to behave 'responsibly'; partly out of deference to Parliament and its political 'masters', as suggested by its early support for the Fourteen-Day Rule. This had become ingrained within the culture of the BBC before the 1950s, but it was not the only interpretation of its role and, by that period, probably not the most appropriate. The BBC's interpretation of public service as serving 'the public interest' had become outmoded. In the years since 1945, the concept has become politicized – no longer is the public interest barely distinguishable from the interests of the state. So it has fallen to television to uphold the public's right to know by providing a forum for the examination of a wide range of social and political issues even when that means challenging the government.[65] Broadcasting did come to occupy a central role in the formation of 'a new and mighty weight of public opinion', as Reith had forecast, although not in the manner in which he conceived it and in a very different social climate.

British political broadcasting: the system in place

For most of the period since 1959, there have been few changes to the regulatory structure of British broadcasting. There has, however, been an enormous expansion of political broadcasting, as television has become the primary channel of communication with the electorate and its main source of news. Consequently, the relationship between parties and broadcasters in this period developed against the context of a relatively fixed system. Earlier deference towards politicians and political institutions has gradually been replaced – particularly since the mid-1970s – by a more confident and autonomous approach. Parties meanwhile have developed a growing sophistication in their techniques of persuasion and media management, accompanied by an increasing concern with image.[66] Television has not only come to provide a forum for politicians, but has become the stage on which politics is played out and politicians called to account. What follows is a brief examination of the range and development of modern-day political broadcasting. It concludes with an assessment of the lessons of the 1997 election and of the prospects for the survival of the system in the future.

News and general programming

In news and current affairs, politics has long been part of the daily routine, going beyond the reporting of events to background analysis of political issues and discussion forums of various kinds. This includes the broadcasting of Parliament, permitted in sound from 1978 and on television from 1985 (House of Lords) and 1989 (House of Commons). Parliament is also covered in its own dedicated programming. Nowadays, broadcasters are able to interpret requirements for impartiality quite loosely. News is largely informed by normal news values and, although attention is paid to maintaining political balance (for example, on the panels of *Question Time* (BBC)), this is commonly done across the schedule as a whole rather than within individual programmes. Particular sensitivity is still applied to programmes such as political interviews with party heavyweights. But politicians or political issues are also a routine feature in programmes as diverse as comedies (including the political satire of *That Was The Week That Was* (BBC) and *Spitting Image* (ITV)), talk shows and documentaries, and occasionally even appear in commercials. Minor politicians sometimes appear as personalities regardless of their political roles (for example, on the news quiz *Have I Got News for You* (BBC)) as though their television exposure has brought them a form of minor celebrity.

But a much stricter interpretation of balance occurs at election time, still governed by regulatory requirements for due impartiality and the RPA.[67] A consequence of the RPA is to render news reporting of constituencies problematic and interviews with individual candidates almost impossible (although devices such as interviewing their agents are sometimes used to circumvent this). More generally, since leading political figures may be interviewed in their national capacity, the RPA effectively intensifies the focus on the national campaign and helps to personalize it by increasing the prominence of leaders. In constituencies where genuinely newsworthy events are taking place (notably Tatton in 1997) the RPA can be a considerable barrier to adequate reporting.[68]

Regulation requires that campaign news coverage should be impartial and 'stopwatching' remains the principal measure of this. Screen time is assigned between parties in the same proportions as for party broadcasts, although newsrooms do pay some attention to the parties' relative prominence in bulletins and the importance of speakers. Balance is measured in a similar way for the multitude of discussion and phone-in programmes, leader interviews and regional programming which abound during the campaign period. Since 1992, ITN claims to have abandoned the stopwatch system in favour of bulletins driven by news values, but the effect – on the content of bulletins and balance between parties – has scarcely been noticeable so far.[69] 'Stopwatching' supposedly makes impartiality measurable, but such rigid adherence to balanced coverage may serve parties', rather than the public's, interests. To maintain parity, broadcasters may have to report campaign events that would not ordinarily be considered newsworthy. Parties have increasingly exploited this to guarantee coverage of positive pseudo-events on the campaign trail – 'the equivalent of junk-mail'.[70] Parity of screen time also fails to ensure that coverage is of equal worth. When an embarrassing, gaffe-strewn day for one party has to be 'balanced' against a smooth campaigning day for another, it is inevitable that news values must intrude. Despite these difficulties, viewers appear comfortable with the impartiality of electoral news.[71]

Politicians, rather than regulators, are nowadays the most alive to the appearance of political partisanship. Such is the perceived power of television that parties are constantly concerned that 'their' policies, achievements, agenda or personnel have been downplayed or ignored in relation to the coverage given to their opponents. There is a lengthy history of party complaints about broadcasting 'bias', including Harold Wilson's attacks on television in 1964–5 and Margaret Thatcher's consummate distrust throughout the 1980s of all that the BBC stood for. Wilson in 1965, Norman Tebbit in 1986 and William Hague in 1999 set up formal media monitoring units to collect examples of television bias against their parties.[72]

The routine of election coverage is usually modified only slightly from one contest to the next. Heavyweight political reporters evaluate the day's campaign news and events, while dedicated correspondents are assigned to follow the party leaders on the campaign trail. News coverage is comprehensive: conscious of its public service responsibilities, the

BBC has extended its main news bulletins during recent campaigns; across all channels viewers could watch up to ten hours of electoral news and comment per day in 1997.[73] The parties' campaign day routine is also predictable: early morning press conferences to introduce the party's theme of the day and to pre-empt the news agenda; occasional morning events such as the unveiling of a new poster for the cameras; afternoon constituency visits and photo-opportunities by the leaders; early evening set-piece speeches. This pattern is timed to provide new material for each of the four main television news bulletins: breakfast, lunchtime, early evening and mid-evening. It also has a ritual quality, enabling reporters to plan their schedules and responses in advance even as it curtails their opportunities to find fresh news angles.[74]

Party broadcasts

The regulations governing party broadcasts – the only permissible form of television political advertising in Britain – have also remained largely unmodified since the 1950s. But the broadcasts themselves have developed greatly.[75] For one thing, they have become much shorter – from 15 to 30 minutes in the 1950s to 10 minutes from 1970 onwards. More recently, parties have generally opted to screen five-minute broadcasts despite additional time being available. Their formats and their place in the parties' campaign strategies have also changed. The Conservatives in 1970 made the first sustained attempt to make livelier and more accessible broadcasts than the 'talking heads' and stilted discussions of the 1950s and 1960s. Their broadcasts were modelled on *News at Ten*, offering plenty to maintain visual interest and 'vox pop' material involving real voters. One featured a specially made film by prominent director Bryan Forbes.[76] The Conservatives' advertisers helped to plan the broadcasts and the main impetus for the further development of party broadcasts came from advertising and marketing. When they took over the Conservative advertising contract in 1978, Saatchi & Saatchi considered the party broadcast as but one element in a unified, research-based promotional strategy geared not to policy but to voter attitude. They devised, wrote and produced most of the Conservative broadcasts for the next 15 years, tying them directly to other promotional activities in the campaign.[77] Although this was a revolutionary step, Labour was following the same strategy by 1987. The broadcasts at least became livelier and better made, if not more popular with viewers.

Of themselves, party broadcasts are not the persuasive tool that they were thought to be before elections received television coverage. However, predictions of their demise have so far been premature. The ending of simultaneous transmission on all channels prior to the 1987 election has been counterbalanced by increasingly slick production and in 1998 the Neill Report rejected broadcasters' pleas for the system to be abandoned, as well as Labour's plan for a system of US-style spot ads.[78] As in commercial advertising, the broadcasts are nowadays used as part of an overall marketing strategy. Much of their value comes from their newsworthiness – they gain regular event-style coverage, especially in the press – and their ability to set the agenda in a very public way. A notable example of this was Labour's 'Jennifer's Ear' broadcast in 1992, which dominated campaign news for three whole days.[79] In recent elections, the style of the broadcasts has drawn on most forms of television programming and advertising, incorporating high production values, music and strong emotional appeals. Common among them have been biographies (Kinnock (1987), Major (1992), Blair and Ashdown (both 1997)) and mini-dramas such as 'Jennifer's Ear'. Parties have also regularly used well-known film directors (including Hugh Hudson, John Schlesinger, Mike Newell and Molly Dineen), partly as a strategy to attract viewers and to gain news coverage. Despite John Major's use of it in 1997, the direct address election broadcast is now rare except for minor parties on small budgets.

The 1997 election and beyond

The 1990s have been marked by the acceleration of trends towards the greater professionalization of party communications and a growing wariness among broadcasters about politicians' promotional methods. The 1997 campaigns were probably the most media-oriented yet. Almost all the parties' promotional activities appeared geared to television and image. Labour, in particular, depended more than ever on strategic planning by media consultants over a long pre-campaign period, control over party messages and the careful 'spinning' of them. Not only did 'spin doctors' control the availability of party information, they also tried to control the media's interpretation of it by 'backstop editing' – bombarding newsrooms with complaints and threats. Innovations included the creation of a vast database, 'Excalibur', for the retrieval of information on opponents and even on the preoccupations of individual journalists. This enabled a rebuttal unit to refute their claims instantly and allowed internal communications to be greatly improved. Fundamental to this was the establishment of Labour's Millbank campaign headquarters in which control over strategy, research and promotion could be exercised centrally.[80]

The broadcasters were equally professional. Their coverage was meticulously planned and its ample funding was justified – at the BBC at least – by an adherence to public service principles. As a corrective to the professionalism of party communications, broadcasters were conscious of the need to maintain their autonomy and to mediate party messages. They set out to deal with a range of issues beyond the parties' preferred narrow agendas and to provide more analysis alongside straight reporting. Parties' pronouncements and themes were not necessarily taken at face value. Positive party visuals (frequently the only visuals available) were often undercut by commentary that was interpretative or disdainful, or which drew attention to the staging or manipulation in their production. Public service principles were also taken to require the inclusion of regionally based reporting and the voices of the public themselves, as well as attempts to prevent political leaders or opinion polls from dominating the coverage. Like Labour, the BBC also moved to Millbank, where it created a specialist political unit to coordinate the whole of its election coverage at the heart of the action and to provide a strong research base.[81] More than ever, the impression given by party–media relations in 1997 was of slick and professional machines almost mirroring one another in their use of the latest technology, mutually interdependent but professionally wary of the tricks the other had in store.

This increasing 'arms race' between parties and the media has led in recent years to charges that political communications are now in crisis – an idea otherwise expressed in the term 'videomalaise' (see Chapter 10).[82] This largely international debate is too wide-ranging to engage with here in detail but it turns on two principal notions. One might be termed a crisis of democratic legitimacy: the media have become so cynical and disdainful towards politicians and the political process in general that public confidence in them is undermined. This in turn has created an electorate who feel increasingly disengaged from politics, less enthusiastic for political information and less likely to vote. The 1997 election provided some evidence for this, including the lowest turnout since the war and a decline in television audiences for election news.[83] Neither, however, was on a scale sufficient to suggest a crisis. To the extent that they do cause concern, it is too easy merely to blame the media. Part of the cause must surely lie with modern forms of party communications. For the most part, in 1997, these were rigidly controlled, superficial and safe – consciously avoiding debates about policy and often intended to undermine public trust in political opponents.

The other aspect of the 'crisis' derives from changes to the structures of broadcasting. Here it is argued that increasingly market-oriented television systems have led to a decline in public service broadcasting and the space which it opens up for civic communication and the formation of consensus. A less well-informed and cohesive electorate, therefore, are less capable of democratic participation. There certainly have been some significant changes to the British broadcasting environment in the 1990s. Following the Broadcasting Act 1990, terrestrial television has become more market-oriented and the public service remit of ITV (and the new Channel 5) weakened. Change has been slow and subtler than predicted but, by 1999, ITV had abandoned its main evening news bulletin *News at Ten* and considerably reduced its current affairs coverage. At the same time, the established broadcasters have faced a challenge from the growth of satellite, cable and digital television which has brought about a proliferation of channels and begun to fragment the UK audience. However, this hardly amounts yet to a full-blown crisis. The British model of public service broadcasting has proved remarkably resilient and is embedded in the political and civic culture of the nation.[84] Terrestrial channels still dominate the nation's viewing habits and public service values are not wholly absent from, for example, the satellite-based Sky News. Despite the temptation to opt for a more populist approach, Sky News's political coverage has generally been responsible and comprehensive. For the 1997 campaign, it billed itself as 'the election station' and exhibited a thoroughly 'public service' approach, being treated by the parties on an equal footing with ITV and the BBC. Arguably, it introduced a significant improvement to election coverage by covering the parties' morning conferences live, and, as a 24-hour news channel, it was able to respond instantly to breaking news.[85]

However, there may be greater threats to the British system ahead. Diminished regulation and audience fragmentation undermine the rationale and funding base of the established channels. And British television has traditionally gained its cultural significance and democratic value by offering a viewing experience shared by millions – in a sense, a vital part of the social 'glue' that helps to construct a broad national consensus. As broadcasting gives way to narrowcasting, television may no longer be able to speak to and for the nation, parties can no longer expect to address an undifferentiated sample of electors through it and, with the growth of the Internet and of channels dedicated to particular programme types, large parts of the electorate are increasingly able to opt out of political coverage and electoral information altogether. The British system of political broadcasting, 35 years in development and flourishing for another 40, has long given the impression of permanence. It is probable that its role in the first election of the new millennium will be similar to that in 1997. Thereafter, however, the future is uncertain. The British broadcasting system may need to adapt to meet changing circumstances. It is capable of this. But unless it can continue to appeal to mass audiences, its role at the heart of British political communications will inevitably be diminished.

8
Referendum Campaigning

Dylan Griffiths

Introduction

As successive volumes of the Nuffield studies testify, general election campaigns have been studied closely in Britain for over half a century. This is easily understandable as general elections are at the core of British democracy and are the context in which voters, parties and politicians orient themselves. General elections punctuate British politics and terms like the 'electoral cycle', 'mid-term blues' or the 'long campaign' are only explicable in terms of regular general election campaigns structuring British political life.

Other electoral campaigns have received, by contrast, much less study. No series of volumes have recorded local election campaigns in Britain in the style of David Butler's books. Referendums have a relatively recent history in the UK (Attlee condemned them as 'alien to all our traditions' in 1945) and to date only one UK-wide referendum has been held, that on membership of the European Economic Community (EEC, now the EU) in 1975. With Uwe Kitzinger David Butler recorded that campaign.[1] At the subnational level, however, we have seen several referendums since the 1970s: two each in Northern Ireland (1973 and 1998), Wales (1979 and 1997) and Scotland (1979 and 1997) and one in London (1998). (See Table 8.1 for a summary of major national and subnational referendums in the UK since 1973.) Referendums have been held frequently on some local government issues.[2] Looking to the future there is the possibility of several more local, regional and national referendums on issues as diverse as electoral reform, membership of the European single currency, the creation of English regional assemblies, the creation of directly elected mayors, the abolition of the remaining grammar schools and even the outlawing of foxhunting. It is time

Table 8.1   Referendums held in the United Kingdom

Date	Location	Subject	% 'Yes' vote	% turnout
8 March 1973	N. Ireland	Stay in UK	98.9	58.7
5 June 1975	UK	Stay in EEC	67.2	64.5
1 March 1979	Scotland	Approve devolution	51.6	63.6
1 March 1979	Wales	Approve devolution	20.9	58.8
11 September 1997	Scotland	Establish Parliament	74.3	60.1
11 September 1997	Scotland	Tax varying power	63.5	60.1
18 September 1997	Wales	Establish Assembly	50.3	51.3
7 May 1998	London	Approve mayoral government	72.0	34.0
22 May 1998	N. Ireland	Approve Good Friday Agreement	71.1	81.0

Source: David Butler and Iain McLean, 'Referendums', in Bridget Taylor and Katarina Thomson, *Scotland and Wales: Nations Again?* (Cardiff: University of Wales Press, 1999).

therefore to study campaigning in referendums more carefully. In this chapter I will draw particularly from the lessons of the 1975 referendum, the only UK-wide referendum held so far and ably chronicled and interpreted by Butler and Kitzinger, and the Welsh Devolution referendum of 1997, the most narrowly won, though not closely fought, referendum campaign held in the UK so far. Academic studies have suggested that the campaign in Wales in 1997 might have had a decisive influence on the result[3] and the Welsh referendum influenced the Neill Committee's inquiry into party funding and the conduct of referendum campaigns.[4] In this chapter I will show that referendum campaigns differ from general (and other election) campaigns in fundamental ways and pose particular challenges for voters, parties, politicians and, not least, electoral law.

Distinguishing characteristics of referendums

Referendums are not legally required

Regular parliamentary elections are a legal requirement in the United Kingdom. The same is true for elections to the European Parliament, the Scottish Parliament and the Welsh Assembly, and local authorities. By contrast there is no obligation on a government or Parliament to hold a referendum before a law takes effect or a bill is introduced into Parliament. This is true even of 'constitutional' acts such as Britain's membership of the European Economic Community (EEC). No referendum was held before Britain became a member of the EEC and the referendum held in 1975 to confirm UK membership on renegotiated terms was necessitated by the politics of the Labour Party not the British constitution. The 1975 referendum was held as it was the only way in which the Labour Party before and after the 1974 general elections could remain united on the issue. In Callaghan's memorable phrase, the promise of a referendum was a 'rubber life raft into which the whole party may one day have to climb'.[5]

Until June 1996 there was no commitment to hold a referendum on Welsh or Scottish devolution. George Robertson and Ron Davies, the Shadow Scottish and Welsh Secretaries, had declared repeatedly that a Labour election victory was a sufficient mandate to legislate for devolution. Then suddenly in June 1996, and apparently without consulting his Scottish and Welsh shadow ministers, Tony Blair declared that a pre-legislative referendum would be held before devolution bills for Scotland and Wales were introduced at Westminster. Political expediency explains this decision. Labour's proposals for a Scottish Parliament gave that body a limited tax varying power. Michael Forsyth, then Conservative Scottish Secretary, portrayed this as a 'tartan tax', a charge that appeared to revive within the electorate fears of Labour's 'tax and spend' past. Nationally, Labour had gone to great lengths to dispel this image and certainly did not want voting for Labour in the forthcoming general election to be associated with voting for higher taxes. Proposing a separate referendum with a separate question within that referendum on the tax varying power seemed to be a way of disassociating a vote for Labour in the general election from the prospect of higher taxes. Announcing a pre-legislative referendum also offered Labour advantages in Wales although its Welsh devolution proposals contained no tax varying powers. In Wales it was clear that some backbench Labour MPs were hostile to the idea of Welsh devolution and might express misgivings about party policy during a general election campaign or seek to wreck a devolution bill during its Commons passage as some Welsh MPs had done in the 1970s. Confirmation of the Welsh electorate's approval of devolution in a pre-legislative referendum would be a useful weapon against such backbench critics as they could no longer claim to be speaking for a silent majority. The passage of the Wales Act 1998 was much more straightforward than the Wales Act 1978 and the admittedly lukewarm endorsement in the referendum may have been one contributory factor.

The power to call a referendum may be expected to strengthen the government of the day at the expense of (other parties in) Parliament. Governments have the power to decide if a referendum campaign need be fought at all. Some critics of 'plebiscitary' democracy reject the referendum for precisely that reason. However, it should not be assumed that referendums are necessarily devices for governments to manipulate party and voter opinion. Firstly, the power to call a referendum does not equal the power to win a referendum as events in Wales in 1979 amply demonstrate. Similarly, the power to dissolve Parliament at a time of its choosing does not necessarily ensure that a government has a decisive advantage in a subsequent general election. Also, formally, it is Parliament not the government that decides whether an issue will go to a referendum or not. Labour's defeat in a vote of no confidence in March 1979 and Callaghan's loss of control over the timing of the general election was brought about by the defeat of the government's devolution proposals in referendums in Scotland and Wales that would not have been held had the government had a majority to pass its measures in the House of Commons.

Referendums are not regular occurrences

One politician, the prime minister, has some discretion (unless defeated in a vote of no confidence in the House of Commons) over the timing of general elections. He or she can call an election at any time within five years of the previous election and is normally assumed to use this discretion so that a general election coincides with a favourable economic climate or other politically propitious circumstances.[6] The timing of local and European parliamentary elections are fixed by law. As there is no requirement to hold a referendum there can be no rules governing their timing. Thus we cannot speak of a referendum cycle in the same sense as a parliamentary electoral cycle as referendums are not regular, long anticipated occurrences in British politics. Just as the decision to hold a referendum is largely made on the grounds of political expediency so the decision when to hold a referendum is made largely on these grounds. The clearest example of this was the timing of the Welsh referendum on 18 September 1997, one week after the Scottish devolution referendum. The Welsh devolution referendum was held a week later in the hope that a strong Yes vote in Scotland would create a bandwagon effect in favour of devolution in Wales. The timing of the campaign was in this instance also a politically contested issue: the first government defeat in the House of Lords after the 1997 general election was on an amendment to hold the Scottish and Welsh referendums on the same day, a politically transparent attempt to frustrate the government's equally politically transparent ploy. Referendums reveal that when a campaign is held can be highly significant for that campaign, whether it is a general election or referendum campaign.

Partisan and candidate cues are absent

In a general, local or European election voters are asked to cast votes for individual candidates and/or political parties. Evaluations of candidates and/or parties can be highly significant in deciding how a voter will cast his or her ballot. In a referendum, however, a voter is asked to vote on a proposition. As Butler and Ranney remind us, this poses particular difficulties for voters in deciding how to vote:

> ... voters in referendums have a cognitive handicap that voters do not have in most other elections. In most elections of candidates to state offices ... the candidates' party labels printed on the ballot provide powerful clues to voters about which alternatives are the most desirable – clues, moreover, that persist from one election to the next and thus grow more useful over time. Referendum electorates have no such clues, and so they probably find it more difficult to translate the information they receive into Yes or No votes on the measures before them.[7]

A referendum campaign tips the voter into a complex world where familiar landmarks may be absent or reveal themselves in strange un-familiar shapes or combinations. Partisanship may be no guide to inter-preting arguments on what may seem remote and complex issues if the party label is absent or prominent party figures are divided on the issue in question and both the 'Yes' and 'No' sides claim to speak for the party and claim the loyalties of its partisans. In the 1975 referendum prominent members of the Labour Party opposed the government's policy (though, just to add to the confusion, the Labour government was itself ignoring the expressed will of the Labour party conference) and several other senior Labour politicians such as Roy Jenkins and Shirley Williams appeared in public on the same side as senior politi-cians from the Conservative and Liberal parties. In the 1979 referendums in Wales and Scotland there were Labour 'No' campaigns recommending the rejection of Labour party policy which had as spokespeople some of the most prominent Labour politicians of the time such as Leo Abse and Neil Kinnock in Wales and Robin Cook and Brian Wilson in Scotland. It is little wonder that voters were confused about the stance of the Labour party on devolution. In Wales barely half the electorate correctly identified the government's stance of recommending a 'Yes' vote in the referendum and only two-fifths of voters believed that Labour MPs favoured this course.[8] By contrast, internal party discipline before and during the 1997 Welsh devolution referendum meant that most Labour identifiers, including those that ignored the party's call to support the devolution proposals, correctly placed the Labour Party's position on the issue. Cognitive dissonance, whereby a voter (deliberately) misperceives a party's stance on an issue in order to bring it (in her mind) closer to her stance on that issue, did not appear to have been a factor in the 1997 referendum for Labour identifiers in Wales, including even those Labour identifiers that voted against the party's proposals or abstained.[9] In both 1979 and 1997 Conservative, Plaid Cymru and SNP supporters followed the clear leads given by their parties by massive margins.[10] Even where a party gives a clear lead voters may fail to heed it. In both 1979 and 1997 there is evidence that Liberal and Liberal Democrat voters in Wales rejected the stance their party espoused by margins of two to one or more.[11] The lesson from the behaviour of Labour identifiers in 1979 and to a lesser extent in 1997 and Liberal (Liberal Democrat) identifiers in both referendums is clear – party identification may be a large factor in referendum voting behaviour but no campaigner should rely upon it alone for success.

Partisan aversion may also be a factor in referendum voting and campaigning. In both 1979 and 1997 the 'Yes' side in the Welsh referendums accused opponents of devolution of being Conservatives or pro-Tory.[12] Relying on partisan aversion may be as unwise in a referendum campaign as assuming that partisan identifiers will automatically support that party's policies. Voters may be no more swayed by an invitation to express their aversion to party than by an invitation to express their support for a party. Although the Conservatives secured less than a fifth of the votes cast in the general election in 1997 in Wales, the 'No' side won almost half of the votes in the referendum four months later even though the Conservatives were the only party associated with a 'No' vote.

Even in the absence of candidates voters may judge an issue in terms of the personalities associated with the issue and look to the leads of well-known and well-regarded politicians. In the 1975 referendum it was argued that the politicians advocating Britain's continued membership of the EEC were relatively popular while those advocating withdrawal were relatively unpopular.[13] Some of the leading names on the 'No' side such as Tony Benn, Ian Paisley and Clive Jenkins appear to have been particularly disliked for their 'extremism'. This bolstered the impression that staying in was the moderate, sensible thing to do.

Alternatively a voter may use her vote in a referendum to express her approval or disapproval of the government or the major parties involved in the referendum.[14] In this way voters may choose to treat referendums in the same way as European or other 'second order' elections and use them as an opportunity to cast judgement on political parties or figures in the national arena.[15] In a referendum campaign, just as much as an election campaign, a party or cause group must have a generally favourable image among the electorate well before the campaign has begun if it is to do well at the conclusion of the campaign.

As with general or other elections attributes such as 'reasonableness', 'moderation' or 'commonsensical' may sway a voter as much as or more than actual policy stances. This may be particularly true in the case of referendums as they may be called to decide issues on which voters are ill informed and have few strong opinions. One of the few things a voter may be certain about is that she can't make her mind up. Hesitant voters may respond sympathetically to other hesitants. Voters may distrust people or organizations that care passionately about issues they hardly care about at all. An image of fanaticism or crankiness is to be avoided and an image of moderation cultivated. In the 1975 EEC campaign Harold Wilson and James Callaghan sought to appear above the fray, to give the impression that their recommendation to stay in the EEC was not born of a principled support of EEC membership but a sober, pragmatic evaluation of Britain's national interests.[16] The European Movement was removed from the centre stage in the 1975 campaign because it 'was suspect. . . . [and] was thought to be too committed to federalism to speak to a sceptical British public'.[17]

Parties and politicians are not the only possible reference group for a voter (see Chapter 2). The opinions of churches, trade unions or business may help the voter decide her opinion on an issue. Much effort in all recent referendums has been expended on getting or claiming support of the CBI or other civil society groups like teachers or the clergy to support one side or another in the debate. After the 'No' side in the Welsh referendum claimed that business was opposed to devolution the Wales CBI had to issue a statement of its neutrality.[18] Both sides in a campaign may vie for the support of prominent groups or claim that the majority of a prominent group is in their camp. Voters may decide how to vote on an issue they know little about themselves by the quality of the spokespeople for each side as much as by the quality of their arguments. Authority and trust as much as good arguments may be decisive attributes in a referendum campaign.[19]

Campaigning resources need not be concentrated solely in political parties

Political parties are not merely associations in voters' minds. As Macartney noted, 'Political parties have headquarters, staff, regular systems of liaison with local activists'.[20] No other organizations are able to command such a large share of the resources necessary for mounting political campaigns. Acquiring campaign resources is a vital task for all protagonists in a referendum campaign. This task is greatly eased if political parties, either nationally or locally, engage in the referendum campaign as happened in both 1975 and 1997. In practice even non-party groups have been heavily dependent on political parties for providing speakers, literature and campaign organization. Referendums open up space for other groups joining the contest. These may be long-established groups that have long been associated with the issue at stake, such as the European Movement or the Parliament for Wales Campaign, or ad hoc groups formed only for the duration of the campaign. Such groups may work independently or may combine in 'umbrella' organizations as happened in 1975. Umbrella groups combine and coordinate the activities of different groups who may agree on little else but this issue. The appearance of consensus and agreement across the normal political divisions may itself become a positive feature in a referendum campaign as the offputting petty party bickering is temporarily discarded.[21] Whether groups combine in this way depends partly on the ideological divisions within different campaigning groups, the perceived advantages of giving an appearance of unity and cooperation and the legal and regulatory framework (which is considered further below). Referendums do not imply the end of parties as campaigning organizations in the United Kingdom. What they may reinforce is a style of campaigning which emphasizes the support of prominent and respected persons and groups, seeks to receive endorsements from the press and generally positive coverage in the media and does not rely on prior partisanship to mobilize voters. Referendums are like dealigned elections, only more so.

Voters' ideological orientations may be particularly important in a referendum

One component of dealignment is the increasing ability of voters to form political judgements independently of parties (see Chapter 2). In a referendum a voter is invited to form a view on an issue unmediated by partisan debate. Svensson noted that voter ideology could be an important element in referendum voting especially if voters had consistent attitudes towards an issue.[22] Voters may have attitudes towards issues in a referendum that are determined by more general political attitudes or orientations. Patriotism, a sense of national identity, a strong attachment to the Welsh language or a distrust of politicians may not be elements of a left–right ideology but may be decisive in determining how a voter may vote in a referendum.[23] Referendums are political contests where the mediating role of party is weaker by definition and this moves the voter and her opinions closer to the heart of the campaign.

The role of local campaigning is changed

In one sense a general election is 659 individual contests in addition to being an occasion where the 'nation decides' (see Chapter 5). The final outcome is the sum of these individual contests. A national referendum such as the 1975 EEC referendum is a very different form of contest. The winner of a national referendum is the recipient of most votes nationally. Marginal seats or wasted votes are redundant terms where the contest is not divided into constituencies. Far less emphasis, it would be assumed, need be paid to local campaigning. However, in both the 1975 EEC referendum and the 1997 Welsh devolution referendum considerable resources were devoted to local campaigning. Local campaigns accompany national referendum campaigns for several reasons. First, this is what many activists are used to and there may be a temptation to recreate a 'traditional' campaign even in changed circumstances. Second, even national campaigns will wish to address local concerns (during the 1975 campaign local campaign literature was produced showing variously that EEC membership would benefit the pea growers in the Borders and shoemakers in Harborough).[24] Third, a local campaign even in a national contest can boost levels of participation and support (and in a closely fought contest every vote might count). The active 'Yes' campaign in Neath Port Talbot in the 1997 referendum campaign appeared to boost turnout and the share of the 'Yes' vote substantially there. A referendum campaign can reveal deficiencies in local campaigning activity that normally remain hidden in general election contests. During the 1997 referendum campaign, where party identification could not be assumed to mobilize voters in itself, the weakness of Labour's campaigning machinery in its Welsh Valleys heartlands was starkly revealed. In a general election, campaigning in safe seats is a waste of time as large majorities are 'wasted votes' as they do not contribute to the national tally of seats. In a referendum every vote counts, no matter where cast and thus campaigning matters everywhere, even in heartland areas.

Electoral rules differ in referendums

The conduct of parties and election campaigns in the United Kingdom is covered by the Representation of the People Act which has been successively amended to reflect and regulate electoral practice. Elaborate conventions over issues like provision of free broadcasting have emerged over time that satisfy the larger political parties at least.[25] Referendums have been relatively infrequent events in British politics hitherto and so no equivalent body of legislation, regulation and convention governing referendums has emerged. The result has been that the conduct of referendums has been ad hoc and arguably unsatisfactory. After the first national referendum in 1975 Butler and Kitzinger were impelled to ask, 'What neutral umpire is to act as gatekeeper to the airwaves, deciding who should put each side of the case? How, if at all, is expenditure to be limited and controlled?'[26] A quarter of a century (and six referendums) later these questions may finally be addressed.

Practice in the interim has remained variable and ad hoc. In the 1975 EEC referendum the government recognized two umbrella organizations, one on each side of the debate, and provided these organizations with limited state funding (in addition to whatever they could raise themselves), free airtime and free distribution to every household of a pamphlet explaining its case. The government also distributed a third pamphlet explaining its view. This was not copied in the 1979 devolution referendums when no umbrella groups existed or were recognized, no funding was given to any campaigning group, no broadcasting facilities were made available and no pamphlets were distributed (not even a summary of the government's own proposals). In the 1997 referendums in Scotland and Wales the government again provided no financial support, pamphlet distribution or free broadcasting time to any group although umbrella groups existed this time, but it did distribute a short summary of the government's proposals to every household and voters could purchase copies of the full White Papers 'Scotland's Parliament' and 'A Voice for Wales' if they wished. In the Northern Ireland referendum in 1998 all households were sent a full copy of the Good Friday Agreement but again no assistance was given to either the 'Yes' or 'No' groups. In the 1998 London referendum on the creation of the Greater London Authority and an elected mayor the government again distributed a summary of its own proposals and gave no assistance or recognition to any side of the debate.

The conduct of the four referendums after 1997 ignored the recommendations of the Constitution Unit's report on the conduct of referendums.[27] It had called for an independent referendum commission (possibly as part of a wider Electoral Commission) which would be responsible for advising the government on the recognition of any umbrella campaigning organizations, the giving of state finance to such organizations and ensuring that each side had equal access to the broadcast media. It had also called for the commission and not the government to have 'responsibility for the publication and management of information relevant to a referendum' and 'for the conventions which require the civil service to avoid engaging in political or public debate, and which limit its actions to the provision of factual information [to] be maintained'.[28]

Whatever the deficiencies of the conduct of the referendums in Scotland, London and Northern Ireland, they were arguably insufficient to call the legitimacy of the outcome into question given the large majorities secured by the winning side in each of these contests. The narrow majority for devolution in the Welsh referendum on a low turnout, however, prompted some doubts as to the legitimacy of the result. The Committee on Standards in Public Life (Neill Committee) noted:

> We were disturbed in particular, by the evidence we heard in Cardiff to the effect that the referendum campaign in Wales in 1997 was very one-sided, with the last-minute 'no' organisation seriously underfunded and having to rely for financial support essentially on a single wealthy donor. The outcome of the Welsh referendum was extremely close, and a fairer campaign might well have resulted in a different outcome.[29]

This view has been echoed in academic research. Evans and Trystan note:

> Referendums in theory invoke the spirit of direct democracy and seek to ascertain the opinions of the electorate on important political issues. On this basis the Welsh referendum result may be called into question – not only is a 50 per cent turnout a poor basis upon which to make a claim of representativeness, but also because by a small majority, the Welsh electorate [as revealed in the Welsh Referendum Survey 1997] actually preferred the constitutional status quo. That they failed to make their voice heard representatively in terms of the referendum vote appears to be as much to do with the

strength of the pro-'yes' political forces and the failure of the 'no' campaign to play its part in mobilising anti-devolution opinion.[30]

To combat this inequality in future referendums the Neill Committee therefore recommended that core funding (at least equivalent to the sums given to the two umbrella groups in the 1975 referendum in any future national referendum) be given by the government to one group on each side of any debate if the Election Commission (which it also recommended be created) ruled that any groups should be recognized as representative groups. It also recommended that broadcasters should give free airtime to any groups recognized by the Election Commission and that these groups, not the parties, should be the basis for allocating airtime to the two sides in a referendum debate. Lastly, it also recommended that the government should not be a participant in any campaign by, for example, distributing literature to households explaining the government's case. In total, these recommendations amount to a significant departure from the way recent referendums have been conducted. If implemented, the side supported by the government in any future referendum would lose a considerable advantage and the opposing side would at least be ensured of the resources to present its case effectively.

The government has responded warmly to most of the contents of the Neill Committee but Jack Straw, the Home Secretary, argued that the Committee's views on the role of governments during referendums were impracticable.[31] A number of backbench MPs, including Martin Bell, the Independent MP for Tatton, introduced a Referendums Bill in 1999 in order to keep up the pressure on the government to enact the recommendations of the Neill Committee. The government's White Paper on *The Funding of Political Parties*[32] published in July 1999 accepted most of the Neill Committee's recommendations with two significant exceptions. First, the Neill Committee had concluded that it was impracticable to try to limit expenditure by any campaign groups during referendum campaigns; the best that could be realized was full disclosure of all expenditure. The government has instead proposed limits of £5 million each for the umbrella groups and limits on expenditure by political parties in referendum campaigns depending on their share of the votes cast at the most recent relevant election, and a limit of £500 000 for other organizations or individuals. Second, in relation to its role in referendums, the government argued that:

In most of the cases in which referendums have been held so far, the purpose of the referendum has been to obtain the endorsement of the electorate for a policy which the government of the day has developed and adopted, and the view has traditionally been that a government has not only a right but a duty to explain and promote its policies. It will clearly be appropriate for it to do so, and to have the assistance of the Civil Service, during the period when a Bill to provide for a referendum is being taken through Parliament. This period, at any rate, cannot reasonably be equated with a general election campaign period.[33]

This position is at variance with the Neill Committee's view. However, the government accepted that 'there ought to be a period leading up to the referendum poll in which the government of the day, as a government, stands aside and the campaigning is left to the political parties and other organisations, with Ministers taking part in their political capacity if they wish' and therefore recommended that 'the government of the day is not to publish material relating to the referendum issue within the period of 28 days leading up to the poll. This will ensure that, in the crucial period when the electors are weighing up the referendum issue, the campaign is not skewed by the expenditure of large sums of taxpayers' money'.[34] This would go some way to address the concerns of the Neill Committee and would prevent a recurrence of the disputes between ministers and Civil Servants over their campaigning role in the Welsh referendum campaign in 1997.[35]

It is possible that the most lasting significance of the Welsh referendum on 18 September 1997 may not be the establishment of a Welsh Assembly but the codification of the rules on the conduct of referendums. Its narrow result and the arguably unequal struggle between the 'Yes' and 'No' camps called into question the desirability of allowing the government of the day to decide the rules for referendums in an ad hoc way. The removal of such flexibility may well influence a government's willingness to test the popular will through a referendum and may have decisively altered the likely terrain of a future referendum on, for example, Britain's membership of the single currency.

Conclusion

Since 1890 when Dicey first recommended the referendum or 'People's Veto' over the issue of Irish Home Rule, referendums have moved from academic fancies, the last refuge of beleaguered politicians and local curiosities to become occasional but important elements of British political life.[36] Referendums have been used to decide major constitutional changes with greater authority than the conventional political process possesses. As further controversial constitutional changes are proposed it is probable that more referendums will be held in the future.

Referendums pose novel challenges to all those involved in British politics. Referendums challenge, or at least qualify, the notion of parliamentary sovereignty which is the basis of the British constitution. They can complicate the policy-making process and add a further obstacle before a government can get its way. Conversely, referendums make it more difficult for future governments to reverse the policies of previous governments. For politicians on the losing side in parliamentary debate they seem to provide a last throw of the dice, an opportunity to reverse defeat in Parliament by an appeal to the people. For party leaders referendums and the promise of referendums can be useful tools of party management or at least preferable to open party splits. Referendums may also be the most effective means available of legitimating or entrenching constitutional change available within the British constitution.

Referendums provide new electoral environments where the usual rules of British (party) politics can be temporarily suspended. Politicians from opposing parties can join together temporarily to promote a cause which unites them. Politicians may find themselves opposing politicians from their own side in a referendum and conventions on how to criticize colleagues publicly may have to be devised. Political parties are not necessarily the key organizations in a referendum. Cause groups or ad hoc campaigning groups may supplement or even overshadow the activities of political parties. Referendums also loosen parties' grip on voters. In a referendum voters are invited to decide on a specific issue, not elect a candidate or a government. Voters may nevertheless choose to follow the lead of a party or of prominent politicians but they are also free to slip the reins of partisanship and decide the issue on its own merits.

Unlike elections the conduct of referendums in the United Kingdom has been comparatively unregulated. Following the Neill Committee's report and the publication of the Home Office's draft bill in the summer of 1999 this is about to change. Future referendums will be conducted according to stricter rules prescribing expenditure limits, access to state funding and the role of the government during referendum campaigns. This may not be enough to ensure a level playing field in future referendum campaigns but it should minimally ensure that all sides get to the campaigning starting block. Greater access to funds, rules ensuring a less one-sided contest and a growing accumulation of recent experience in the UK and elsewhere of referendums will ensure that referendum campaigning in this country will continue to evolve.

9
Assessing Communications and Campaign Effects on Voters

John Bartle

Introduction

The major political parties spend a great deal of time and energy in an effort to communicate their ideas, policies, achievements and leadership qualities to voters. They invest enormous sums of money to produce elaborate election broadcasts, eye-catching posters, newspaper adverts and leaflets. They spend large sums on information technologies and employ highly paid consultants from the worlds of advertising, television or marketing to communicate their message. The parties invest all this time and energy in the expectation that some or all of these activities will influence the final decisions of a significant portion of the electorate. Moreover, if theories of class and partisan dealignment are correct, more voters than ever should be 'up for grabs' and responsive to short-term factors such as those that are emphasized during campaigns.[1] Political communications therefore ought to be of *increasing* importance and parties that run poor campaigns should be placed at *increasing* disadvantage.

In this chapter, I will examine two basic approaches to assessing the effect of both specific communications and campaigns as a whole on voting behaviour. The first approach, associated with contemporary histories such as the Nuffield studies, provides a great deal of contextual information about the campaign. These studies record the assessments of those most intimately involved in it – the politicians and campaign professionals – and then the authors provide their own reasoned assessments on the basis of the evidence. The aim of this approach is to provide some understanding of a specific election campaign and draw parallels with previous elections. The second approach relies far more on the 'hard' evidence of panel studies, controlled experiments and evidence from the polls to test hypotheses. The main aim of this approach is to provide generalizations about communications and campaign effects.[2]

In the final section of this chapter I examine the history of the study of campaign effects in order to understand just how little is known about the formation of short-term political preferences. The early theoretical studies thought that mass propaganda would undermine the very existence of democracy and facilitate the rise of demagogues.[3] Later research calmed such fears suggesting that most propaganda merely served to reinforce voters' prior predispositions and had 'minimal effects' on voters.[4] However, a new group of scholars has challenged this orthodoxy. They have argued that political communications influence voters through long-term processes and that the effects of political communications are conditional.[5] Rather than presenting any single orthodoxy, therefore, this chapter will assess the advantages and disadvantages of several methods. This will enable readers to assess the burgeoning literature in the field.

Contemporary history and communications effects

Contemporary histories of election campaigns, such as the Nuffield studies, represent an invaluable resource to political scientists. Each volume has meticulously documented the events leading up to the election: the changes in party policy, fluctuations in the economy, trends in the opinion polls and the gradual evolution of party organizations. They have also provided a detailed 'blow-by-blow' account of the short campaign itself, documenting every major speech, gaffe, event or campaign stunt, together with the reaction of the public as indicated by fluctuations in the daily opinion polls.

In recent years, the Nuffield studies have been joined by other contemporary histories. In February 1974 the *Britain at the Polls* series was launched.[6] These volumes, written by academics working in the field of electoral politics, again provide a great deal of background information about the election. However, they also provide much more by way of analysis and interpretation.[7] In 1979, they were joined by yet another volume, *Political Communications*. This series contains articles written by academics and pundits. However, most importantly, *Political Communications* contains the reflections of campaigners themselves: senior politicians, pollsters and other advisers.[8] Together with the autobiographies of campaigners and politicians, these volumes provide assessments of the campaign from an elite level – from inside the belly of the beast, so to speak.[9]

The insights provided by the campaigners and politicians themselves are often revealing. After their electoral disaster in 1997, one senior Conservative strategist attributed their defeat, at least in part, to 'the successful use by the Labour Party of certain campaign techniques'.[10] John Major suggested that in 1997 'most voters had made up their minds about how they were going to vote long before I asked the Queen for a dissolution of Parliament'.[11] He also concluded that 'our "New Labour: New Danger" approach did not work'.[12] For Labour, Philip Gould emphasized the apparent softness of the Labour vote, almost suggesting that the election turned on a 'last minute' decision.[13] For the Liberal Democrats Richard and Alison Holme attributed their success to 'conducting a straightforward, convincing and trustworthy campaign'.[14]

The evidence of the campaigners is worth taking very seriously. They have experienced the election campaign at first hand, attended many meetings, and monitored television output and newspaper stories very carefully. They have had access to inside information, such as private polls, that others are denied. Moreover, they desperately need to know the relationship between what they do and how voters behave. They therefore have incentive to correctly estimate the effect of communications on voters. There is yet another reason for taking these interpretations seriously: they will inevitably influence how campaigns develop in the future. Even if what is learnt is incorrect, it is likely to have profound implications for the conduct of future campaigns.

These advantages aside, there are also reasons to take their interpretations with a pinch of salt. Many informants were closely involved in the campaign and may either wish to overstate their own importance (if their side won) or distance themselves from criticism (if their side lost). They may therefore have incentives to distort their public statements. Even if they represent genuine assessments, the campaigners can be disadvantaged by the sheer amount of information available to them. As Butler and Kavanagh point out, the 'danger is that [a] detailed analysis of the campaign, analogous to the ball-by-ball radio commentary of a cricket match, may result in an exaggeration of the effects of the bits and pieces of a campaign'.[15] In the 1992 campaign, for example, John Major's decision to emphasize the 'threat to the Union' was, at the time, generally interpreted as the last throw of the dice by a desperate man. Yet, in hindsight, 'Paddy Ashdown and senior Labour figures concluded that it had been a masterstroke by John Major',[16] even though there is precious little evidence that it had any effect. Those directly involved in the campaign may be unduly influenced by their personal experiences, which are – almost by definition – unrepresentative. Rather than providing information about the effect of the campaign, we may simply be observing fluctuations in morale among 'increasingly exhausted and nervous people'.[17]

Experienced contemporary historians such as the authors of the Nuffield studies and *Britain at the Polls* therefore know that the personal opinions of the campaigners themselves are sometimes an unreliable guide as to what actually happened. They therefore weigh the available evidence in order to arrive at a reasoned evaluation of the effect of a particular communication or campaign. These accounts by experienced commentators are often highly persuasive and, given the speed with which they are published, quickly become regarded as the 'orthodoxy'. It is only later, when the full body of evidence becomes available, that political scientists seek to challenge that orthodoxy.

Behavioural studies of campaign effects

Most studies of political communications effects in Britain have been heavily influenced by the 'behavioural revolution' that swept through political science in the 1950s. Its two fundamental principles are that (1) only the *observable* behaviour of voters, parties and the media is a legitimate subject of analysis, and (2) any explanation (or causal account) of such behaviour should be capable of *empirical testing*.[18]

Most researchers in the field of political communications rely primarily upon socially representative large-scale surveys of the population. This enables them to simultaneously examine a large number of competing or complementary hypotheses. The socially representative nature of the samples also enables researchers to generalize from the sample to the population as a whole, subject to the standard principles of statistical inference. Established bodies, such as the NES in America, the BES, BEPS and BSA in Britain, carry out most such studies. These are occasionally supplemented by more specialist surveys such as Miller et al.'s study of the 1987 general election campaign or Norris and Sanders' experimental study of the effects of television news.[19]

The data resulting from these surveys is used primarily to assess the relationship between political communications and *voters' sense of civic engagement* (political knowledge), *their political priorities* (what they are thinking about as they arrive at their vote decision) and *their political preferences* (vote, opinions on policy proposals, evaluations of party leaders and assessments of party competence).[20] However, as the following sections demonstrate, while it is straightforward to demonstrate an association between variables, it is far more difficult to establish that the relationship is causal. Researchers must use a wide range of evidence from both individual and aggregate level sources. It is to this distinction that I now turn.

Individual level data

'Individual level' data contains information about individuals: their age, gender, social class and a wide range of political attitudes, opinions and evaluations. In this section I will explore how three types of individual level data (panel studies, cross-sectional studies and experimental studies) can be used to assess the effect of both specific political communications and campaigns as a whole.

Panel studies

Panel studies collect data from repeated interviews, known as 'waves', with the same individuals. They are primarily used in voting research to establish the amount of vote switching that takes place.[21] In addition, the data can be used to draw causal inferences. This is most easily demonstrated in a three-wave panel study design where changes in an explanatory variable (X_n) between t_1 and t_2 may be assumed to cause subsequent changes in dependent variable (Y) between t_2 and t_3, since cause precedes effect.[22] Thus:

- If voters switch from a tabloid newspaper in t_1 to a 'quality' newspaper in t_2 and their political knowledge increases between t_2 and t_3, then we may conclude that the increased quality of the newspaper has caused the increase in knowledge.
- If voters switch from a 'pro' European newspaper in t_1 to an 'anti' European newspaper in t_2 and the importance they attach to the European issue increases between t_2 and t_3, then we may conclude that the change of newspaper caused them to think the issue was more important.
- If voters change from reading a pro-Conservative newspaper to a pro-Labour newspaper between t_1 and t_2 and their evaluations of Tony Blair are enhanced between t_2 and t_3 then we may conclude that the change of newspaper has caused them to think more favourably of Tony Blair.[23]

In each case I have added the caveat 'may conclude' since, in practice, a great many variables change simultaneously. In order to assess the effect on Y *uniquely* attributable to X_n we must 'control for' all those variables that may influence *both* Y and X_n. Ideally therefore the data set should contain all those variables that are of theoretical relevance to the processes we are examining. We can still make causal inferences in the absence of a complete data-set, but the uncertainty attached to those estimates increases since it is unclear whether including the missing variable would have altered our findings.[24]

Panel studies offer a large number of advantages to social scientists. First and most obviously they provide a plausible means of drawing causal inferences.[25] Second, many of the variables of interest in social surveys are measured inaccurately. Some portion of their observed variation is therefore attributable to the inadequacy of the instrument rather than to real change.[26] If such flawed measures are used as explanatory variables this will bias any estimate of their causal effect. Although not essential for the purpose, panel data enable analysts to perform a relatively straightforward adjustment of the data to remove this random component of observed change and produce unbiased estimates of causal effect. Third, since *prior* attitudes and beliefs are used to explain *subsequent* attitudes and beliefs, panel study data are far less vulnerable to the problem of 'rationalization' (more on which below).[27]

Despite these undoubted advantages, panel studies, however, are not ideal for assessing specific communications effects. Although we observe voters' responses, in the form of a changed opinion or vote, we do not observe the precise stimulus to which voters respond. Researchers must therefore use their knowledge of external events to establish a link between observed response and some plausible stimulus. This can be a dangerous practice, particularly since the interviews take place a year or so apart. Researchers must therefore wait for 'natural experiments' to take place. When they do, the resulting data are compelling, but analysts must learn to be patient in the meantime.[28]

There is another limitation with using panel studies to examine communication effects. Many researchers believe that if the political communications influence voters, they do so over long periods of time, via the steady 'drip, drip' of communications. They have therefore sought to extend panel studies over longer periods of time. However, efforts to extend the temporal dimension of the panel study have been frustrated by two practical problems. The first of these is that panel members are often reluctant to be re-interviewed, prove difficult to trace or die. This 'panel attrition' progressively reduces the sample size, increasing the 'standard errors' and thus reducing the statistical significance of observed relationships. It can also lead to biased inferences if those who leave the panel are drawn disproportionately from specific groups such as the poor or the politically apathetic.[29] One practical effect is often to reduce the effective sample to two waves, making causal inference problematic since all that is observed is a correlation between changes at two time points. The second general problem is 'panel conditioning'. The experience of being repeatedly interviewed may induce otherwise 'representative' individuals to behave in very unrepresentative ways.[30] In order to appear consistent they may become more interested in politics. Previous studies, for example, have demonstrated that political awareness is associated with greater opinion stability and issue voting.[31] To be sure, we can assess the extent of both 'panel attrition' and 'panel conditioning' by comparing responses from the new wave in the panel with responses to a fresh cross-section. We can even develop a model to formally estimate these effects.[32] Yet both these solutions are expensive. Collecting parallel cross-sectional data greatly increases the cost of panel studies, while modelling these effects absorbs data that could otherwise be used to estimate substantive effects.[33]

Panel studies therefore represent a valuable source of evidence about campaigns, but give us little information about specific communications. Any conclusions based on panel studies data should therefore be viewed in conjunction with other available evidence, such as that from cross-sectional, experimental and aggregate studies.

Cross-sectional studies

The BES, the longest-running series of studies on British general elections, has primarily relied upon cross-sectional studies of the electorate to draw inferences about political communications. These consist of 'snap-shots' of the electorate's social characteristics, media usage and political attitudes at a particular point in time. Although such data lack any observable dynamic element, cross-sectional studies enable researchers to establish the association between media usage and political attitudes or behaviour and thus provide the stimulus to further research.

Cross-sectional studies offer a number of advantages to researchers and parties alike. First, these studies do not suffer from the problems of panel 'attrition' or 'conditioning' that plague panel studies. Second, researchers do not have to anticipate what might happen in a particular campaign, as in a panel study, since cross-sectional studies can be commissioned at a moment's notice. In 1995, for example, a Gallup poll suggested that the 'demon eyes' posters, that showed Tony Blair with evil red eyes, were highly unpopular among both Conservative and Labour voters alike.[34] This enabled campaigners to rapidly gather information on the success or failure of the campaign.

Cross-sectional data can be used to draw descriptive inferences about the relationship between two variables. However, as every social scientist has been taught, 'correlation is not causation' and they must be wary of leaping to causal inferences. This is well illustrated by the long-established correlation between newspaper readership and vote. Readers of Conservative newspapers tend to vote Conservative, while readers of Labour newspapers vote Labour. Naively one might infer that newspaper causes vote. However, the statistical association may well be the result of another causal process altogether, whereby identifiers with a particular party – or those who are ideologically predisposed to one party – tend to choose a newspaper compatible with those predispositions.[35] The association may therefore simply result from the fact that partisan predispositions cause *both* newspaper readership and vote. This 'self-selection bias' results in greater uncertainty as to the validity of any causal statements based on cross-sectional data alone.

A further problem with cross-sectional data is that they tend to encourage a degree of 'rationalization'. For example, voters are often asked to judge which of the parties fought the best campaign.[36] In 1997 most voters reported that Labour had 'fought the best campaign' and the Conservatives the worst. Yet, given what we know about the 'remoteness of politics' for most voters (see Chapter 2), it must be doubted whether voters readily distinguish between the campaign and voting behaviour. It is likely that a large number of voters reasoned that, since *they* had voted for party X, party X must have fought the best campaign. Others may have reasoned that 'X won the election, therefore X must have won the campaign'. In such cases we cannot conclude that those who voted Labour did so because they fought the 'best campaign', since vote may well have caused the evaluation. Alternatively, some may have merely been repeating journalists' judgements that Labour had fought the best campaign.

There are other problems with asking voters to assess the appeal of specific campaigns such as the 'demon eyes' posters that undermine the use of social surveys in general. Butler and Kavanagh suggest that, 'People do not like to appear supportive of appeals to fear' and may conceal their responses to negative advertisements.[37] For that reason some advertising agencies insist that their posters and broadcasts should not be pre-tested on voters.[38] However, such possibilities raise larger issues that we do not have space to explore here.

Cross-sectional surveys are extraordinarily flexible instruments that can be adapted to assess either the campaign in general or specific communications. The results provide clues for future research. However, the causal inferences drawn from such studies are subject to a high degree of uncertainty as a result of rationalization and partisanship. Researchers must therefore strive to validate their findings from other studies that contain a dynamic element, such as panel, aggregate or experimental studies.

Controlled experimental studies

Researchers have no control over the timing of their 'natural experiments' in panel studies and do not observe change in cross-sectional studies. One obvious solution to both these problems therefore is to carry out a controlled experiment in which the conditions are manipulated so that we can directly observe voters' responses to stimuli.[39] While the method has seldom been used in the past, recent studies by Cappella and Jamieson,[40] Norris and Sanders[41] and Iyengar[42] have revived interest in it. Norris and Sanders, for example, used it to estimate the effect of various aspects of television coverage during the 1997 general election. In particular they wished to examine various hypotheses about the effect of:

- *directional bias of news coverage* (the hypothesis that 'positive' reports about a party will enhance voters' evaluations of the party while 'negative' reports will lower evaluations);
- *differences in stopwatch coverage* (the hypothesis that greater coverage of a party will enhance voters' evaluations);
- *differences in the news agenda* (the hypothesis that greater coverage of an issue will increase its importance to voters and benefit the party most favourably associated with that issue).

Before the experiments began respondents were asked to complete a short questionnaire about their interest in politics, evaluations of the parties' images, which issues were most important to them and their personal backgrounds. They were then randomly allocated to 'control' and 'treatment' groups and given videos to watch. These consisted of a 30-minute 'sandwich'. The first ten minutes and the last ten minutes of the video were the same for both groups. However, while the control groups were given a non-political report in the middle section, the treatment groups were given a political report that had been constructed to test one of the three basic hypotheses. After watching, the video respondents were again asked to record their evaluations of the parties and the importance of various issues.

The great advantage of the experiment is that, since respondents are allocated at random to the control and treatment groups, then any observed change in their responses can only be attributable to the stimulus to which they are exposed.[43] It therefore permits analysts to arrive at causal statements. Moreover, unlike panel studies, analysts need not wait for 'natural experiments', since they have it within their power to produce the necessary conditions to test their hypotheses.

The controlled experiment is often held to represent *the* ideal method of assessing the effect of *specific* campaign communications. However, it does have limitations. It is far from clear, for example, how long any observed 'effects' last. Voters may be observed reacting strongly to biased broadcasts, but if that effect is so ephemeral that it has dissipated by the following week or month, it may be of little substantive importance. The 'solution' of course is to extend the temporal dimension of the experiment by adopting a repeated test research design.[44] However, this solution produces its own problems. First, it would be extremely difficult – if not impossible – for researchers to maintain any degree of control. Short of imprisoning subjects, it is inevitable that they will be exposed to stimuli other than those that are part of the experimental design. Second, the longer an experiment lasts, the more likely those subjects are to be 'conditioned' by the process itself. The hurdles to a repeated test design are therefore formidable. To date no researchers have grasped the nettle and sought to extend the temporal dimension of experiments.

There are further limitations with experimental methods. Research such as that conducted by Norris and Sanders provides plausible evidence about the effect of a single stimulus on various dependent variables *if other things are equal*. Their evidence demonstrates that *if* television news contained a preponderance of messages favourable to a particular party, then it would receive an electoral reward. Yet studies of television news indicate that this counterfactual is not particularly relevant. Broadcasters take the task of providing fair and impartial coverage very seriously.[45] There is usually some attempt to present an opposing view within the programme itself and, even if coverage within programmes may be favourable to one party, balance is achieved across a series of broadcasts. The experimental findings could therefore be simply viewed as 'unrealistic', since in the real world coverage is balanced over a period of time.

A more general problem with experiments is that human beings, unlike chemicals or other animals, are quite capable of changing their behaviour if they are aware that they are being experimented on. Respondents may anticipate analysts' expectations and alter their behaviour either to gratify – or to confound – those expectations. If this is a real danger, respondents can be given misleading information about the aims of the research and prior expectations. Norris and Sanders, for example, told their respondents they 'were primarily interested in selective perception, that is, whether young people and older people, or men and women are interested in different stories in the news', when in fact they were interested in other issues altogether.[46] This raises some thorny ethical issues for researchers.

Even this most 'scientific' of methods is therefore of somewhat limited use when studying communication effects. Experiments allow analysts to make a direct link between observed stimulus and response, but it is unclear how far one can generalize from such findings to the 'real world'. Yet again such evidence needs to be viewed in conjunction with a wider portfolio of evidence, such as that from aggregate level studies.

Aggregate level studies

As the name implies, 'aggregate level' data contains information about aggregates or groups of individuals. Aggregate studies can be divided into those that use monthly poll data and those that use the daily poll data from the campaign itself. In recent years political scientists have made increasing use of such data and have applied sophisticated techniques, borrowed from econometrics, to establish the causal relationship between the state of the economy (as indicated by the rate of inflation, unemployment and economic expectations) and party support.[47] More recently such techniques have been applied to examine the relationship between the balance of political communications and party support.

Monthly opinion polls

Most aggregate studies of party support have focused on monthly data taken from the national opinion polls, such as those shown in Figure 9.1. These models assume that variations in party popularity are caused by: *the objective state of the economy* (measured by inflation, unemployment and interest rates), *economic perceptions* (measured by prospective and retrospective evaluations of household finances), *major political events* (such as the ERM crisis of September 1992) and *evaluations of party leaders* (measured by responses to the questions about who would make the 'best Prime Minister').

This approach to public opinion has largely focused on the electorate's response to changing *economic* circumstances. The results have tended to support a simple 'reward/punishment' hypothesis: that governments

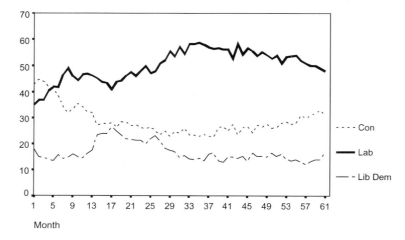

Figure 9.1 Monthly opinion polls (1992–97).

are rewarded for producing 'good times' and punished for producing 'bad times'. More recently, however, political scientists have also begun to use aggregate data to examine the effect of political communications by including measures of the extent to which media coverage was favourable to one party or another. In a 1984 study, for example, Mosley, found that he could explain 35 per cent of the variation in government popularity using the official measures of economic performance.[48] However, simply by replacing the official rate of inflation with the *Daily Mirror*'s Shopping Clock Index, he found that he could explain 47 per cent of the variation. It therefore appeared that the communications from the newspaper were influencing some portion of the electorate. This study was subject to the obvious limitation that it appeared to assume that everyone either read the *Daily Mirror* or had access to the Index. Yet it clearly suggested that the national press might play a major role in communicating national economic conditions to the public. This research was extended in 1993 by Sanders et al. when they examined press coverage of the economy over a period from 1979 to 1987.[49] Their findings suggested that, although newspaper coverage of the economy did not appear to have any direct influence on government popularity, it did affect personal financial expectations: the 'better' the coverage for the government, the higher the expectations of voters. Moreover, since financial expectations were in turn related to government popularity, newspaper coverage could be said to have an indirect effect on party support, just like the indirect effects discuss in Chapter 2 and outlined in Figure 2.1. Similarly, in their 1996 study, Gavin and Sanders found that the balance of television coverage exerted a small, but statistically significant, effect on support for the Conservatives over a 12-month period from 1993 to 1994.[50] They also found that the balance of coverage exerted a statistically significant effect on perceptions of comparative economic competence: a variable that in turn has strong effects on party support. Yet again the balance of media coverage was found to have a significant indirect effect on party support.

This approach offers several advantages to analysts of communications and public opinion. First, because the time series contains a dynamic element, it allows analysts to establish the causal relationship between any pair of variables, either by a simple visual inspection of the time series or by more complex statistical methods.[51] Second, time series data permit researchers to estimate the effect of specific political events that must be assumed constant across individuals (such as the ERM crisis in 1992). Third, this general species of model has proved remarkably successful in forecasting election outcomes several months before an election. Indeed, one such model correctly forecast the Conservatives' share of the vote in 1992, some 18 months before the election.[52]

Despite these advantages aggregate studies are subject to some major limitations. The models have to make some heroic assumptions about the psychological processes that are going on in individuals' minds. In addition, many of the measures of political communications are, as yet, unsophisticated. In their study of the effects of newspapers, for example, Sanders et al. relied on a very simple system of coding. Articles were divided into five categories relating to the economy and then each article was coded as 'sympathetic', 'neutral' or 'antipathetic'. The *balance* of coverage was then calculated by simply summing articles over the month and calculating the net balance. No allowance was made for the prominence of the articles or the strength of each article: each one counted the same. The challenge for future research is therefore to establish a way of coding variables according to their tone and prominence.

Campaign polls

The logic of the aggregate studies based on monthly opinion poll data can also be applied to opinion polls taken during the formal campaign itself when, it is assumed, most voters are tuned into politics, attentive to the political debate and eagerly gather information from the media. However, researchers have so far failed to establish any link at all between the day-to-day balance of television coverage and support for any of the parties. In the 1997 election, for example, the only major

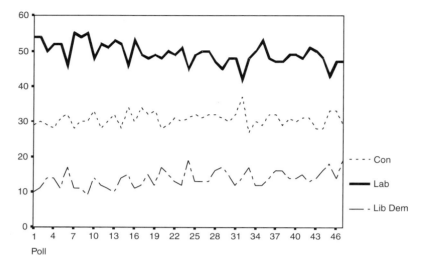

Figure 9.2   The campaign polls in 1997.

change in party support during the formal campaign was a gradual
decline in support for Labour and an equally gradual rise in support for
the Liberal Democrats (see Figure 9.2). Norris et al. conclude that the
rise in support for Liberal Democrats 'appears to have resulted from
factors other than their exposure to positive or negative television news
coverage'.[53]

These negative results are unsurprising. In Chapter 2 we established
that most voters enter an election predisposed to support a particular
party, so that only around 25 per cent of voters claim to 'make up their
minds' during the campaign itself. During the campaign television
makes every effort to provide unbiased coverage, so that there is little
reason to expect that the coverage will affect voters. Moreover, although
a great deal of information is available, much of it flies above the heads
of voters who do not follow the campaign closely. These are hardly the
sort of conditions where one might expect there to be important
communications effects.

The tendency of support for the Liberal Democrats to increase during
the campaign has been quite pronounced in three out of four recent
elections and is worth explaining.[54] Three factors appear to be at work
here. First, the media tend to focus on the two major parties outside
election campaigns and this may give the voters the impression that

they must choose between the two main parties: Conservative or Labour. During the formal campaign television pays more serious attention to the centre party and reminds voters of their existence and the tactical voting opportunities. Second, it may well be that voters are responding against the negative campaign styles of the major parties. It may not therefore be the amount of coverage that matters, but the nature of the campaign itself that helps the 'moderate' party. Third, the Liberal Democrats are most voters' 'second choice' party and receive a high proportion of tactical votes. The steady increase in support for the Liberal Democrats might therefore simply reflect the crystallization of tactical vote decisions.

Constituency campaigns

In Chapter 5 we saw that it is also possible to assess the effect of local campaigns on election outcomes. This method combines aggregate data (actual votes obtained by the parties in each constituency) with survey evidence on the 'intensity' of the campaign (the number of canvassers, use of computers and so on). This ingenious use of a wide variety of evidence has demonstrated that local campaigns can influence the size of the swing in individual constituencies and is indicative of what the scientific imagination can achieve by employing a wide range of data and methods.

Multi-method studies

I have indicated on several occasions that no single method is likely to produce correct estimates of the effect of political communications. It is therefore wise to examine a wide range of data and to use a whole range of methods to ensure that our conclusions are not an artefact. In their study of the 1997 general election, for example, Norris et al. used cross-sectional studies, panel studies and aggregate data to gauge the electoral response.[55] They also used content analysis of major television news programmes and the front pages of leading newspapers to measure the balance of media messages. Finally, they used the party manifestos as a measure of the parties' ideal agenda, while press releases and party election broadcasts were taken to indicate their actual agenda. This allowed them to assess the effect of television coverage on the public's agenda, the extent to which citizens shared the parties' agenda and the extent to which parties stuck to their 'ideal agenda' and thus provide an overall assessment of communications effects.

With the arrival of such multi-method studies, the study of political communications is likely to be transformed from a 'patchwork of disparate, very specific and highly context bound findings lacking generalisability' into a more coherent programme of systematic research and replication.[56] To illustrate why this may be so I will briefly examine earlier studies of campaign effects.

The history of campaign effects

Lippmann and mass propaganda

Early studies of public opinion tended to suggest that mass communications represented a grave threat to democracy. In *Public Opinion*, published in 1922, Walter Lippmann argued that most voters had only limited experience of the political world. Much of what they 'knew' was therefore based on stereotypes, misunderstanding and rumour. He argued that political leaders were able to 'manufacture consent' for their policies by applying the sophisticated techniques of 'psychological warfare' developed during the First World War. These reduced debate to the repetition of slogans and demonized the opposition. Lippmann's work implied that the public was more responsive to the emotional appeals of the demagogue than to the reasoned arguments of the statesman.

Lippmann claimed that the 'the practice of democracy has turned a corner. A revolution is taking place, infinitely more significant that any shifting of economic power'.[57] His concerns appeared well founded as the authoritarian regimes of Nazi Germany and Soviet Russia made extensive use of propaganda. However, his writings were largely based on a priori theorizing and the use of selective historical examples, rather than on any hard evidence about the effect of propaganda on individuals' attitudes and behaviour. While many of his theoretical insights inspired later generations of researchers, his gloomy conclusions about democracy were later questioned.

Lazarsfeld and minimal effects

Paul Lazarsfeld, Bernard Berelson and Hazel Gaudet reported on one of the most famous panel studies in *The People's Choice*. These authors outlined an early version of the 'aligned voter' model. This suggested that most voters had relatively stable partisan attachments that were the product of parental affiliations, childhood socialization and the accumulated political experiences of groups to which they belonged (see Chapter 2). They demonstrated that the votes of those people who were undecided before the campaign could be predicted from a few

social characteristics and concluded that social pressures led to con-
formity between their attitudes and those of people like themselves.[58]

Lazarsfeld et al. suggested that election campaigns served essentially
three functions: they *activated* those who were indifferent to politics,
reinforced the partisan and *converted* those who were doubtful. However,
they argued that by far the most important of these processes was
reinforcement. Most voters sought out information that reinforced their
predispositions and screened out that which did not. Campaign propaganda therefore largely served to reinforce, validate and strengthen
decisions made a long time ago and provided loyal party supporters
with arguments to justify their behaviour.[59] They went on to argue that
'even those who had not yet made a decision exposed themselves to
propaganda to fit their not-yet-conscious political predispositions'.[60]
They concluded that campaigns were important, but they were important
largely because they activated latent predispositions.[61]

Contemporary studies of political communications

The People's Choice has had an enormous effect on all subsequent studies
of political communications. In general, most analysts have agreed with
the conclusions that political communications have had only a minimal
effect on voters. *The People's Choice* was followed by a whole host of
studies that attested to the relative inattentiveness of most citizens,
the conserving effects of partisanship and the neutrality of television
coverage. In recent years, however, this orthodoxy has been severely
criticized. The all-pervasive nature of the modern media has made it less
plausible to suggest that communications and campaigns have 'minimal
effects'. It is widely believed that communications effects are 'more fugitive
than minimal'.[62] Indeed, one eminent analyst has suggested that 'the
state of research on media effects is one of the most notable embarrass-
ments of modern social science'.[63] Certainly the 'minimal effects' school
of thought rests uneasily beside many politicians' faith in the efficacy of
electioneering.

Researchers have responded to this embarrassment in several ways.
First, researchers have adopted a multi-method approach to the study of
communications effects (discussed above). Second, researchers have
paid increasing attention to causal structure and to the indirect effects of
political communications. This is well-illustrated by Gavin and Sanders'
study of television. Third, increasing attention has been paid to the
conditional effects of political communications. Zaller, for example, has
demonstrated that the effect of political communications varies with
both political predispositions and political awareness.[64] This is because

although those with high levels of awareness are most likely to receive communications, they also tend to have the strongest predispositions and are therefore less likely to accept information that contradicts their predispositions. Those with low levels of awareness on the other hand tend to have weaker predispositions and are therefore open to influence, but are less likely to receive the communication. The relationship between political awareness and attitude change is thus non-monotonic. It is therefore those voters with medium levels of awareness who are most affected by communications.[65] Research has therefore moved on to establish under what conditions political communications can influence voters.[66] Fourth, researchers have begun to examine the effect of political communications in a wider range of contexts, such as referendums and local elections (see Chapter 8). Finally, most researchers accept that political communications may exert most of their influence over a long period of time as the result of a constant drip-drip of propaganda. Attention is therefore shifting towards the influence of communications on voters' long-term predispositions: their basic sense of party identity and values. However, as we have demonstrated, extending the temporal dimension raises numerous methodological challenges for panel studies and experimental methods alike.

In the meantime politicians and political campaigners alike will continue to arrive at their own conclusions as to the effect of political communications, to identify 'mistakes' and the 'turning points' of the campaign. It is these evaluations that will shape future party policy and the conduct of campaigns. While every effort must be made to improve the scientific study of communications effects, political scientists would be wise to pay close attention to the evaluations of politicians and other campaigners. It is their beliefs about the effect of political communications that continue to transform political communications.

10
Political Communications and Democratic Politics
Pippa Norris

Introduction

Previous chapters have demonstrated how professional spin doctors, hired political consultants, advertising experts and sophisticated party web pages appear to have gradually displaced traditional forms of party campaigning, like local party volunteers, constituency rallies and door-to-door canvassing. The professionalization of political communications is becoming evident in many established and newer democracies.[1] One common perspective has conceptualized these changes as representing the 'rise of political marketing', where the primary development involves the way candidates, parties, government, lobbyists and groups have borrowed communication techniques from the private sector in an attempt to achieve strategic objectives like gaining votes, driving public opinion or influencing legislation.[2] Yet this perspective remains limited, since political agents may be responding to changes in the news media, electorate or wider political system as much as initiating developments. The rise of the Internet, for example, or the loosening of party–voter bonds provide problems and opportunities for politicians seeking to control the news agenda in a more complex, unpredictable and fragmented communication environment. Another alternative perspective has often regarded recent changes as the 'Americanization' of campaigning, if seen as originated in the United States. Yet rather than a specifically American development, with practices like negative advertising, personalized politics or high campaign expenditures which are subsequently exported in a pre-packaged box to other countries, it seems more accurate to understand this process as an 'import–export' shopping model with campaigners borrowing whatever techniques are believed to work.[3] Developments in campaign communications can therefore best be understood as part of the modernization process rooted in technological, economic and political developments common to many societies. This process simultaneously transforms party organizations, the news media and the electorate.[4]

The key issue this chapter addresses is whether the modernization of political communications described throughout this book has proved detrimental to the quality of democracy, as so many fear. The first section briefly summarizes theories of media malaise, which suggest that changes in the news industry and in party campaigns have transformed the structure and contents of political communications and that this, in turn, has contributed towards civic disengagement among the public. Theories of 'videomalaise' or 'media malaise', suggesting that exposure to political coverage contributed towards political alienation, first emerged in the early 1970s in Robinson's studies of American television news, and were expanded in Miller et al.'s analysis of newspaper readers.[5] In the post-Vietnam and post-Watergate era theories of media malaise seemed to provide a plausible reason for growing public disillusionment with government. In the 1990s, following another wave of disenchantment, this perspective has launched a deluge of popular books. The core argument is that public faith in representative institutions and leaders has been eroded by developments in political communications, including tabloidization of the news media and the adoption of political marketing techniques by parties.

The chapter goes on to examine evidence for these claims, drawing on the 1964 and 1997 British Election Studies. Far from supporting this theory, the chapter demonstrates a consistent and positive relationship between attention to party and news messages and indicators of civic knowledge, political efficacy and voting participation. This evidence lends further confirmation to patterns found throughout Western Europe and the United States.[6] The conclusion theorizes that this positive relationship is open to a number of interpretations but it can best be explained by the theory of a 'virtuous circle'. Attention to campaign communications function in this account as a two-way flow to activate the politically interested, progressively strengthening and reinforcing political information, interest and involvement. This is understood as a long-term process operating at a diffuse level: it is the cumulative impact of regular and repeated exposure and attention to the news media and to party campaigns, the steady drip, drip, drip of political communications, that gradually influences the public. Through this process, those already most engaged acquire further information that facilitates practical political choices. In contrast, the disengaged are less affected since they are less disposed to pay attention to political coverage. The conclusion considers the implications of this theory for understanding the rise of post-modern campaigns and the future of British democracy.

Changes in the structure and organization of party campaigns

In understanding the modernization of campaign communications we need to make a clear analytical distinction between changes in the structure and organization of parties and the news industry, changes in the contents of political messages and changes in the potential effects of these messages.

The impact of developments on changing the balance of power within party structures is most persuasive (see Chapter 3). Pre-modern campaign organizations were based primarily upon direct forms of interpersonal communications between candidates and citizens at the constituency level (see Figure 10.1). In these campaigns, local party volunteers selected the candidates, rang the doorbells, posted the pamphlets, targeted the wards, planned the resources and generally provided all the grassroots machinery linking voters and candidates, supplemented by some professional party agents working in particular constituencies (see Chapter 5). Planning by the party leadership was largely short term and ad hoc and most activity like leadership speeches and rallies was essentially constituency-focused, although the rise of radio broadcasts and newsreels started to change this pattern as early as the 1920s. In the news media, the partisan-leaning press acted as the core intermediary between politicians and the public (see Chapter 6). And the electorate was anchored to parties by strong loyalties (see Chapter 2).

The era from the late 1950s until the late 1980s was characterized by the predominance of the modern campaign, defined as having a party organization coordinated more closely at national level by politicians and press officers at central office and advised by part-time external professional media consultants, opinion pollsters and advertising gurus. Active planning and policy presentations lengthened well beyond the period of the official campaign. For the major parties the principal forum of campaign events moved to the battle to dominate news agendas on television and in the national press. The daily campaign used morning press conferences, policy launches, leadership tours, party election broadcasts and key leadership speeches to influence a relatively small group of editors, producers and journalists who were the key gatekeepers in a

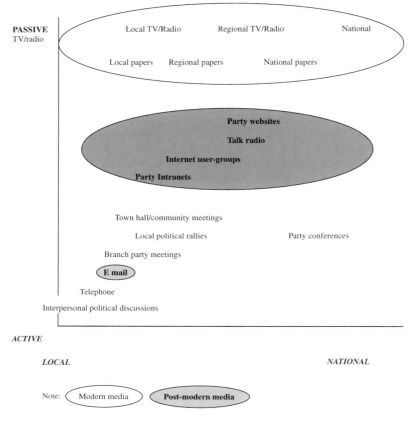

Figure 10.1   Typology of campaign media.

limited range of national newspapers and TV studios. And the electorate became increasingly decoupled from party and group loyalties. At the heart of the campaign, for the major parties, a team of political leaders and party staff, supplemented by external advisers, handled the press, commissioned polls and advertisements, and scheduled the *thème du jour*, leadership tours, news conferences and photo opportunities in the attempt to frame the news.

The process continues to evolve and since the mid-1990s Britain has been experiencing the gradual emergence of post-modern campaigns. In these contests, parties have become more proactive, coordinated and systematic in their news management and election targeting. The coterie of professional consultants expert in advertising, public opinion, marketing and strategic news management has become more co-equal actors with politicians, assuming a more influential role within government (cf. Chapter 5). Local activity has been coordinated more tightly from national party headquarters by beepers, fax and Internet. A 'permanent' campaign has been developing, where the techniques of electioneering and governing become intertwined. The news media is becoming increasingly fragmenting into a more complex and incoherent environment of multiple channels, outlets and levels, ending the days of the captive audience for the BBC and ITN evening news or the loyal and predictable readership on the right for the *Mail* or on the left for the *Mirror*. New information technologies, notably the explosion in Internet use, as well as the use of techniques like 'town-hall meetings', daily tracking polls and focus groups, are gradually facilitating more interactive formats between the news media, parties and the public. Newspaper–party linkages are weakening, as the press responds to a more autonomous 'media logic' of sales rather than traditional political loyalties. And as Chapter 2 demonstrates, the electorate may become further dealigned, or 'up for grabs', in their voting choices as social and political identities are constructed rather than given.[7] The characteristics of post-modern campaigns are continuing to evolve in Britain, along with political uses of the web. As shown in Figure 10.1, in many regards post-modern campaigns facilitate a return to some earlier forms of interactivity, placing these channels between the techniques that predominated in the pre-modern and modern era.

Previous chapters have demonstrated how this process has transformed party organizations: tipping the balance of power from elected representatives towards professional consultants, and from constituency party activists towards Westminster HQs (Chapter 3). Increased professionalization has placed additional strains on party revenues: the Neill report estimated that for the major parties the real costs of campaigning quadrupled from 1983 to 1997.[8] There has also been a substantial increase in the costs of press offices during routine periods of government. It is estimated that 60 people, many of these paid by public funds, are employed for research, media and campaigning purposes in the newsroom of CCO. It is also estimated that over 70 special advisers are employed in Whitehall by the Blair government.[9]

These developments have affected Westminster politics but have they contributed towards public cynicism? Here there is much speculation that the rise of political marketing with its techniques of 'spin', selling and persuasion may have undermined the credibility of political leaders and institutions but the evidence is far from clear-cut.[10] Bob Franklin provides one of the clearest statements of this thesis, decrying the 'packaging of politics', the manipulation of the public by official government advertising campaigns and the rise of image over substance in Britain, which he believes may have contributed towards public cynicism.[11] Jay Blumler argues that the use of public relations techniques by Conservative and Labour governments may have altered the tone of political news, producing a more adversarial journalist–politician relationship, producing a 'crisis' in civic communication.[12] American research about the use of 'negative' or attack political advertising has raised worries that this practice may demobilize the electorate.[13] This literature suggests that if everything in politics is designed for popular appeal, with 'catch-all' parties adopting whatever slogan, message or image will resonate with today's focus groups, rather than authentic and deep-rooted ideological beliefs, then the public may become more sceptical of party campaign messages.

Changes in the contents of political coverage

There is also much speculation, but little systematic evidence, that changes in the news coverage of government and public affairs have contributed towards political cynicism and disengagement. As discussed in earlier chapters, many believe that declining sales and intense headline-to-headline competition for readers have increased the 'tabloidization' of the press (see Chapter 6). 'Tabloidization' can refer to either the style or substance of news. The main worry is that this process has 'dumbed down' serious political coverage in the broadsheets as well as the popular end of the market, shrinking international news and parliamentary coverage, producing popular headlines focusing more on Blur than Blair.[14] At least until recently, British television has been insulated from downmarket pressures through regulated competition, but there are widespread anxieties that the dam is about to break producing a deluge of tabloid TV with the growing fragmentation of terrestrial, digital, satellite, cable and broadband television outlets (see Chapter 7). The abolition of the flagship ITN *News at Ten* is regarded as indicative of these dangers. The emerging Internet age has produced an even greater diversity of places to go and things to do, now that about a fifth of the British public is online.[15]

It is feared that changes in the news industry mean that standards of British television are about to plunge headlong into a wasteland exemplified by imported sitcoms, Schwarzenegger action movies and

Swedish soft porn. Many in Europe believe that growing competition from commercial channels in the 1980s has undermined the quality and diversity of public service television. The multiplication of media outlets, chasing the mass-market audience with low-cost, low-quality scheduling, is believed to have reduced the choice of programme types.[16] For Peter Dahlgren, the displacement of public service television by commercial channels has impoverished the public sphere.[17] Many worry that Britain may be following down the path of American television, where concern about the quality of serious political coverage has produced a Greek chorus lamenting the modern state of journalism. To mention just a few of the critics, for Entman the free press falls far short of its ideals, leaving too much of the public ignorant and disconnected from politics.[18] For Neil Postman the major networks, driven by their haemorrhage of viewers to cable, have substituted entertainment-oriented, crime, celebrity and consumer-obsessed tabloid television for serious political coverage of national and world affairs.[19] Neil Gabler echoes these claims, arguing that entertainment has come to be the predominant value on television news, with the result that the political process has been repackaged into show business.[20] For Roderick Hart, television creates illusions of political participation, while encouraging passivity, thereby seducing America.[21] Larry Sabato warns of the dangers of pack journalism, with all the press corp focusing obsessively on a few sensationalist stories producing a 'feeding frenzy'.[22] For Thomas Patterson, the press, in its role as election gatekeeper, has become a 'miscast' institution, out of order in the political system. Where America goes, in the multi-channel, mega-complex, entertainment-oriented, Disney Corp and Microsoft-dominated world, it is often feared that other countries will quickly follow (see Chapter 1).

Yet many of the more dire predictions seem exaggerated. Structural changes have radically transformed the news industry during the last half-century but rather than simply moving the news media downmarket, as so many assume, this has produced a diversification of communication outlets, formats, levels and audiences in Europe and the United States.[23] In Britain, real-audio *BBC News Online* now coexists a click away from real-audio Amsterdam porn, the worthy 7 p.m. *Channel 4 News* broadcasts along with *Live TV's* news bunny, *MTV* is available alongside the *Parliamentary Channel,* and the *Independent* sits on the same stands as the *Sunday Sport.* Television programmes commonly allow those who are interested to drill down for further information in related websites. In post-industrial societies more political information is available than ever before and the structure of the news industry in Europe is not necessarily following the commercially dominant and television-centric American model.

Moreover, in Europe the news audience has not narrowed over time, as some fear; rather, recent decades have seen the development of a wider and more socially diverse news audience. During the last fifty years on average across all post-industrial societies newspaper sales have not declined: the proportion of regular readers of European newspapers has doubled in the last three decades, and the social profile of readers has broadened.[24] The fall noted in earlier chapters in Britain, especially among Sunday papers, is not therefore an inevitable or universal secular trend. Three-quarters of all Europeans now watch TV news every day, up from half three decades earlier. In post-industrial societies the amount of news and current affairs broadcast on public service TV has tripled in the last thirty years, not shrunk. Use of the Internet has exploded so that by the end of the twentieth century a fifth of all Europeans were online, as were half of all Americans and Scandinavians. The new forms of campaigning provide a wide range of alternative channels for parties to connect with the public, from traditional house-to-house canvassing, national press conferences and party political broadcasts, to intranet and Internet web pages, e-mail lists and 'virtual' conferences. Even in the United States, where perhaps post-modern campaigns have developed furthest, newer forms of campaign communications complement, rather than replace, older ones. For example, the proportion of Americans contacted by the major parties during the campaign was higher in the mid-1990s than in the mid-1950s. Just as in warfare the poor bloody foot soldiers continue to be deployed alongside the Stealth bombers, so local volunteers contacting voters continue to work alongside sophisticated party websites.

The impact on public engagement

Parties have adopted far more sophisticated techniques of political marketing, and the news media have diversified in channels and levels, but have these developments eroded citizen engagement with democracy, as many suggest? Many of the more exaggerated fears reflect a deeply conservative and nostalgic tendency to believe in a 'golden age' of face-to-face electioneering when, as in Lake Wobegon, all the politicians were articulate, all the voters were well-informed and all the party activists were above average. In this mythical Britain, knowledgeable citizens enthusiastically debated Suez with parliamentary candidates at local campaign rallies, discussed the latest balance of payments crisis over tea and Spam sandwiches in the factory canteen, and read worthy parliamentary speeches on the Cuban crisis or the Rhodesian problem in the *Daily Mail* or *Daily Herald*. Campaigns, like Hovis and Marmite and Lipton's and Lucky Strikes, were widely believed to be good for you. Too often commentators slide far too easily, like a street gambler's sleight of hand, from discussing changes in party campaigns or the news industry (which have happened) to assumptions about their effects upon the public (which have not).

The number of sceptics questioning the evidence for all these claims has been growing in recent years. Earlier studies by the author found that, contrary to videomalaise theory, although TV watching was related to some signs of apathy, attention to the news media was associated with positive indicators of civic engagement in the United States and Britain, as well as in other countries.[25] Evidence from a battery of Eurobarometer surveys and the American NES surveys demonstrates that people who watch more TV news, read more newspapers, surf the net and pay attention to campaigns are consistently more knowledgeable, trusting of government and participatory.[26] Repeated tests confirm this positive relationship, even after controlling for factors that characterize the news audience, like their prior education and political interest. In a wide range of post-industrial societies, attention to the news media and party campaigns was found to be positively associated with political knowledge, trust and activism, rather than generating cynicism and disengagement, as many fear. Along similar lines, Kenneth Newton found that reading a broadsheet newspaper in Britain, or watching a lot of television news, was associated with high levels of political knowledge, interest and understanding of politics.[27] Christina Holtz-Bacha reported similar positive effects from attention to the news media in Germany.[28] The most recent examination of the American NES evidence, by Stephen Earl Bennett and his colleagues, found that trust in politics and trust in the news media went hand in hand, with no evidence that use of the news media caused political cynicism.[29] But so far these voices have been published as scattered scholarly studies and thereby drowned out by the Greek chorus of popular lament for the state of modern journalism.

Civic engagement and campaign communications in Britain

To extend this work further we can examine whether similar patterns are found in Britain. Unfortunately we lack consistent items that would allow us to analyse systematic trends over time in British general election campaigns but we can compare campaign communications in the 1964 BES, at the start of the series, with evidence for the most recent pattern in the 1997 BES.

The 1964 survey monitored three main categories of campaign messages. Media communications include coverage of the election in television news and current affairs, radio news and newspapers. Party-initiated communications include campaign leaflets, canvassing by party workers and local election meetings. Lastly, personal communications include talking about the campaign with family, friends or colleagues. Table 10.1 shows that in the mid-1960s, the news media were the most popular source of information: 82 per cent reported following the campaign on TV or radio news while two-thirds followed events in newspapers. Reading party leaflets (64 per cent) and talking to others during the campaign (60 per cent) were also fairly common activities. In contrast only about a third (37 per cent) reported contact with a party canvasser, while few (8 per cent) said that they attended a political meeting during the campaign. Even in the mid-1960s, therefore, although television election coverage was a relatively recent innovation, the news media had quickly come to dominate the main channels of campaign communications.

We can examine the association between exposure to campaign communication and three indicators of civic engagement included in the 1964 survey: reported voting turnout, campaign interest and political efficacy. Table 10.1 presenting zero order correlations, without any social controls, shows that exposure to the news media and to personal discussions was consistently associated with civic engagement. The differences between groups were positive and significant on most of the indicators except for being canvassed, which was insignificantly related to civic engagement. In no case was use of the news media or party communications associated negatively with these indicators.

Are similar patterns evident today or has this positive association weakened over the years due to changes in campaign communications? The BES post-election cross-sectional survey in 1997 lets us compare exposure and attention to national and local television and newspapers, as well as whether the respondent was contacted at home or by telephone by party workers. We can also examine six indicators of 'civic engagement', broadly defined, including attitudes towards democracy, political trust, internal political efficacy, political knowledge, political interest and voting turnout. The specific items are all outlined in the appendix to the chapter and scales were developed using principal

Table 10.1   Zero-order correlations between civic engagement and campaign communications, 1964 British general election

Types of campaign communication	% 'Yes'	Voting turnout	Campaign interest	Political efficacy
News media				
Regular TV/radio news	82	0.09**	0.29**	0.17**
Regular newspaper reader	64	0.10**	0.31**	0.12**
Party contact				
Canvassed by party worker	37	0.02	0.01	0.01
Read party leaflet	64	0.07**	0.28**	0.12**
Attended party meeting	8	0.04	0.16**	0.08**
Interpersonal communications				
Discussed politics with family and friends	59	0.04	0.30**	0.14**

Note: Significant at the 0.01 (**) or the 0.05 (*) level. For all items and scales see appendix to chapter.

Sources: 1964 BES.

components factor analysis (not reproduced here). Since the wording of these items is not identical to those used earlier the results of the analysis in 1964 and 1997 are not strictly comparable, nevertheless we can compare the direction of the associations.

Table 10.2 presents the zero-order correlations between these indicators and types of campaign communication without any control. The results show that attention to political news was strongly related to the propensity to vote, satisfaction with British democracy, political interest and political knowledge. A similarly positive albeit weaker correlation was evident in terms of exposure to the news media. The only exceptions concerned political efficacy where, contrary to the other findings, regular viewers of local television news and regular readers of a national paper have a lower sense that they could influence the political process.

Of course it could be that these correlations are spurious if prior social background influences both use of the news media and civic engagement. Accordingly a series of regression models were run to examine the earlier associations controlling for age, gender, education and social class. These standard social variables have commonly been found to be strongly related to political participation, interest and knowledge, although to be more weakly associated with political trust. The aim was not to develop comprehensive models explaining patterns of civic engagement, which would require many other factors to be considered,

Table 10.2 Zero-order correlations between civic engagement and campaign communications, 1997

Types of campaign communication	Satisfaction with democracy	Political trust	Political efficacy	Political interest	Political knowledge	Voting turnout
Television						
Regular viewer national TV news	0.11**	0.04*		0.15**	0.13**	0.12**
Regular viewer local TV news	0.06**		−0.06**	0.03*		0.05**
High attention to political news on TV	0.17**	0.06**	0.24**	0.69**	0.40**	0.20**
Newspapers						
Regular reader national morning paper	0.07**		−0.08**		0.06**	0.08**
Regular reader local paper				0.05*		0.05**
High attention to political news in paper	0.16**		0.27**	0.67**	0.41**	0.20**
Party contract						
Canvassed by party at home or by phone		0.04*				0.11**

Note: Only correlations significant at the 0.01 (**) or the 0.05 (*) level are reported. For all items and scales see appendix to chapter.

Source: BES 1997.

but rather to examine the standardized regression coefficients for the communication variables after entry of the social controls. To simplify the analysis, because of the intercorrelations between the media variables, the measures of exposure and attention were combined into a single scale for TV news and another for newspapers. The weakness of the party contact correlations meant that these were dropped from the analysis.

Table 10.3 demonstrates that even after entry of these social controls, the communication variables proved to be strong and positive predictors of political efficacy, interest, knowledge and turnout. The only dimension where these factors proved to be insignificant concerned political trust, which has often been found to be poorly related to social and news variables. Again in no case was there a significant negative relationship between civic engagement and exposure and attention to campaign communications.

Table 10.3 Association between civic engagement and campaign communications with social controls, 1997

Types of campaign communication	Satisfaction with democracy	Political trust	Political efficacy	Political interest	Political knowledge	Voting turnout
Social background						
Gender (male)	0.11**	–0.02	0.01	0.10**	0.20**	–0.04*
Age (years)	0.18**	0.08*	–0.13**	–0.03	0.23**	0.11**
Education (highest qualification)	0.07	0.03	0.19**	0.08**	0.23**	0.00
Social class (non-manual)	0.04	–0.01	0.05*	0.13**	0.10**	0.00
Campaign communications						
Exposure and attention to TV news	0.06*	–0.01	0.14**	0.32**	0.13**	0.08**
Exposure and attention to newspapers	0.04	–0.01	0.10**	0.37**	0.16**	0.08**
Adjusted R^2	0.06	0.01	0.12	0.44	0.25	0.07

Note: The coefficients represent standardized beta coefficients in regression models controlling for age (years), gender (0/1), education and class (manual/non-manual). Ordinary least squared regressions are used for the scales in columns 1–4. Logistic regressions are used for the models of voting turnout in column 7. Only coefficients significant at the 0.01 (**) or the 0.05 (*) level are reported. For all items and scales see appendix to chapter.

Source: BES 1997.

Conclusions: a virtuous circle

The evidence that we have analysed in Britain lends further confirmation to the pattern found in other European countries and in the United States. That is, attention to the news media and party messages is positively associated with levels of political knowledge and participation. This account also strengthens the conclusions presented earlier in previous studies of the 1992 general election,[30] and of the 1997 British general election campaign panel survey: 'Those most attentive to news on television and in the press, and regular viewers and readers', *On Message* concluded, 'were significantly more knowledgeable than the average citizen about party policies, civics and the parliamentary candidate standing in their constituency. They were also more likely to turn out.'[31] Although there was minimal short-term attitudinal change during the 12-month run-up to the 1997 general election, the persistent pattern suggests that in the long term repeated attention to the news media functions as a socialization process similar to the effects of the family, class and community.

Of course this persistent pattern in cross-sectional surveys does not demonstrate the causal direction of this relationship. There are three possible interpretations of this association, which cannot be resolved using the available survey evidence. The pattern could be explained as a one-way flow from prior political attitudes towards media use. That is, it could that because I'm interested and involved in public affairs I regularly turn on the news or read a paper to follow the campaign. This explanation fits the 'uses and gratifications' theory of use of the mass media. Or, alternatively, the pattern may be the result of a one-way flow from media use to political attitudes. In this case, because I usually catch the news, for whatever reason, I could gradually become more interested in, and informed about, politics. Both these interpretations cannot be ruled out based on the evidence presented in this chapter. Correlations, no matter how persistent, do not help us unravel complex issues of causality. Cross-sectional surveys provide limited insights into these familiar 'chicken-and-egg' issues (see Chapter 9).

But it does seem more plausible to interpret this consistent pattern as a diffuse process of two-way interactive flows, or a long-term virtuous circle. According to this theory, those who are interested and engaged in politics are most likely to pay attention to news and information about public affairs in newspapers, television, the Internet and from party messages. And, in turn, those who frequently pay attention to these sources are most likely to acquire information that facilitates learning about public affairs, practical political choices and therefore further engagement in the political process. In this regard, repeated exposure to campaign communications functions as a long-term socialization process, analogous to the influence of parents or friends. Cross-sectional surveys cannot prove that the persistent links between the party support of parents and siblings are the product of socialization processes but this seems a likely inference.

Yet if the news media crystallizes and strengthens prior predispositions, why are the more cynical and disengaged not similarly reinforced in their disengagement? The reason is that this group is naturally immunized from the positive or negative messages of the news media by a triple process. Given the diversification of media sources, the disengaged are less likely to catch the political news; if they do catch the news (perhaps out of habit) they probably pay less attention to political coverage; and if they catch the news and pay attention to politics they are less likely to trust the messages, since trust in the news media and in government commonly goes hand in hand. Even if the news and party messages have become more negative over the years, even if campaign communications focus increasingly on the horse race and less on issues of substance, even if tabloidization has reduced serious political coverage of serious issues, as critics suggest, the effect of exposure and attention to political messages still proves healthy for civic engagement.

Therefore the public is not simply passively responding to political communications being presented to them, in a naive 'stimulus–response' model; instead they are critically and actively sifting, discarding and interpreting the available information from politicians and journalists. According to the virtuous circle theory, the more educated and literate public in post-industrial societies are capable of using the more complex range of news sources and party messages available in post-modern campaigns to find the information they need to make practical political choices. This suggests that there are many reasons to be sceptical about many of the stronger claims of media malaise. If the public is disenchanted with their leaders and institutions, if citizens are making greater demands on governments, as seems evident in many countries, then we should look more directly at the performance of representative democracy and less at the surface reflections.[32]

Recent years have seen a revival in concern about civic engagement, notably low levels of turnout in the 1997 British general election (71.6 per cent), the lowest level in the postwar period. The erosion of turnout evident in the June 1999 elections to the European Parliament has set widespread alarm bells ringing in Brussels, Strasbourg and Luxembourg as further evidence that the public is becoming disenchanted and disengaged with European politics. The level of voting participation across the EU fell from almost two-thirds (63 per cent) of the electorate in the first direct elections in 1979 to just under half (49.2 per cent) of European citizens in June 1999, its historical nadir. Britain also has the lowest turnout of any the EU states; in June 1999 (90 per cent) of Belgian citizens voted compared with only one quarter (23 per cent) of the British electorate.

Yet before we can consider the pros and cons of alternative policy initiatives, like the introduction of leadership debates during the campaign, changes to the system of party political broadcasts or other reforms to the news media, we need to demonstrate that it is political communications per se which are at the root of any 'problem'. It is true that turnout has declined in recent British elections but this can best be explained by a combination of political factors. As Heath and Taylor demonstrate, one of the main reasons why voting participation varies over the years is the changing electoral context, notably the closeness of the race in conjunction with large ideological differences between the major parties.[33] If the outcome seems in doubt, as in 1992, then people tend to flock to the polls. If, as in 1997, all indicators predict an easy victory so that there are few doubts about the result, this encourages the leading party's voters to stay at home, particularly in safe seats. Moreover, many assume that most established democracies have experienced a general secular decline in voter participation but in fact in these countries levels of turnout have remained fairly stable during the last two decades; on average 71 per cent of voting age population participated in elections in these states in the 1990s, down only 3 per cent from the 1970s.[34] British turnout in the last election was therefore about what we might expect for established democracies rather than lower than average. The major systematic variations in turnout between countries can best be explained by institutional factors, such as the frequency of elections (producing British voter fatigue in the succession of elections and referendums from 1997 to 1999), the type of electoral system and compulsory voting. Certainly institutional reforms might help boost British turnout including changes to the facilities for registration and voting, the frequency, level and timing of elections, and the competitiveness of electoral politics.[35] Comparative studies of 22 democracies by Jackman and Miller,[36] research on the European elections by Franklin, van der Eijk and Oppenhuis,[37] and Wolfinger and Rosenstone's work in the United States,[38] all confirm that political institutions and electoral laws provided the most plausible explanation for variations in voter turnout. Devices like the introduction of online registration and voting facilities, supplementing not replacing conventional ballot boxes, seem like one of the most important steps towards boosting participation levels.

But any 'problems' of civic engagement in Britain should be addressed directly by institutional reforms that can serve to boost voter turnout at the polls, not by introducing major changes to the process of political communications. The system clearly isn't perfect. We all have our own list of things which, if we could play God for a day, we might want to change. Of course tabloids should, in the best of all possible worlds, devote more attention to politics and less to porn. Cheque-book journalism and tacky scandal-driven 'exclusives' about the personal sex lives of politicians are unfortunate, albeit entertaining. Party broadcasts should probably spend more time presenting positive policy options rather than negative critiques of the other side. Minor parties should have a more level financial playing field, and all parties should be more transparent in their financial dealings, a major problem that has already been addressed by the Neill Committee. And dutiful citizens should, of course, pay more serious attention to the campaign and civic affairs, watching the *Panorama* specials and reading the election supplements, as well as turning out on wet and windy nights to cast their ballot. The new communication environment created by the digital and broadband convergence of technologies will pose major challenges to British campaign communications as we have known them since the war. Similar to the television revolution in the late 1950s, the Internet will transform e-politics, like e-commerce. But any potential policy reforms to political communications are probably worse than leaving things alone, given the problems of freedom of speech and publication inherent in regulating these matters, the need for the press to act as an unfettered watchdog for the abuse of power and the unintended consequences which often accompany the best-meaning policy reforms. In the last analysis, caution seems preferable to meddling in the process of political communications, and in the old adage, if it's not broken, we shouldn't attempt to fix it.

Appendix – survey items and scales (BES, 1997)

Democratic satisfaction – 9-point scale

'On the whole, how satisfied are you with the way democracy works in Britain. Are you . . . satisfied, fairly satisfied, not very satisfied, or not at all satisfied?'

'In some countries, people believe their elections are conducted fairly. In other countries, people believe their elections are conducted unfairly. Thinking of the last general election in Britain, where would you place it on this scale? Last election was conducted fairly (1) . . . Last election was conducted unfairly (5).'

Political trust – 8-point scale

'How much do you trust British governments of any party to place the needs of the nation above the interest of their own political party.' Just about always, most of the time, only some of the time, almost never.

'How much do you trust politicians of any party in Britain to tell the truth when they are in a tight corner.' Just about always, most of the time, only some of the time, almost never.

Political efficacy – 15-point scale

'People like me have no say in what the government does.'

'Parties are only interested in people's votes, not in their opinions.'

'It doesn't really matter which party is in power, in the end things go on much the same.'

Agree strongly, agree, neither agree nor disagree, disagree, strongly disagree.

Political knowledge – 6-point scale

'Here is a quick quiz. For each thing I say, tell me if it is true or false. If you don't know, just say so and we will skip to the next one.

- The number of members of parliament is about 100? (F)
- The longest time allowed between general elections is four years? (F)
- Britain's electoral system is based on proportional representation? (F)
- MPs from different parties are on parliamentary committees? (T)
- Britain has separate elections for the European Parliament and the British-Parliament? (T)
- No one may stand for Parliament unless they pay a deposit?' (T)

Newspaper use and attention

'About how often do you read [name of daily morning newspaper]? Every day, four or five days a week, two to three days a week, one day a week or less.' [PAPSCALE]

'People pay attention to different parts of newspapers. When you read [name of paper] how much attention do you pay to stories about politics? A great deal, quite a bit, some, a little, or none?' [PAPERATT]

'About how often, if at all, do you read a morning, evening or weekly local newspaper?' [LOCAL]

TV use and attention

'On average, how many days a week do you watch all or part of any national news programme on any television channel?' 0–7. [TVSCALE]

'On average, how many days a week do you watch or listen to all or part of any local news programme on radio or television?' 0–7. [LOCALTV]

'People pay attention to different parts of the television news. When you watch the news on television, how much attention do you pay to stories about politics? A great deal, quite a bit, some, a little, or none?' [TVATT]

Party contact

'Did a canvasser from any party call at your home to talk to you during the election campaign? Yes (1) No (0).' [CANV]

'Were you contacted by anyone on the telephone during the election campaign asking you how you might vote? Yes (1) No (0).' [TELCANV]

Notes

Chapter 1: Introduction

1. Colin Seymour-Ure, *The British Press and Broadcasting Since 1945* (Oxford: Blackwell, 1996).
2. Paul M. Sniderman, Richard A. Brody, Philip E. Tetlock with Henry E. Brady, *Reasoning and Choice: Explorations in Political Psychology* (Cambridge: Cambridge University Press, 1991); Arthur Lupia and Matthew D. McCubbins, *The Democratic Dilemma: Can Citizens Learn What they Need to Know?* (Cambridge: Cambridge University Press, 1998) and Bernard Grofman (ed.), *Information, Participation and Choice: An Economic Theory of Democracy in Perspective* (Ann Arbor: University of Michigan Press, 1995).
3. Susan Herbst, *Reading Public Opinion: How Actors View the Democratic Process* (Chicago: Chicago University Press, 1998).
4. Bob Franklin, *Packaging Politics: Political Communications in Britain's Media Democracy* (London: Edward Arnold, 1994).
5. Robert Huckfeldt and John Sprague, 'Social Order and Political Chaos: The Structural Setting of Political Information', in John A. Ferejohn and James H. Kuklinski (eds), *Information and Democratic Processes* (Chicago: University of Illinois Press, 1990).
6. However, see Robert Dahl, 'Minorities Rule', in Leonard J. Fein (ed.), *American Democracy: Essays on Image and Realities* (London: Holt, Rinehart & Winston, 1964), p. 126.
7. Dennis Kavanagh, *Constituency Electioneering in Britain* (London: Longman, 1970), ch. 1.
8. David Butler, *The McCallum Lecture*, 1 November 1997.
9. Cf. Michael Cockerell, *Live From Number 10: The Inside Story of Prime Ministers and Television* (London: Faber & Faber 1989), who makes the claim for 1955 as the 'first television election', ch. 4.
10. Pippa Norris, 'The Battle for the Campaign Agenda', in Anthony King (ed.), *New Labour Triumphs: Britain at the Polls* (Chatham, NJ: Chatham House, 1998), p. 115.
11. Ronald B. McCallum and Alison Readman, *The British General Election of 1945* (Oxford: Geoffrey Cumberlege, 1947), p. 134.
12. David Butler, 'The Changing Nature of British Elections', in Ivor Crewe and Martin Harrop (eds), *Political Communications: The General Election Campaign of 1983* (Cambridge: Cambridge University Press, 1986), p. 4.
13. David Butler and Richard Rose, *The British General Election of 1959* (London: Macmillan, 1960), p. 1.
14. McCallum and Readman, *The British General Election of 1945*, p. 155.
15. David Butler, *British General Elections Since 1945* (Oxford: Blackwell, 1989), p. 79.
16. Anthony Mughan, 'Party Leaders and Presidentialism in the 1992 Election: A Post-War Perspective', in David Denver, Colin Rallings and David Broughton

(eds), *British Elections and Parties Yearbook 1993* (Hemel Hempstead: Harvester Wheatsheaf, 1993), pp. 193–204.

17. McCallum and Readman, *The British General Election of 1945*, p. 129.
18. Kenneth Harris, *Attlee* (London: George Weidenfeld & Nicolson, 1982), p. 259.
19. Colin Munro, 'Legal Constraints, Real and Imagined', in Ivor Crewe, Brian Gosschalk and John Bartle (eds), *Political Communications: Why Labour Won the General Election of 1997* (London: Frank Cass, 1998), pp. 236–48.
20. Butler and Rose, *The British General Election of 1959*, p. 22.
21. Butler and Rose, *The British General Election of 1959*, p. 23.
22. Butler and Rose, *The British General Election of 1959*, p. 25.
23. Mark Abrams and Richard Rose, *Must Labour Lose?* (Harmondsworth: Penguin, 1960).
24. Butler and Rose, *The British General Election of 1959*, pp. 52–3.
25. Butler and Rose, *The British General Election of 1959*, p. 84.
26. Butler and Rose, *The British General Election of 1959*, p. 78.
27. David Butler and Anthony King, *The British General Election of 1964* (London: Macmillan, 1965), p. 76.
28. Butler and Rose, *The British General Election of 1959*, p. 59.
29. Butler and Rose, *The British General Election of 1959*, pp. 59–60.
30. Butler and Rose, *The British General Election of 1959*, p. 60.
31. Butler and Rose, *The British General Election of 1959*, p. 58.
32. Butler and Rose, *The British General Election of 1959*, p. 19
33. David Butler, *British General Elections since 1945* (Oxford: Blackwell, 1989), p. 79.
34. Butler and Rose, *The British General Election of 1959*, p. 21 and p. 28.
35. John Bartle, 'Market Analogies, the Marketing of Labour and the Origins of New Labour', in Nicholas J. O'Shaughnessy (ed.), *Readings in Political Marketing* (Westport, CT: Praeger, forthcoming); Dominic Wring, *The Marketing of the Labour Party* (London: Palgrave, forthcoming).
36. David Butler and Dennis Kavanagh, *The British General Election of 1997* (London: Macmillan, 1997), p. ix.
37. Colin Hughes and Patrick Wintour, *Labour Rebuilt: The New Model Party* (London: Fourth Estate, 1990); Eric Shaw, *The Labour Party Since 1979: Crisis and Transformation* (London: Routledge, 1994).
38. Anthony King, 'Why Labour Won – At Last', in King, *New Labour Triumphs*, p. 200.
39. Keith Alderman and Neil Carter, 'The Labour Party and the Trade Unions: Loosening the Ties', *Parliamentary Affairs* (1994), pp. 321–37.
40. Philip Gould, *The Unfinished Revolution: How Modernisers Saved the Labour Party* (London: Little Brown, 1998).
41. The Labour Party, *Partnership in Power* (London: Labour Party, 1997); David Manion, 'The Business of Power', *The Chartist* (October 1997), pp. 14–15; Ann Black, 'For Better and for Worse', *The Chartist* (October 1997), pp. 12–13.
42. Richard Burden, ' Time to Renew New Labour', *New Statesman and Society*, 11 August 1995.
43. Jay G. Blumler and Michael Gurevitch, 'Change in the Air: Campaign Journalism at the BBC', Crewe et al., *Political Communications*, pp. 176–94.

44. Kirsty Milne, 'Falling on Their Sword', *New Statesman*, 18 July 1997.
45. Daniel Finkelstein, 'Why the Conservatives Lost', in Crewe et al., *Political Communications*, pp. 11–15.
46. Nicholas Jones, *Campaign 1997: How the General Election was Won and Lost* (London: Indigo, 1997); Ewan MacAskill, 'Millbank's Part in Major's Downfall', *The Guardian*, 3 May 1997.
47. David McKie, 'Swingers, Clingers, Waverers, Quaverers: The Tabloid Press in the 1997 General Election', in Crewe et al., *Political Communications*, pp. 115–30.
48. Norris, 'The Battle for the Campaign Agenda', pp. 120–1.
49. Blumler and Gurevitch, 'Change in the Air'.
50. David Butler and Dennis Kavanagh, *The British General Election of 1992* (London: Macmillan, 1992), ch. 7.
51. See http://www.official-documents.co.uk/document/cm40/4057/volume-1/volume-1.pdf. Table 3.5, p. 36 and Table 3.7, p. 37.
52. See http://www.official-documents.co.uk/document/cm40/4057/volume-1/volume-1.pdf, ch. 10.
53. The Conservative Party, *The Fresh Future* (London: Conservative Party, 1997).
54. Margaret Scammell, *Designer Politics: How Elections are Won* (London: Macmillan, 1995).
55. Bruce I. Newman, *The Marketing of the President: Political Marketing as Campaign Strategy* (London: Sage, 1994); Bruce I. Newman, *The Mass Marketing of Politics: Democracy in an Age of Manufactured Images* (London: Sage, 1999); Dan Nimmo, *The Political Persuaders: The Techniques of Modern Election Campaigns* (Englewood Cliffs, NJ: Prentice Hall, 1970).
56. Richard R. Lau, Lee Sigelman, Caroline Heldman and Paul Babbit, 'The Effects of Negative Political Advertisements: A Meta-Analytic Assessment', *American Political Science Review*, 93 (1999), 851–75; Larry M. Bartels, 'Partisanship and Voting Behaviour, 1952–1996', *American Journal of Political Science*, 44 (2000), 35–50; Warren E. Miller and J. Merrill Shanks, *The New American Voter* (Cambridge, MA: Harvard University Press, 1996).
57. See Munro, 'Legal Constraints, Real and Imagined'.
58. Peter Goddard, Margaret Scammell and Holli A. Semetko, 'Too Much of a Good Thing? Television in the 1997 Election Campaign', in Crewe et al., *Political Communications*.
59. Lawerence Rees, *Selling Politics* (London: BBC, 1992), p. 43.
60. Blumler and Gurevitch, 'Change in the Air'.
61. Ivor Crewe and Anthony King, *SDP: The Birth, Life and Death of the Social Democratic Party* (Oxford: Oxford University Press, 1995), p. 9.
62. Jay G. Blumler, Dennis Kavanagh and Tom J. Nossiter, 'Modern Communications versus Traditional Politics in Britain: Unstable Marriage of Convenience', in David L. Swanson and Paolo Mancini (eds), *Politics, Media and Modern Democracy* (Westport, CT: Praeger Press, 1996), pp. 49–72.
63. MacAskill, 'Millbank's part in Major's Downfall'.
64. Stephen Ward and Rachel Gibson, 'The First Internet Election? United Kingdom Political Parties and Campaigning in Cyberspace', in Crewe et al., *Political Communications*, pp. 96–114.

Chapter 2:   Changing Voters or Changing Models of Voting?

1. The author would like to thank Jack Kneeshaw and Samantha Laycock of the University of Essex for very helpful comments on previous drafts of this chapter.

2. See Ivor Crewe, Bo Sarlvik and James Alt, 'Partisan Dealignment in Britain 1964–74', *British Journal of Political Science*, 7 (1977), 129–90; Mark Franklin, *The Decline of Class Voting in Britain: Changes in the Basis of Electoral Choice* (Oxford: Oxford University Press, 1985); Ivor Crewe, 'Great Britain', in Ivor Crewe and David Denver (eds), *Electoral Change in Western Democracies: Patterns and Sources of Electoral Volatility* (London: Croom Helm, 1985), pp. 100–50; Richard Rose and Ian McAllister, *Voters Begin to Choose: From Closed Class to Open Elections in Britain* (London: Sage, 1986); Mark Franklin, Tom Mackie, Henry Valen et al., *Electoral Change: Responses to Evolving Social and Attitudinal structures in Western Countries* (Cambridge: Cambridge University Press, 1992); David Denver, *Elections and Voting Behaviour in Britain* (London: Harvester Wheatsheaf, 1994), ch. 4; Pippa Norris, *Electoral Change since 1945* (Oxford: Blackwell, 1996), ch. 4.

3. Russell J. Dalton, *Citizen Politics in Western Democracies: Public Opinion and Political Parties in the United States, Great Britain, West Germany and France* (Chatham, NJ: Chatham House, 1996).

4. David Butler and Donald Stokes, *Political Change in Britain: The Evolution of Electoral Preference*, 2nd edn (London: Macmillan, 1974), pp. 20–3.

5. Butler and Stokes, *Political Change in Britain*, pp. 323–37.

6. Butler and Stokes, *Political Change in Britain*, pp. 316–23.

7. Butler and Stokes, *Political Change in Britain*, p. 47.

8. The survey question reads, 'How long ago did you decide that you would definitely vote the way you did? A long time ago, some time last year, some time this year, during the campaign'.

9. Martin Harrop and William L. Miller, *Elections and Voters: A Comparative Introduction* (London: Macmillan, 1987), p. 101; Ivor Crewe, 'Voting and the Electorate', in Patrick Dunleavy, Andrew Gamble, Ian Holiday and Gillian Peele (eds), *Developments in British Politics 4* (London: Macmillan, 1993), pp. 92–122.

10. Angus Campbell, Philip E. Converse, Warren E. Miller and Donald E. Stokes, *The American Voter* (Chicago: Chicago University Press, 1976), ch. 12.

11. Paul F. Lazarsfeld, Bernard Berelson and Hazel Gaudet, *The People's Choice: How the Voter Makes Up His Mind in A Presidential Campaign* (New York: Columbia University Press, 1948), p. 27.

12. Butler and Stokes, *Political Change in Britain*, chs 4, 5, 8 and 9.

13. Peter Pulzer, *Political Representation and Elections in Britain* (London: Allen & Unwin, 1967), p. 98.

14. Butler and Stokes, *Political Change in Britain*, ch. 2.

15. Butler and Stokes, *Political Change in Britain*, p. 51.

16. Campbell et al., *The American Voter*, pp. 140–4.

17. Pippa Norris, 'Theories of Political Communications', in Pippa Norris, John Curtice, David Sanders, Margaret Scammell and Holli A. Semetko, *On Message: Communicating the Campaign* (London: Sage, 1999), p. 6.

18. Robert Worcester and Roger Mortimore, *Explaining Labour's Landslide* (London: Politicos, 1999), p. 119.
19. David Butler and Richard Rose, *The British General Election of 1959* (London: Macmillan, 1960), p. 24.
20. Arthur Lupia and Matthew D. McCubbins, *The Democratic Dilemma: Can Citizens Learn What They Need to Know?* (Cambridge: Cambridge University Press, 1998).
21. Ivor Crewe, 'Do Butler and Stokes Really Explain Political Change in Britain?', *European Journal of Political Research*, 2 (1974), 47–92.
22. Anthony Downs, *An Economic Theory of Democracy* (New York: Harper & Row, 1957).
23. Christopher H. Achen, 'Social Psychology, Demographic Variables and Linear Regression: Breaking the Iron Triangle in Voting Research', *Political Behaviour*, 14 (1992), 195–211, at p. 198.
24. Morris P. Fiorina, *Retrospective Voting in American National Elections* (New Haven, CT: Yale University Press, 1981), p. 190.
25. Anthony Heath, Geoffrey Evans and Jean Martin, 'The Measurement of Core Beliefs and Values: The Development of Socialist/Laissez Faire and Libertarian/Authoritarian Scales', *British Journal of Political Science*, 24 (1993), 115–32.
26. Heath et al., 'The Measurement of Core Beliefs and Values'.
27. Donald Stokes, 'Spatial Models of Party Competition', in Angus Campbell, Philip E. Converse, Warren E. Miller and Donald Stokes, *Elections and the Political Order*. (London: John Wiley, 1966), pp. 161–79; Donald Stokes, 'Valence Politics', in Dennis Kavanagh (ed.), *Electoral Politics* (Oxford: Clarendon Press, 1992), pp. 141–64.
28. David Sanders, 'Why the Conservatives Won – Again', in Anthony King (ed.), *Britain at the Polls 1992* (Chatham, NJ: Chatham House, 1993), pp. 171–222; Michael S. Lewis-Beck, *Economics and Elections: The Major Western Democracies* (Ann Arbor: University of Michigan, 1990).
29. Sanders, 'Why the Conservatives Won – Again', p. 213.
30. Lewis-Beck, *Economics and Elections*, pp. 37–8.
31. Geoff Evans, 'Economics, Politics and the Pursuit of Exogeneity: Why Pattie, Johnston and Sanders are Wrong', *Political Studies*, 47 (1999), 933–6.
32. Sanders, 'Why the Conservatives Won – Again', p. 200.
33. Butler and Rose, *The British General Election of 1959*, p. 18.
34. David Sanders, 'Economic Performance, Management Competence the Outcome of the Next General Election', *Political Studies*, 44 (1996), 203–31.
35. Anthony King, 'Why Labour Won – At Last', in Anthony King (ed.), *New Labour Triumphs: Britain at the Polls* (Chatham, NJ: Chatham House, 1998), pp. 185–92.
36. Cf. Anthony Mughan, 'Party Leaders and Presidentialism in the 1992 Election: A Post-War Perspective', in David Denver, Colin Rallings and David Broughton (eds), *British Elections and Parties Yearbook 1993* (Hemel Hempstead: Harvester Wheatsheaf, 1993), pp. 193–204.
37. John Bartle, Ivor Crewe and Anthony King, *Was it Blair Who Won It? Leadership Effects in the 1997 British General Election*, University of Essex, Essex Papers in Politics and Government No. 128.

38. John R. Zaller, *The Nature and Origins of Mass Opinion* (Cambridge: Cambridge University Press, 1992), p. 6.
39. Franklin, *The Decline of Class Voting in Britain*, p. 152.
40. Butler and Stokes, *Political Change in Britain*, ch. 9.
41. David Sanders, 'The Voters', in Patrick Dunleavy, Andrew Gamble, Ian Holiday and Gillian Peele (eds), *Developments in British Politics 5* (London: Macmillan, 1997), p. 55.
42. Ivor Crewe and Katarina Thomson, 'Party Loyalties: Realignment or Dealignment?', in Geoffrey Evans and Pippa Norris (eds), *Critical Elections: British Parties and Voters in Long-Term Perspective* (London: Sage, 1999), pp. 64–86, Figure 4.1, p. 71.
43. Ian Budge, Ivor Crewe, David McKay and Ken Newton, *The New British Politics* (Harlow: Longman, 1998), p. 363; Rose and McAllister, *Voters Begin to Choose*, ch. 3.
44. Dalton, *Citizen Politics in Western Democracies*, pp. 21–7.
45. Dalton, *Citizen Politics in Western Democracies*, p. 21.
46. Crewe et al., 'Partisan Dealignment in Britain 1964–74'; Franklin, *The Decline of Class Voting in Britain*; Crewe, 'Great Britain'; Rose and McAllister, *Voters Begin to Choose*.
47. Ivor Crewe, 'Introduction: Electoral Change in Western Democracies: A Framework for Analysis', in Crewe and Denver, *Electoral Change in Western Democracies*, pp. 1–22, at p. 8.
48. This conclusion concurs with Norris, *Electoral Change Since 1945*, pp. 110–11; Denver, *Elections and Voting Behaviour in Britain*, pp. 73–8.
49. Crewe, 'Introduction: Electoral Change in Western Democracies', p. 10.
50. Anthony Heath et al., *Understanding Political Change: the British Voter 1964–1987* (Oxford: Pergamon Press, 1991), p. 14.
51. John Bartle, 'Heterogeneity in Models of Vote Choice: Some Evidence from the British Election Study', in Charles Pattie, David Denver, Justin Fisher and Steve Ludlam (eds), *British Elections and Parties Review, Volume 7* (London: Frank Cass, 1997), pp. 1–27.
52. The BES introduced a measure of political knowledge in 1992 and 1997.
53. Eric R. A. N, Smith, *The Unchanging American Voter* (Berkeley: University of California Press, 1989).
54. The question is, 'Which of the reasons on this card comes closest to the main reason you voted for the party you chose? I always vote that way, I thought it was the best party, I really preferred another party but it had no chance of winning in this constituency, other'.
55. Geoffrey Evans, John Curtice and Pippa Norris, 'New Labour, New Tactical Voting? The Causes and Consequences of Tactical Voting in the 1997 General Election', in David Denver, Justin Fisher, Philip Cowley and Charles Pattie (eds), *British Elections and Parties Review, Volume 8. The 1997 General Election* (London, Frank Cass, 1998), pp. 65–79.
56. Franklin, *The Decline of Class Voting in Britain*; Richard Rose and Ian McAllister, *Voters Begin to Choose: From Closed-Class to Open Elections in Britain* (London: Sage, 1986); Heath et al., *Understanding Political Change*.
57. Heath et al., *Understanding Political Change*, ch. 2.
58. Zaller, *The Nature and Origins of Mass Opinion*.

Chapter 3: Power as well as Persuasion: Political Communication and Party Development

1. Austin Mitchell, *Election '45: Reflections on the Revolution in Britain* (London: Bellew/Fabian Society, 1995), p. 42.
2. Pippa Norris, John Curtice, David Sanders, Margaret Scammell and Holi A. Semetko, *On Message: Communicating the Campaign* (London: Sage, 1999).
3. Richard Rose, *The Problem of Party Government* (London: Macmillan, 1974), p. 90.
4. Ronald McCallum and Alison Readman, *The British General Election of 1945* (Oxford: Oxford University Press, 1947); Mitchell, *Election '45*, pp. 41–80.
5. Herbert George Nicholas, *The British General Election of 1950* (London: Macmillan, 1951); David Butler, *The British General Election of 1951* (London: Macmillan, 1952); David Butler, *The British General Election of 1955* (London: Macmillan, 1955).
6. David Farrell, 'Campaign Strategies and Tactics', in Lawrence LeDuc, Richard G. Niemi, Pippa Norris (eds), *Comparing Democracies: Elections and Voting in Global Perspective* (Thousand Oaks, CA: Sage, 1996), pp. 160–83.
7. Pippa Norris, *Electoral Change since 1945* (Oxford: Blackwell, 1997), pp. 193–211.
8. Jay Blumler and Dennis Kavanagh, 'The Third Age of Political Communication: Influences and Features', *Political Communication*, 16 (1999), 209–30.
9. Avraham Shama, 'The Marketing of a Political Candidate', *Journal of the Academy of Marketing Sciences*, 4 (1976), 764–77.
10. Dominic Wring, 'Political Marketing and Party Development: a "Secret" History', *European Journal of Marketing*, 30 (1996), 100–11.
11. Moisei Ostrogorski, *Democracy and the Organization of Political Parties* (Chicago: Quadrangle, 1902).
12. Neal Blewett, *The Peers, the Parties and the People: the General Elections of 1910* (London: Macmillan, 1972), p. 312.
13. John Antcliff, 'The Politics of the Airwaves', *History Today* (1984), March.
14. Timothy Hollins, 'The Presentation of Politics: the Place of Publicity, Broadcasting and Film in British Politics, 1918–39' (Leeds University: unpublished PhD, 1981).
15. Dominic Wring, 'From Mass Propaganda to Political Marketing: the Transformation of Labour Party Election Campaigning', in Colin Rallings, David M. Farrell, David Denver and David Broughton (eds), *British Parties and Elections Yearbook 1995* (London: Frank Cass, 1996), pp. 105–24.
16. Harold Croft, *A Handbook of Party Organization* (London: Labour Party, 1931).
17. Timothy Hollins, 'The Presentation of Politics', p. 37.
18. Wring, 'From Mass Propaganda to Political Marketing', p. 109.
19. Bernard Donoghue and George W. Jones, *Herbert Morrison: Portrait of a Politician* (London: Weidenfeld & Nicolson, 1973), pp. 109–11.
20. Colin Seymour-Ure, *The British Press and Broadcasting since 1945* (Oxford: Blackwell, 1996).
21. David Butler and Richard Rose, *The British General Election of 1959* (London: Macmillan, 1960), p. 17.

22. Richard Rose, *Influencing Voters: A Study of Campaign Rationality* (London: Faber & Faber, 1967).

23. David Butler and Anthony King, *The British General Election of 1964* (London: Macmillan, 1965); Richard Rose, in Butler and King, *The British General Election of 1964*; Lord Windlesham, *Communication and Political Power* (London: Jonathan Cape, 1966).

24. Andrew Taylor, 'The Conservative Party, Electoral Strategy and Public Opinion Polling, 1945–64', in Charles Pattie, David Denver, Justin Fisher and Steve Ludlam (eds), *British Elections and Parties Review: Volume 7* (London: Frank Cass, 1997).

25. Windlesham, *Communication and Political Power*.

26. Rose, *Influencing Voters*; Dennis Kavanagh, *Election Campaigning: the New Marketing of Politics* (Oxford: Blackwell, 1995).

27. Margaret Scammell, *Designer Politics: How Elections Are Won* (London: Macmillan, 1995).

28. Hilde Himmelweit, Patrick Humphreys and Marianne Jaeger, *How Voters Decide* (Milton Keynes: Open University Press, 1981).

29. Scammell, *Designer Politics*, pp. 65–70; Kavanagh, *Election Campaigning*, pp. 57–65.

30. Scammell, *Designer Politics*, p. 76.

31. Nicholas O'Shaughnessy, *The Phenomenon of Political Marketing* (London: Macmillan, 1990), p. 212.

32. Adrian Sackman, 'The Learning Curve Towards New Labour: Neil Kinnock's corporate party 1983–92', *European Journal of Marketing*, 30 (1996), 147–58.

33. David Butler and Dennis Kavanagh, *The British General Election of 1987* (London: Macmillan, 1988).

34. David Butler and Dennis Kavanagh, *The British General Election of 1992* (London: Macmillan, 1992).

35. Dave Hill, *Out for the Count* (London: Macmillan, 1992).

36. David Butler and Dennis Kavanagh, *The British General Election of 1997* (London: Macmillan, 1997).

37. Richard Cockett, 'The Party, Publicity and the Media', in Anthony Seldon and Stuart Ball (eds), *Conservative Century: The Conservative Party since 1900* (Oxford: Oxford University Press, 1994), pp. 547–77.

38. J. Ferris and U. Bar-Joseph, 'Getting Marlowe to Hold his Tongue: the Conservative Party, the Intelligence Services and the Zinoviev Letter', *Intelligence and National Security*, 8 (1993), 100–37.

39. Scammell, *Designer Politics*, p. 31.

40. Michael Cockerell, *Live from Number 10: The Inside Story of Prime Ministers and Television* (London: Faber & Faber, 1989), p. 15.

41. Cockerell, *Live from Number 10*, p. 24.

42. Windlesham, *Communication and Political Power*.

43. Cockett, 'The Party, Publicity and the Media', pp. 569–70.

44. See Steve Hilton, 'The Conservative Party's Advertising Strategy', in Ivor Crewe, Brian Gosschalk and John Bartle (eds), *Political Communications: Why Labour Won the General Election of 1997* (London: Frank Cass, 1998), pp. 45–52.

45. Rose, *Influencing Voters*, p. 70.

46. Cockerell, *Live from Number 10*, p. 71.
47. Mark Abrams and Richard Rose, *Must Labour Lose?* (Harmondsworth: Penguin, 1960).
48. Butler and King, *The British General Election of 1964*, p. 57.
49. David Butler and Anthony King, *The British General Election of 1966* (London: Macmillan, 1966).
50. David Butler and Michael Pinto-Duschinsky, *The British General Election of 1970* (London: Macmillan, 1971).
51. Robert Worcester, *British Public Opinion* (London: Blackwell, 1991), pp. 51–2.
52. Kavanagh, *Election Campaigning*, p. 86.
53. David Butler and Dennis Kavanagh, *The British General Election of 1983* (London: Macmillan, 1984), pp. 57–8.
54. Butler and Kavanagh, *The British General Election of 1987*, p. 50.
55. Paul Webb, 'Election Campaigning, Organisational Transformation and the Professionalisation of the Labour Party', *European Journal of Political Research*, 18 (1991), 9–28.
56. Butler and Kavanagh, *The British General Election of 1987*, p. 59.
57. Colin Hughes and Patrick Wintour, *Labour Rebuilt: The New Model Party* (London: Fourth Estate, 1990); Philip Gould, *The Unfinished Revolution: How the Modernisers Saved the Labour Party* (London: Little Brown, 1998).
58. Timothy Hollins, *The Presentation of Politics*, pp. 213–14.
59. Kevin Swaddle, 'Hi-Tech Elections: Technology and the Development of Electioneering since 1945', *Contemporary Record* (1988), Spring.

Chapter 4:   The Rise of Campaign Professionalism

1. Max Weber, 'Politics as a Vocation', in Hans Heinrich Gerth and Charles Wright Mills (eds), *From Max Weber: Essays in Sociology* (New York: Oxford University Press, 1946), pp. 77–128.
2. Richard Cockett, 'The Party, Publicity and the Media', in Anthony Seldon and Stuart Ball (eds), *Conservative Century: The Conservative Party since 1900* (Oxford: Oxford University Press), pp. 547–78.
3. Margaret Scammell, *Designer Politics: How Elections Are Won* (London: Macmillan, 1995), p. 54.
4. Philip. Gould, P. Herd and Chris Powell, 'The Labour Party's Campaign Communications', in Ivor Crewe and Martin Harrop (eds), *Political Communications: The General Election Campaign of 1987* (Cambridge: Cambridge University Press), p. 72.
5. Dennis Kavanagh, *Election Campaigning: The New Marketing of Politics* (Oxford: Blackwell, 1995), p. 128. Kavanagh notes a connection between Abrams and Tucker. Early in 1959, Tucker attended a talk by Abrams to the Bow Group on 'The Conservative Party and the Working Class'. On the basis of the talk, Tucker wrote a memo outlining how ambitious working-class voters might be detached from the Labour Party, a document which was circulated to the Cabinet.
6. Mark Abrams, *Social Surveys and Social Action* (London: Heinemann, 1951).
7. Mark Abrams and Richard Rose, *Must Labour Lose?* (Harmondsworth: Penguin, 1960).

8. Attlee averaged seven or eight meetings a day, speaking without notes, and continued to deal with official business. See Trevor Burridge, *Clement Attlee: A Political Biography* (London: Cape, 1985), p. 293.
9. Miss Hornby Smith's contribution is acknowledged in David Butler, *The British General Election of 1951* (London: Macmillan, 1952), p. 67.
10. These figures are calculated from the Nuffield studies.
11. Herbert George Nicholas, *The British General Election of 1950* (London: Macmillan, 1951), p. 115.
12. Cockett, 'The Party, Publicity and the Media', p. 564.
13. David Butler and Richard Rose, *The British General Election of 1959* (London: Macmillan, 1960), p. 21.
14. David Butler and Anthony King, *The British General Election of 1964* (London: Macmillan, 1965), p. 70.
15. Butler and King, *The British General Election of 1964*, pp. 150–1.
16. David Butler and Michael Pinto-Duschinsky, *The British General Election of 1970* (London: Macmillan, 1971), p. 98.
17. Kavanagh, *Election Campaigning*, p. 143. We should, however, make an exception for MORI's swansong election in 1987, when 'the link between pollster and party was one of the closest and most intelligent that has been achieved in recent British politics'. See David Butler and Dennis Kavanagh, *The British General Election of 1987* (London: Macmillan, 1988), p. 133.
18. Butler and King, *The British General Election of 1964*, p. 76.
19. Richard Rose and Ian McAllister, *Voters Begin To Choose* (London: Sage, 1986).
20. David Butler and Dennis Kavanagh, *The British General Election of 1979* (London: Macmillan, 1980), pp. 138–9.
21. J. Sharkey, 'Saatchi's and the 1987 Election', in Crewe and Harrop (eds), *Political Communications: The General Election Campaign of 1987*, p. 64. See also Scammell, *Designer Politics*, p. 120.
22. David Butler and Dennis Kavanagh, *The British General Election of 1992* (London: Macmillan, 1992), p. 81.
23. David Butler and Dennis Kavanagh, *The British General Election of 1983* (London: Macmillan, 1984), p. 35.
24. Steve Hilton, 'The Conservative party's Advertising Strategy', in Ivor Crewe, Brian Gosschalk and John Bartle (eds), *Political Communications: Why Labour Won the General Election of 1997* (London: Frank Cass, 1998), pp. 45–52.
25. Tim Delaney, 'Labour's Advertising Campaign', in Robert Worcester and Martin Harrop (eds), *Political Communications: The General Election Campaign of 1979* (Cambridge: Cambridge University Press), p. 31.
26. In David Butler and Dennis Kavanagh, *The British General Election of October 1974* (London: Macmillan, 1975), p. 154.
27. As a child, Gould used to pace round his suburban garden, planning Labour's campaigns. In 1959, at the age of nine, he was stunned by his party's defeat. See Philip Gould, *The Unfinished Revolution: How the Modernisers Saved the Labour Party* (London: Little Brown, 1998), p. 1.
28. Johnny Wright, 'Advertising the Labour Party in 1983', in Ivor Crewe and Martin Harrop (eds), *Political Communications: The General Election Campaign of 1983* (Cambridge: Cambridge University Press, 1986), pp. 75–81.

29. David Butler and Dennis Kavanagh, *The British General Election of 1997* (London: Macmillan, 1997), p. 230.
30. Quoted in Gould, *The Unfinished Revolution*, p. 316.
31. Shaun Bowler and David Farrell, 'The Contemporary Election Campaign', in Shaun Bowler and David Farrell (eds), *Electoral Strategies and Political Marketing* (London: Macmillan, 1992), p. 225.
32. Angelo Panebianco, *Political Parties: Organization and Power* (Cambridge: Cambridge University Press, 1988).

Chapter 5: The Fall and Rise of Constituency Campaigning

1. See David Denver and Gordon Hands, *Modern Constituency Electioneering* (London: Frank Cass, 1997), pp. 184–5.
2. See David Butler, *The British General Election of 1951* (London: Macmillan, 1952); David Butler and David Kavanagh, *The British General Election of 1951* (London: Macmillan, 1992).
3. David Butler and Donald Stokes, *Political Change in Britain* (London: Macmillan, 1974).
4. Butler, *The British General Election of 1951*, p. 4.
5. *The Times*, 24 March 1992.
6. John M. Bochel and David Denver, 'Canvassing, Turnout and Party Support: an Experiment', *British Journal of Political Science*, 1 (1971), 257–69; Robert T. Holt and John E. Turner, *Political Parties in Action* (New York: Free Press), 1968.
7. See David Denver, *Elections and Voting Behaviour in Britain* (Hemel Hempstead: Harvester Wheatsheaf, 1994), p. 152.
8. See Denver, *Elections and Voting Behaviour*, ch. 3.
9. Ivor Crewe, 'The Electorate: Partisan Dealignment Ten Years On', in Hugh Berrington (ed.), *Change in British Politics* (London: Frank Cass, 1984), p. 211.
10. Ron J. Johnson and Charles J. Pattie, 'The Impact of Spending on Constituency Campaigns at Recent British General Elections', *Party Politics*, 1 (1995), 261–73.
11. Paul Whiteley and Patrick Seyd, 'Labour's Vote and Local Activism', *Parliamentary Affairs*, 45 (1992), 582–95; Paul Whiteley, Patrick Seyd and Jeremy Richardson, *True Blues: The Politics of Conservative Party Membership* (Oxford: Clarendon Press, 1994).
12. Denver and Hands, *Modern Constituency Electioneering*, ch. 9; David Denver and Gordon. Hands, 'Constituency Campaigning in the 1997 General Election: Party Effort and Electoral Effect', in Ivor Crewe, Brian Gosschalk and John Bartle (eds), *Why Labour Won the General Election of 1997* (London: Frank Cass, 1998), pp. 75–92.
13. Don MacIver, *The Liberal Democrats* (London: Harvester Wheatsheaf), ch. 10.
14. The data are derived from our questionnaire studies of the 1992 and 1997 general elections, funded by the ESRC (1992: Y304253004; 1997: R000222027). These figures are based on responses from party election

agents; the numbers are 410 for the Liberal Democrats, 450 for Labour and 434 for the Conservatives.

15. Figures from Office of Population, Censuses and Surveys, *The General House-hold Survey 1975* (London: HMSO, 1978), Table 4.28; Office of Population, Censuses and Surveys, *Living in Britain: Results for the 1994 General House-hold Survey* (London: HMSO, 1994), Table 6.8

16. David Denver and Gordon Hands, 'Triumph of Targeting? Constituency Campaigning in the 1997 Election', in David Denver, Justin Fisher, Philip Cowley and Charles Pattie (eds), *British Elections and Parties Review, Volume 8* (London: Frank Cass, 1998), pp. 171–90.

17. For further discussion see Denver and Hands, *Modern Constituency Election-eering*; Denver and Hands, 'Triumph of Targeting?'; Denver and Hands, 'Constituency Campaigning in the 1997 General Election'.

18. David Denver and Gordon Hands, 'Constituency Campaigning in the 1992 General Election: The Peculiar Case of the Conservatives', in David M. Farrell, David Broughton, David Denver and Justin Fisher (eds), *British Elections and Parties Yearbook* (London: Frank Cass, 1996), pp. 85–105.

19. Quoted in Paul Whiteley and Patrick Seyd, 'Labour's Grassroots Campaign in 1997', in Denver et al., *British Elections and Parties Review, Volume 8*, pp. 191–207.

Chapter 6: The National Daily Press

1. David Butler and Richard Rose, *The British General Election of 1959* (London: Macmillan, 1960), p. 110.

2. This claim excludes a number of relaunches, such as that of the *Daily Herald/Sun* in 1964 and the Murdoch *Sun* in 1969.

3. The legislation prevented people picketing in disputes with which they were not directly involved – so-called secondary picketing. Murdoch's adroitness in comprehensively outwitting the unions is succinctly described in Jeremy Tunstall, *Newspaper Power* (Oxford: Clarendon Press, 1996), ch. 2.

4. Price wars in the 1990s, plus a deliberate move downmarket by *The Times*, blurred but did not eliminate the difference.

5. For background on the Downing Street press office see Michael Cockerell, Peter Hennessy and David Walker, *Sources Close to the Prime Minister* (London: Macmillan, 1984). Bernard Ingham's memoirs, *Kill the Messenger* (London: HarperCollins, 1991), give detail on the Thatcher era.

6. A Canadian law of 1919 bans citizens from accepting foreign honours such as a British peerage unless they give up their Canadian citizenship. Roy Thomson did so; Black appeared unwilling.

7. Herbert George Nicholas, *The British General Election of 1950* (London: Macmillan, 1951), p. 175.

8. David Butler, *The British General Election of 1955* (London: Macmillan, 1955), p. 103.

9. David Butler and Donald Stokes, *Political Change in Britain* (Harmonds-worth: Penguin, 1971), p. 284.

10. David Butler and Dennis Kavanagh, *The British General Election of 1983* (London: Macmillan, 1984), p. 215; David Butler and Dennis Kavanagh, *The British General Election of 1987* (London: Macmillan, 1988), p. 187.

11. Colin Seymour-Ure, 'National Daily Papers and the Party System', in O. Boyd-Barrett, Colin Seymour-Ure and Jeremy Tunstall, *Studies on the Press*, Royal Commission on the Press Working Paper 3 (London: HMSO, 1977).
12. The 'noose trial' took place at Cowley motor works, where eight men were 'tried' before several hundred colleagues with a noose on display in the background and were fined £3.00 for not joining an unofficial strike. David Butler and Anthony King, *The British General Election of 1966* (London: Macmillan, 1966), pp. 108–10. In the 1992 case, Labour's broadcast claimed a little girl ('Jennifer') was queue-jumped by a private patient for treatment of an ear infection. The accuracy of the details was hotly contested. David Butler and Dennis Kavanagh, *The British General Election of 1992* (London: Macmillan, 1992), pp. 122–4.
13. Butler and Kavanagh, *The British General Election of 1987*.
14. A detailed analysis of the *Sun*'s 1992 campaign, contrasted with the *Daily Mirror*'s, is in Colin Seymour-Ure, 'Characters and Assassinations', in Ivor Crewe and Brian Gosschalk (eds), *Political Communications: the General Election Campaign of 1992* (Cambridge: Cambridge University Press, 1995).

Chapter 7: Political Broadcasting in Britain: System, Ethos and Change

1. See Pippa Norris, John Curtice, David Sanders, Margaret Scammell and Holli A. Semetko, *On Message: Communicating the Campaign* (London: Sage, 1999), pp. 97–9.
2. Martin Harrop, 'Political Marketing', *Parliamentary Affairs*, 43 (1990), 277–91; Margaret Scammell, 'Political Marketing: Lessons for Political Science', *Political Studies*, XLVII (1999), 718–39.
3. Margaret Scammell and Holli A. Semetko, 'Political Advertising on Television – The British Experience', in Lynda Lee Kaid and Christine Holtz-Bacha (eds), *Political Advertising in Western Democracies: Parties and Candidates on TV* (London: Sage, 1995), p. 28.
4. Jay G. Blumler and Michael Gurevitch, *The Crisis of Public Communication* (London: Routledge, 1995), pp. 182–99.
5. Sykes Committee, *Broadcasting Committee Report*, Cmnd. 1951 (London: HMSO, 1923), pp. 11, 15.
6. Paddy Scannell, 'Public Service Broadcasting: the History of a Concept', in Andrew Goodwin and Garry Whannel (eds), *Understanding Television* (London and New York: Routledge), p. 14.
7. Described as 'Victorian ideals of service laced with Arnoldian notions of culture' (Scannell, 'Public Service Broadcasting', p. 23).
8. John Reith, 'Memorandum of Information on the Scope and Conduct of the Broadcasting Service' (evidence to the Crawford Committee, 1925), quoted in Scannell, 'Public Service Broadcasting', p. 14.
9. Asa Briggs, *The History of Broadcasting in the United Kingdom, Volume I: The Birth of Broadcasting* (London: Oxford University Press, 1961), pp. 268–9; Asa Briggs, *The History of Broadcasting in the United Kingdom, Volume II: The Golden Age of Wireless* (London: Oxford University Press, 1965), pp. 132–4.

10. 25 January 1929, quoted in Briggs, *The Golden Age of Wireless*, p. 134.
11. Clifford Sharp, quoted in Briggs, *The Golden Age of Wireless*, p. 140.
12. See Briggs, *The Golden Age of Wireless*, pp. 140–1.
13. In the absence of legal provision, allocation is formally the responsibility of broadcasters but is exercised through consultation with parties. See Colin Munro, 'Legal Constraints, Real and Imagined', in Ivor Crewe, Brian Gosschalk and John Bartle (eds), *Political Communications: Why Labour Won the General Election of 1997* (London: Frank Cass, 1998), p. 241.
14. Asa Briggs, *The History of Broadcasting in the United Kingdom, Volume IV: Sound and Vision* (London: Oxford University Press, 1979), pp. 605–6; but see also pp. 632–3.
15. Ronald B. McCallum and Alison Readman, *The British General Election of 1945* (London: Oxford University Press, 1947), pp. 139–43, 154–5.
16. Briggs, *Sound and Vision*, pp. 650–2.
17. Michael Cockerell, *Live From Number 10: The Inside Story of Prime Ministers and Television* (London: Faber & Faber, 1988), p. 9.
18. Sir William Haley, quoted in Briggs, *Sound and Vision*, p. 664, fn.
19. Briggs, *Sound and Vision*, pp. 649–50.
20. Cockerell, *Live From Number 10*, p. 28; David. E. Butler, *The British General Election of 1955* (London: Macmillan, 1955), p. 47; but see Briggs, *Sound and Vision*, pp. 678–9.
21. Cockerell, *Live From Number 10*, p. 20.
22. Butler, *The British General Election of 1955*, p. 48.
23. Cockerell, *Live From Number 10*, pp. 28–36; Butler, *The British General Election of 1955*, p. 110.
24. Cockerell, *Live From Number 10*, pp. 15, 32–3.
25. Cockerell, *Live From Number 10*, p. 16.
26. Briggs, *Sound and Vision*, pp. 673–6.
27. Bernard Sendall, *Independent Television in Britain: Volume 1 – Origin and Foundation, 1946–62* (London: Macmillan, 1982), p. 123.
28. See Sendall, *Independent Television in Britain: Volume 1*, pp. 233–43; Briggs, *Sound and Vision*, pp. 605–8.
29. Cockerell, *Live From Number 10*, pp. 44–51.
30. Sendall, *Independent Television in Britain: Volume 1*, pp. 242–3.
31. Geoffrey Cox, *Pioneering Television News* (London: John Libbey, 1995), p. 121.
32. Sendall, *Independent Television in Britain: Volume 1*, p. 243; Asa Briggs, *The History of Broadcasting in the United Kingdom, Volume V: Competition* (London: Oxford University Press, 1995), pp. 115–16.
33. For an account of the RPA 1949, applicable in 1958 and 1959, see David. E. Butler and Richard Rose, *The British General Election of 1959* (London: Macmillan, 1960), pp. 77, 280–1. The Act was amended in 1969, giving existing broadcasting practice the force of law, and again in 1983.
34. See Briggs, *Sound and Vision*, pp. 663–4.
35. Sendall, *Independent Television in Britain: Volume 1*, p. 351.
36. *Daily Mail*, 14 February 1958, quoted in Briggs, *Competition*, p. 238.
37. Joseph Trenaman and Denis McQuail, *Television and the Political Image* (London: Methuen, 1961), p. 14, fn.
38. Butler and Rose, *The British General Election of 1959*, p. 76–7.
39. Briggs, *Competition*, p. 239.

40.   Cockerell, *Live From Number 10*, p. 53.
41.   Cockerell, *Live From Number 10*, p. 55.
42.   Cockerell, *Live From Number 10*, p. 57.
43.   Robin Day, *Grand Inquisitor* (London: Pan, 1989), p. 3
44.   *Daily Express*, quoted in Cockerell, *Live From Number 10*, p. 62.
45.   *Daily Telegraph*, quoted in Cockerell, *Live From Number 10*, p. 62.
46.   Day, *Grand Inquisitor*, p. 3.
47.   Cockerell, *Live From Number 10*, pp. 64–8; Butler and Rose, *The British General Election of 1959*, p. 77.
48.   Butler and Rose, *The British General Election of 1959*, p. 41.
49.   Colin Seymour-Ure, *The British Press and Broadcasting Since 1945* (Oxford: Blackwell, 1991), p. 162.
50.   Butler and Rose, *The British General Election of 1959*, p. 78.
51.   Cockerell, *Live From Number 10*, p. 69.
52.   Butler and Rose, *The British General Election of 1959*, pp. 78–9.
53.   Butler and Rose, *The British General Election of 1959*, p. 78; Seymour-Ure, *The British Press and Broadcasting Since 1945*, p. 162.
54.   Butler and Rose, *The British General Election of 1959*, pp. 78–80.
55.   Butler and Rose, *The British General Election of 1959*, p. 79.
56.   Cockerell, *Live From Number 10*, p. 69.
57.   See Cockerell, *Live From Number 10*, pp. 69–74; Butler and Rose, *The British General Election of 1959*, pp. 84–90.
58.   Blumler and Gurevitch, *The Crisis of Public Communication*, p. 186.
59.   Cockerell, *Live From Number 10*, p. 68.
60.   Butler and Rose, *The British General Election of 1959*, pp. 82–3.
61.   (Sir) Denis Forman, quoted in Cockerell, *Live From Number 10*, p. 68.
62.   Briggs, *Competition*, pp. 252–3.
63.   Butler and Rose, *The British General Election of 1959*, p. 189.
64.   Independent Television Commission, successor since the 1990 Broadcasting Act to the ITA and, from 1968, the IBA.
65.   See Scannell, 'Public Service Broadcasting', pp. 23–5, for a fuller discussion of this shift.
66.   For more detail on developments in broadcasters' and parties' approaches, see Blumler and Gurevitch, *The Crisis of Public Communication*, pp. 185–90, and Seymour-Ure, *The British Press and Broadcasting Since 1945*, pp. 170–6.
67.   Now Section 93 of the 1983 Act. See Crewe et al., *Political Communications*, pp. 217–34, and Richard Tait, 'Anatomy of a Turn-off', *Guardian*, 20 May 1997, p. 17.
68.   See Peter Goddard, Margaret Scammell and Holli A. Semetko, 'Too Much of a Good Thing? Television in the 1992 Election Campaign', in Ivor Crewe and Brian Gosschalk (eds), *Political Communications: The General Election Campaign of 1992*, (Cambridge: Cambridge University Press, 1995), p. 163; Martin Bell, 'The Accidental Hero', *Guardian*, 6 May 1997, G2, pp. 1–5.
69.   Stephen Perkins, 'Regulations, the Media and the 1997 General Election: The ITC Perspective', in Ivor Crewe, Brian Gosschalk and John Bartle (eds), *Political Communications Why Labour Won the General Election of 1997* (London, Frank Cass, 1998), p. 230.
70.   David Butler and Dennis Kavanagh, *The British General Election of 1987* (London: Macmillan, 1987), p. 244.

71. Perkins, 'The ITC Perspective', pp. 229–30.
72. Cockerell, *Live From No. 10*, pp. 113–16; Margaret Scammell, *Designer Politics: How Elections are Won* (London: Macmillan, 1995), p. 129; Rachel Sylvester, 'Tories Hire Media Watchdog to Monitor Bias at Dyke's BBC', *Independent on Sunday*, 27 June 1999.
73. See Jay G. Blumler and Michael Gurevitch, 'Change in the Air: Campaign Journalism at the BBC, 1997', in Crewe et al., *Political Communications*, pp. 181–3; Holli A. Semetko, Margaret Scammell and Peter Goddard, 'Television', in Pippa Norris and Neil T. Gavin (eds), *Britain Votes 1997* (Oxford: Oxford University Press, 1997), pp. 101–2.
74. For an account of this routine in 1997, see Butler and Kavanagh, *The General Election of 1997*, pp. 93–4.
75. For a thorough account of these developments up to 1992, see Scammell and Semetko, 'Political Advertising on Television'.
76. Cockerell, *Live From Number 10*, pp. 147–9.
77. Scammell, *Designer Politics*, pp. 70–1; Kavanagh, *Election Campaigning*, pp. 57–74.
78. Neill Report, *5th Report of the Committee on Standards in Public Life: The Funding of Political Parties in the United Kingdom*, Cm 4057-I (London: Stationery Office, 1998).
79. See Scammell and Semetko, 'Political Advertising on Television', pp. 32–3.
80. Butler and Kavanagh, *The General Election of 1997*, pp. 56–9.
81. Blumler and Gurevitch, 'Campaign Journalism at the BBC, 1997', pp. 181–7; Goddard et al., 'Too Much of a Good Thing?', esp. pp. 153–5, 169–70.
82. In the British context, see, for example, Norris et al., *On Message*, pp. 97–9; Blumler and Gurevitch, *The Crisis of Public Communication*, pp. 203–12; James Curran, 'Crisis of Public Communication: A Reappraisal', in Tamar Liebes and James Curran (eds), *Media, Ritual and Identity* (London: Routledge, 1998), pp. 175–202.
83. Perkins, 'The ITC Perspective', p. 228.
84. Curran, 'Crisis of Public Communication: A Reappraisal', pp. 176–9.
85. Adam Boulton, 'Television and the 1997 Election Campaign: A View from Sky News', in Crewe et al., *Political Communications*, pp. 195–204.

Chapter 8:   Referendum Campaigning

1. David Butler and Uwe Kitzinger, *The 1975 Referendum*, 2nd edn (London: Macmillan, 1996).
2. Stanley Alderson, *Yea or Nay? Referenda in the United Kingdom* (London: Cassell, 1975).
3. Laura McAllister, 'The Welsh Devolution Referendum: Definitely, Maybe?', *Parliamentary Affairs*, 51 (1999), 149–65; Geoffrey Evans and Dafydd Trystan, 'Why Was 1997 Different?', in Bridget Taylor and Katarina Thomson (eds), *Scotland and Wales: Nations Again?* (Cardiff: University of Wales Press, 1999).
4. Committee on Standards in Public Life, *Fifth Report of the Committee on Standards in Public Life*, Cm 4057-I (London: HMSO, 1998).
5. Butler and Kitzinger, *The 1975 Referendum*, p. 12.

6. Dennis Kavanagh, 'The Timing of Elections: The British Case', in Ivor Crewe and Brian Gosschalk and Martin Harrop (eds), *Political Communications: The General Election of 1987* (Cambridge: Cambridge University Press, 1989), pp. 3–14.
7. David Butler and Austin Ranney, 'Theory', in David Butler and Austin Ranney (eds), *Referendums: A Comparative Study of Practice and Theory* (London: Macmillan, 1996), p. 19.
8. Denis Balsom, 'Public Opinion and Welsh Devolution', in David Foulkes, John Barry Jones and Richard Wilford (eds), *The Welsh Veto: The Wales Act 1978 and the Referendum* (Cardiff: University of Wales Press, 1983).
9. Richard Wyn Jones and Dafydd Trystan, 'The 1997 Welsh Referendum Vote', in Bridget Taylor and Katarina Thomson (eds), *Scotland and Wales: Nations Again?* (Cardiff: University of Wales Press 1999).
10. Jon Bochel, David Denver and Alan Macartney, *The Referendum Experience Scotland 1979* (Aberdeen: Aberdeen University Press, 1981); Foulkes et al., *The Welsh Veto*; Taylor and Thomson, *Scotland and Wales: Nations Again?*
11. Denis Balsom, 'Public Opinion and Welsh Devolution', in Foulkes et al., *The Welsh Veto*; Wyn Jones and Trystan, 'The 1997 Welsh Referendum Vote'.
12. John Barry Jones, 'The Development of the Devolution Debate', in Foulkes et al., *The Welsh Veto*; Leighton Andrews, *Wales Says Yes: The Inside Story of the Yes for Wales Referendum Campaign* (Bridgend: Seren Press, 1999).
13. Philip Goodhart, *Full Hearted Consent: The Story of the Referendum Campaign – and the Campaign for the Referendum* (London: Davis-Poynter, 1976); Butler and Kitzinger, *The 1975 Referendum*.
14. Mark Franklin, Carl van der Eijk and Michael Marsh, 'Referendum Outcomes and Trust in Government: Public Support for Europe in the Wake of Maastricht', *West European Politics*, 18 (1995), 101–17.
15. Anthony Heath, 'Were the Welsh and Scottish Referendums Second-Order Elections?', in Taylor and Thomson, *Scotland and Wales: Nations Again?*
16. Butler and Kitzinger, *The 1975 Referendum*, p. 95.
17. Butler and Kitzinger, *The 1975 Referendum*, p. 69.
18. Andrews, *Wales Says Yes*, p. 129.
19. See also Arthur Lupia and Matthew D. McCubbins, *The Democratic Dilemma: Can Citizens Learn What They Need to Know?* (Cambridge: Cambridge University Press, 1998).
20. Alan Macartney, 'The Protoganists', in Bochel et al., *The Referendum Experience Scotland 1979*, p. 25.
21. Butler and Kitzinger, *The 1975 Referendum*; Andrews, *Wales says Yes*.
22. P. Svensson, 'Class, Party and Ideology: A Danish Case Study of Electoral Behaviour in Referendums', *Scandinavian Political Studies*, 7 (1984), 175–96.
23. Taylor and Thomson, *Scotland and Wales: Nations Again?*
24. Butler and Kitzinger, *The 1975 Referendum*, p. 122.
25. Richard Katz and Peter Mair, 'Changing Models of Party Organization and Party Democracy – The Emergence of the Cartel Party', *Party Politics*, 1, (1995) 5–28
26. Butler and Kitzinger, *The 1975 Referendum*, p. 225.
27. Constitution Unit, *Report of the Commission on the Conduct of Referendums* (London: Constitution Unit, 1996).

28. Constitution Unit, *Report of the Commission on the Conduct of Referendums*, p. 75.
29. Committee on Standards in Public Life, *Fifth Report of the Committee on Standards in Public Life*, para. 12.32.
30. Geoffrey Evans and Dafydd Trystan, 'Why Was 1997 Different?', pp. 113–14.
31. House of Commons Hansard Session 1997–1998, Vol. 319 9–11–98 column 57 Political Parties (Funding).
32. Home Office, *The Funding of Political Parties in the UK: The Government's Proposals for Legislating in Response to the Fifth Report of the Committee on Standards in Public Life*, Cm 4413 (London: HMSO, 1999).
33. Home Office, *The Funding of Political Parties in the UK*, para. 8.16.
34. Home Office, *The Funding of Political Parties in the UK*, para. 8.16.
35. Andrews, *Wales Says Yes*, pp. 102–3.
36. Vernon Bogdanor, *The People and the Party System: The Referendum and Electoral Reform in British Politics* (Cambridge: Cambridge University Press, 1981).

Chapter 9:   Assessing Communications and Campaign Effects on Voters

1. Ivor Crewe, Bo Sarlvik and James Alt, 'Partisan Dealignment in Britain 1964–74', *British Journal of Political Science*, 7 (1977), 129–90.
2. David Sanders, 'Behavioural Analysis', in David Marsh and Gerry Stoker (eds), *Theory and Methods in Political Science* (London: Macmillan, 1995).
3. Joseph A. Schumpeter, *Capitalism, Socialism and Democracy* (London: Unwin, 1987); Walter Lippmann, *Public Opinion*, (New York: Free Press, 1997).
4. Paul F. Lazarsfeld, Bernard Berelson and Hazel Gaudet, *The People's Choice: How the Voter Makes up His Mind in a Presidential Campaign* (New York: Columbia University Press, 1963).
5. Larry M. Bartels, 'Messages Received: The Political Impact of Media Exposure', *American Political Science Review*, 87 (1993), 267–85; Steven E. Finkel, 'Reexamining the "Minimal Effects" Model in Recent Presidential Campaigns', *Journal of Politics*, 55 (1993), 1–21.
6. Howard R. Penniman (ed.), *Britain at the Polls: the Parliamentary Election of February 1974* (Washington: American Enterprise Institute for Public Policy Research, 1974); Howard R. Penniman (ed.), *Britain at the Polls, 1979: a Study of the General Election* (Washington, DC: American Enterprise Institute for Public Policy Research, 1981); Austin Ranney (ed.), *Britain at the Polls, 1983: a Study of the General Election* (Washington, DC: American Enterprise Institute for Public Policy Research, 1984); Anthony King (ed.), *Britain at the Polls, 1992* (Chatham, NJ: Chatham House Publishers, 1993); Anthony King (ed.), *New Labour Triumphs: Britain at the Polls 1997* (Chatham, NJ: Chatham House Publishers, 1998).
7. King, *Britain at the Polls 1992*, p. vii.
8. Robert M. Worcester and Martin Harrop (eds), *Political Communications: The General Election Campaign of 1979* (London: George Allen & Unwin, 1982); Ivor Crewe and Martin Harrop (eds), *Political Communications: The General Election Campaign of 1983* (Cambridge: Cambridge University Press, 1986); Ivor Crewe and Martin Harrop (eds), *Political Communications: The*

General Election Campaign of 1987 (Cambridge: Cambridge University Press, 1989); Ivor Crewe and Brian Gosschalk (eds), *Political Communications: The General Election Campaign of 1992* (Cambridge: Cambridge University Press, 1995); Ivor Crewe, Brian Gosschalk and John Bartle (eds), *Political Communications: Why Labour Won the General Election of 1997* (London: Frank Cass, 1998).

9. See Philip Gould, *The Unfinished Revolution: How the Modernisers Saved the Labour Party* (London: Little Brown, 1998); Sarah Hogg and Jonathan Hill, *Too Close to Call: Power and Politics – John Major in No.10* (London: Little Brown, 1995).

10. Daniel Finkelstein, 'Why the Conservatives Lost', in Crewe et al., *Why Labour Won the General Election of 1997*, p. 14.

11. John Major, *John Major: The Autobiography* (London: HarperCollins, 1999), p. 690.

12. Major, *The Autobiography*, p. 696.

13. Gould, *The Unfinished Revolution*, chapter 11.

14. Richard Holme and Alison Holme, 'The Role of the Liberal Democrats', in Crewe et al., *Political Communications: Why Labour Won the General Election of 1997*, p. 27.

15. David Butler and Dennis Kavanagh, *The British General Election of 1992* (London: Macmillan, 1992), p. 249.

16. Butler and Kavanagh, *The British General Election of 1992*, p. 261.

17. David Butler and Dennis Kavanagh, *The British General Election of 1987* (London: Macmillan, 1987), p. 251.

18. Sanders, 'Behavioural Analysis', p. 58.

19. William L. Miller, Harold D. Clarke, Martin Harrop, Lawrence LeDuc and Paul F. Whiteley, *How Voters Change: The British Election Campaign in Perspective* (Oxford: Clarendon Press, 1990).

20. Pippa Norris, John Curtice, David Sanders, Margaret Scammell and Holli A. Semetko, *On Message: Communicating the Campaign* (London: Sage Publications, 1999), pp. 14–18.

21. See Table 2.1 above.

22. It is possible to draw limited causal inferences from a two-wave design, but this is not our concern in this chapter. James A. Davis, *The Logic of Causal Order*, Sage University Paper Series on Quantitative Applications in the Social Sciences, Series No. 007–55 (Beverley Hills, CA: Sage Publications, 1985). Also see Warren E. Miller, 'Temporal Order and Causal Inference', *Political Analysis*, 8 (1999), 119–40.

23. Panel study data can be used in more complex causal models to extract estimates of causal effect. See Steven E. Finkel, *Causal Analysis with Panel Data*, Sage University Paper Series on Quantitative Applications in the Social Sciences, Series No. 07–105 (Newbury Park, CA: Sage, 1995).

24. Gary King, Robert O. Keohane and Sidney Verba, *Designing Social Inquiry: Scientific Inference in Qualitative Research* (Princeton, NJ: Princeton University Press, 1994), pp. 31–3.

25. Larry Bartels, 'Panel Effects in American National Election Studies', *Political Analysis*, 8 (1999), 1–20.

26. John R. Zaller, *The Nature and Origins of Mass Opinion* (Cambridge: Cambridge University Press, 1992).

27. Larry Bartels, 'Panel Effects in American National Election Studies', p. 3.
28. Warren E. Miller and J. Merrill Shanks, *The New American Voter* (Harvard: Harvard University Press, 1996), p. 138.
29. Larry Bartels, 'Panel Effects in American National Election Studies', pp. 3–4.
30. Larry Bartels, 'Panel Effects in American National Election Studies', pp. 4–5.
31. John Bartle, 'Political Awareness and Heterogeneity in Models of Voting Choice: Some Evidence from the British Election Studies', in Charles Pattie, David Denver, Justin Fisher and Steve Ludlam (eds), *British Elections and Parties Review, Volume 7* (London: Frank Cass, 1997), pp. 1–20.
32. Bartels, 'Panel Effects in American National Election Studies', pp. 8–18.
33. Bartels, 'Panel Effects in American National Election Studies', p. 18–19.
34. David Butler and Dennis Kavanagh, *The British General Election of 1997* (London: Macmillan, 1997), p. 38.
35. Kenneth Newton, 'Do People Believe Everything They Read in the Papers? Newspapers and Voters in the 1983 and 1987 Elections', in Ivor Crewe, Pippa Norris and David Denver (eds), *British Elections and Parties Yearbook* (Hemel Hempstead: Harvester Wheatsheaf, 1991), pp. 51–74.
36. Butler and Kavanagh, *The British General Election of 1997*, p. 238.
37. Butler and Kavanagh, *The British General Election of 1997*, p. 43.
38. Butler and Kavanagh, *The British General Election of 1997*, p. 43.
39. See Carl I. Hovland, Arthur A. Lumsdaine and Fred Sheffield, *Experiments on Mass Communication* (New York: John Wiley & Sons, 1949).
40. Joseph N. Cappella and Kathleen Hall Jamieson, *Spirals of Cynicism* (New York: Oxford University Press, 1997).
41. David Sanders and Pippa Norris, 'Does Negative News Matter? The Effect of Television News on Party Images in the 1997 British General Election', in David Denver, Justin Fisher, Philip Cowley and Charles Pattie (eds), *British Elections and Parties Review, Volume 8: The 1997 General Election* (London: Frank Cass, 1998), pp. 150–70.
42. Shanto Iyengar, *Is Anyone Responsible? How Television Frames Political Issues* (Chicago: Chicago University Press, 1991).
43. Norris et al., *On Message*, p. 51.
44. Norris et al., *On Message*, p. 149.
45. See Jay G. Blumler and Michael Gurevitch, 'Change in the Air: Campaign Journalism at the BBC, 1997', in Crewe et al., *Political Communications*, pp. 176–194.
46. Norris et al., *On Message*, p. 51.
47. Harold D. Clarke and Marianne C. Stewart, 'Economic Evaluations, Prime Ministerial Approval and Governing Party Support: Rival Models Reconsidered', *British Journal of Political Science*, 25 (1995), 145–70.
48. Paul Mosley, 'Popularity Functions and the Media: A Pilot Study of the Popular Press', *British Journal of Political Science*, 12 (1982), 118–28.
49. David Sanders, David Marsh and Hugh Ward, 'The Electoral Impact of Press Coverage of the British Economy, 1979–87', *British Journal of Political Science*, 23 (1993), 175–210.
50. David Sanders and Neil Gavin, 'The Impact of Television News on Public Perceptions of the Economy and Government, 1993–94', in David M. Farrell, David Broughton, David Denver and Justin Fisher (eds), *British Elections and Parties Yearbook 1996* (London: Frank Cass, 1996), pp. 68–84.

51. Sanders, 'Behavioural Analysis', p. 64.
52. David Sanders, 'Government Popularity and the Next General Election', *Political Quarterly*, 62 (1991), 235–61.
53. Norris et al., *On Message*, p. 150.
54. Regressing support for the Liberal Democrats (or SDP/Liberal Alliance) against time during the campaign reveals that support rose significantly in 1983, 1992 and 1997. Only in 1987 did support fall (as indicated by the negative B coefficient). See below:

	1983	1987	1992	1997
Constant	16.22	24.06	15.16	11.69
B-coefficient	0.22	–0.06	0.10	0.09
T-ratio	[8.97]	[–4.39]	[6.26]	[3.82]

55. Norris et al., *On Message*, ch. 3.
56. David Farrell and Rudiger Schmitt-Beck, 'Do Campaigns Matter? The Political Consequences of Modern Electioneering': http://www.essex.ac.uk/ecpr/ jointsessions /Copenhagen/LM3.htm.
57. Lippmann, *Public Opinion*, p. 158.
58. Lazarsfeld et al., *The People's Choice*, p. xviii.
59. Lazarsfeld et al., *The People's Choice*, p. 88.
60. Lazarsfeld et al., *The People's Choice*, p. 80.
61. Lazarsfeld et al., *The People's Choice*, p. 73.
62. Bartels, 'Messages Received', p. 267.
63. Bartels, 'Messages Received', p. 267.
64. Zaller, *The Nature and Origins of Mass Opinion*, pp. 19–21.
65. Zaller, *The Nature and Origins of Mass Opinion*, pp. 16–21.
66. John R. Zaller, 'Monica Lewinsky's Contribution to Political Science', *PS: Political Science and Politics*, XXXI (1998), 182–9.

Chapter 10:   Political Communications and Democratic Politics

1. For accounts of campaigning in different nations see Frederick Fletcher (ed.), *Media, Elections and Democracy* (Toronto: Dundurn Press, 1991); David Butler and Austin Ranney (eds), *Electioneering* (Oxford: Clarendon Press, 1992); Shaun Bowler and David M. Farrell (eds), *Electoral Strategies and Political Marketing* (New York: St. Martin's Press, 1992); Richard Gunther and Anthony Mughan, *Democracy and the Media: A Comparative Perspective* (New York: Cambridge University Press, 2000).
2. See, for example, Bruce I. Newman (ed.), *Handbook of Political Marketing* (Thousand Oaks, CA: Sage, 1999).
3. For the debate on 'Americanization' see Dennis Kavanagh, *Electioneering* (Oxford: Blackwell, 1995); Ralph Negrine and Stylianos Papathanassopoulos, 'The "Americanization" of Political Communications: A Critique', *Harvard International Journal of Press/Politics*, 1 (1996), 45–62; David Farrell, 'Campaign Strategies and Tactics', in Lawrence LeDuc, Richard G. Niemi and Pippa Norris (eds), *Comparing Democracies: Elections and Voting in Global Perspective* (Thousand Oaks, CA: Sage, 1996), pp. 160–83; David Swanson and Paolo

Mancini (eds), *Politics, Media and Modern Democracy* (New York: Praeger, 1996); Margaret Scammell, *The Wisdom of the War Room: U.S. Campaigning and Americanization*, Joan Shorenstein Center Research Paper R-17 (Cambridge, MA: Harvard University, 1997). For the 'shopping' model see Fritz Plassner, Christian Scheucher and Christian Senft, 'Is There a European Style of Political Marketing?', in Bruce I. Newman (ed.), *Handbook of Political Marketing* (Thousand Oaks, CA: Sage, 1999).

4. For a fuller discussion see Pippa Norris, *Electoral Change since 1945* (Oxford: Blackwell, 1997).
5. Michael Robinson, 'Public Affairs Television and the Growth of Political Malaise: The Case of "the Selling of the President"', *American Political Science Review*, 70 (1976), 409–32; Arthur Miller, Edie H. Goldenberg, and Lutz Erbring, 'Type-Set Politics: The Impact of Newspapers on Public Confidence', *American Political Science Review*, 73 (1979), 67–84.
6. Pippa Norris, *A Virtuous Circle: Political Communications in Post-Industrial Societies* (New York: Cambridge University Press, 2000).
7. See also Geoffrey Evans and Pippa Norris (eds), *Critical Elections: British Parties and Voters in Long-term Perspective* (London: Sage, 1999).
8. Note this is based on estimates of constant prices. *5th report of the Committee on Standard in Public Life* chaired by Lord Neill, Cm 4057 (London: Stationery Office, 1998), Table 3.11.
9. Jill Sherman, 'Taxpayer funds Tory army of spin-doctors', *The Times*, 23 September 1999.
10. See, for example, Nicholas Jones, *Soundbites and Spin Doctors* (London: Cassell, 1995); Martin Rosenbaum, *From Soapbox to Soundbite: Party Political Campaigning since 1945* (London: Macmillan, 1997).
11. Bob Franklin, *Packaging Politics* (London: Edward Arnold, 1994).
12. Jay Blumler, 'Origins of the Crisis of Communication for Citizenship', *Political Communication*, 14 (1997), 395–404.
13. Stephen Ansolabehere and Shanto Iyengar, *Going Negative: How Political Advertisments Shrink and Polarize the Electorate* (New York: Free Press, 1995); Lynda Lee Kaid and Christina Holtz-Bacha, *Political Advertising in Western Democracies* (Thousand Oaks, CA: Sage, 1995); Kathleen H. Jamieson, *Dirty Politics* (Oxford: Oxford University Press, 1992); Kathleen H. Jamieson, *Packaging the Presidency: A History and Criticism of Presidential Advertising* (New York: Oxford University Press, 1984); Karen S. Johnson-Cartee and Gary A. Copeland, *Negative Political Advertising: Coming of Age* (Hillsdale, NJ: Erlbaum, 1991).
14. See, for example, the discussion by Steven Barnett, 'Dumbing Down or Reaching Out', in Jean Seaton (ed.), *Politics and the Media* (Oxford: Blackwell, 1998).
15. Pippa Norris, 'The Internet in Europe: A New North-South Divide?', *Harvard International Journal of Press/Politics*, 5 (2000), 1–12.
16. Y. Achille and J. I. Bueno, *Les télévisions publiques en quête d'avenir* (Grenoble: Presses Universitaires de Grenoble, 1994).
17. Jürgen Habermas, *The Theory of Communicative Action* (London: Heinemann, 1984); Jürgen Habermas, *The Structural Transformation of the Public Sphere* (Cambridge, MA: MIT Press, 1998); Peter Dahlgren and Colin Sparks, *Communication and Citizenship* (London: Routledge, 1995); Peter Dahlgren,

Television and the Public Sphere (London: Sage, 1995); Tony Weymouth and Bernard Lamizet, *Markets and Myths: Forces for Change in European Media* (London: Longman, 1996).

18. Robert Entman, *Democracy without Citizens: Media and the Decay of American Politics* (Oxford: Oxford University Press, 1989).
19. Neil Postman, *Entertaining Ourselves to Death* (New York: Viking, 1985).
20. Neil Gabler, *Life the Movie* (New York: Alfred A. Knopf, 1989).
21. Roderick Hart, *Seducing America* (New York: Oxford University Press, 1994); Roderick Hart, 'Easy Citizenship: Television's Curious Legacy', in Kathleen Hall Jamieson (ed.), 'The Media and Politics', *Annals of the American Academy of Political and Social Science*, 546 (1996).
22. Larry Sabato, *Feeding Frenzy: How Attack Journalism has Transformed American Politics* (New York: Free Press, 1988).
23. Norris, *A Virtuous Circle*.
24. Norris, *A Virtuous Circle*.
25. Pippa Norris, 'Does Television Erode Social Capital? A Reply to Putnam', *P.S.: Political Science and Politics*, XXIX (1996); Norris, *Electoral Change since 1945*; Pippa Norris, 'Television and Civic Malaise', in Susan J. Pharr and Robert D. Putnam (eds), *What's Troubling the Trilateral Democracies* (Princeton, NJ: Princeton University Press; 2000); Pippa Norris, John Curtice, David Sanders, Margaret Scammell and Holli Semetko, *On Message* (London: Sage, 1999).
26. Pippa Norris, *A Virtuous Circle*.
27. Kenneth Newton, 'Politics and the News Media: Mobilisation or Videomalaise?', in Roger Jowell, John Curtice, Alison Park, Katarina Thomson and Lindsay Brook (eds), *British Social Attitudes: the 14th Report, 1997/8* (Aldershot: Ashgate, 1997), pp. 151–68.
28. Christina Holtz-Bacha, 'Videomalaise Revisited: Media Exposure and Political Alienation in West Germany', *European Journal of Communication*, 5 (1990), 73–85.
29. See Stephen Earl Bennett, Staci L. Rhine, Richard S. Flickinger and Linda L. M. Bennett, 'Videomalaise Revisited: Reconsidering the relation between the public's view of the media and trust in government', *Harvard International Journal of Press/Politics*, 4 (1990), 8–23.
30. Norris, *Electoral Change Since 1945*.
31. Norris et al., *On Message*, p. 113.
32. Pippa Norris, *Critical Citizens: Global Support for Democratic Governance* (Oxford: Oxford University Press, 1999).
33. Anthony Heath and Bridget Taylor, 'New Sources of Abstention', in Evans and Norris *Critical Elections*, pp. 164–80.
34. IDEA, 'Voter Turnout from 1945 to 1998': www.int-idea.se.
35. See Ivor Crewe, 'Electoral Participation', in Austin Ranney and David Butler (eds), *Democracy at the Polls* (Washington, DC: AEI Press, 1981), pp. 216–63; Arend Lijphart, 'Unequal Participation: Democracy's Unresolved Dilemma', *American Political Science Review*, 2 (1981), 1–14.
36. Robert W. Jackman and Ross A. Miller, 'Voter Turnout in the Industrial Democracies During the 1980s', *Comparative Political Studies*, 27 (1995), 467–92. See also Richard Katz, *Democracy and Elections* (Oxford: Oxford University Press, 1997).

37. Mark Franklin, Cess van der Eijk and Erik Oppenhuis, 'The Institutional Context: Turnout', in Cess van der Eijk and Mark Franklin (eds), *Choosing Europe? The European Electorate and National Politics in the Face of Union* (Ann Arbor, MI: University of Michigan Press, 1996), pp. 306–31.
38. Raymond Wolfinger and Steven Rosenstone, *Who Votes?* (New Haven, CT: Yale University Press, 1980).

Index